# The Spiritual Exercises Reclaimed

UNCOVERING
Liberating Possibilities
FOR WOMEN

Katherine Dyckman, S.N.J.M.

Mary Garvin, S.N.J.M.

Elizabeth Liebert, S.N.J.M.

PAULIST PRESS New York/Mahwah, N.J.

The Publisher gratefully acknowledges use of the following: Excerpts from *The Love of Christ Impels Us: Providence Retreat in Everyday Life* by the Sisters of Providence. Copyright 1990. Used by permission of the Sisters of Providence Provincial Administration, Spokane, Washington. Excerpts from *Ignatius of Loyola: Spiritual Exercises and Selected Works* (Classics of Western Spirituality series), edited by George E. Ganss, S.J., with the collaboration of Parmananda R. Divarkar, S.J., Edward J. Malatesta, S.J., and Martin E. Palmer, S.J. Copyright 1991. Used by permission of Paulist Press.

*Cover & interior design by Lynn Else*
*Cover & interior art created by Terry Mullen, S.N.J.M. Used by permission of the artist.*

Copyright © 2001 by The Sisters of the Holy Names

Library of Congress Cataloging-in-Publication Data

Dyckman, Katherine Marie, 1931–
    The spiritual exercises reclaimed : uncovering liberating possibilities for women / Katherine Dyckman, Mary Garvin, and Elizabeth Liebert.
        p. cm.
    Includes bibliographical references (p.   ).
    ISBN 0-8091-4043-8 (alk. paper)
    1. Ignatius, of Loyola, Saint, 1491–1556. Exercitia spiritualia. 2. Catholic women—Religious life. 3. Spiritual exercises. I. Garvin, Mary, 1939– II. Liebert, Elizabeth, 1944– III. Title.

BX2179.L8 D3 2001
248.8′43—dc21
                                                                                    2001036451

Published by Paulist Press
997 Macarthur Boulevard
Mahwah, New Jersey 07430

www.paulistpress.com

Printed and bound in the
United States of America

# The Spiritual Exercises Reclaimed

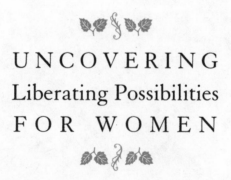

UNCOVERING

Liberating Possibilities

FOR WOMEN

# Table of Contents

# Acknowledgments

The process of writing this work has been an exercise in collaborative scholarship unlike any other previously encountered. Our method developed as we worked together. Our first act was simply to read, ponder and discuss the text of the *Spiritual Exercises* together, trying to let surface in our consciousness the issues for women as we had experienced them personally and ministerially. We tried, as well, to notice what the text *really* said, not what we remembered that it said or thought that it said or hoped that it said. Here we moved back and forth between various translations, noting the nuances each preserved.

Next we sought to increase the range of our personal experience with the Spiritual Exercises. Consultations, largely comprised of women who give the Spiritual Exercises to other women and men, helped us sharpen our questions and convictions. We continued, each in her setting, to work with the Spiritual Exercises, teaching, directing and supervising, trying to pay attention to anomalies, conversions, energy, enthusiasm—and the opposite. We tried to generalize without losing the particularity of individual experience, a process that seemed endless. We prayed as we worked, our common prayer emerging from and feeding into our insights about the Exercises; as we did so, our prayer became a living part of our laboratory.

Eventually we began writing, each of us addressing parts of the Exercises that held energy for us, either because we were attracted to it or repelled somehow by the language or interpretation we had encountered. The drafts came back to the group of three for comment, discussion, argument, acclaim, celebration—whatever it took so that each could assent to all. Finally, the entire text was edited (more than once) for consistency in language, style and voice.

In this long, long process, we have had many collaborators, beginning with those who introduced us to the Spiritual Exercises and accompanied us through their powerful dynamic. We acknowledge those whom we ourselves have accompanied through the Exercises, who have gifted us with profound insights into the Spiritual Exercises. Our consultants in Seattle, Spokane and the San Francisco Bay area grounded us in a reality bigger than our own experience and always spurred us on by saying, "When are you going to be done?" Those who critiqued our manuscript saved us from the more egregious oversights and errors and offered us gems to consider. Our various communities put up with our alternating presence and absence, depending upon where we could gather for our next collaborative session. We acknowledge our families as well, and especially those loved members who went to God during the time in which we have been struggling to bring this book to birth. Those institutions to which we are professionally accountable—San Francisco Theological Seminary and the Graduate Theological Union, Gonzaga University, Seattle University and the Sisters of the Holy Names of the Washington Province—provided us with encouragement, time and/or funds, encouraging us in multiple and concrete ways. Two Sisters of the Holy Names deserve our special thanks: Theresa Mullen for the illustrations that grace these pages and Phyllis Taufen for her masterful editorial assistance through several versions of this manuscript. Finally, we acknowledge the presence of the Holy Spirit in this entire enterprise of "apostolic community." We rejoice that our friendship has deepened immeasurably during this project. With gratitude to the many persons and institutions indicated so briefly above, we dedicate this work to all those women who have entered into the Spiritual Exercises and who have been moved into mission on behalf of others as a result.

# Preface

Our work illumines a centuries-old spiritual process that grew out of Ignatius of Loyola's spiritual experience and out of the pastoral experience he gleaned while working with women and men of his time. Over some years, Ignatius established a pattern of spiritual exercises that invited people into a profound experience of God and frequently evoked a deep conversion and a renewed sense of mission.

Eventually, Ignatius distilled this process into the text of the *Spiritual Exercises* so others might enter into their own dynamic spiritual transformation. As Ignatius intended, the *Exercises* have been adapted to a wide range of persons, time frames, theologies and cultures. Insofar as these adaptations have addressed the spiritual situation of those entering into them, they have continued to speak deeply to human hearts and desires.

Our purpose, then, is to invite others into a direct experience of God, to create parameters within which radical transformation might occur through the action of the Holy Spirit. We examine this dynamic transformational process and illumine it in light of contemporary culture. The lens through which we focus our interpretation is the experience of women: women of the past, to understand their presence during the formative years of the *Spiritual Exercises,* but primarily women in the present, to invite their voices into the interpretive task. In so doing, we situate the *Spiritual Exercises* within our time so they might continue their transformative work in women and men engaged in today's world.

We write for various circles of people whose common bond is the Spiritual Exercises. We speak to those who are captured by the vision and spirit of the Spiritual Exercises and who seek to deepen their life and ministry in the midst of their everyday situations. We also write for those who passionately resist elements of the Spiritual Exercises or the ways they have been interpreted. We believe that in using women's experience as our hermeneutical key to understanding the dynamic of the Spiritual Exercises, we can address the situation of many contemporary women and men who seek radical spiritual transformation. Thus, while we begin with the text of the *Spiritual Exercises,* we continually try to illumine it in light of our experience as women and with women.

Even more significantly, we believe women are impoverished when their unique perspective remains invisible within some area of human discourse.[1] But men are also poorer when women's experience has been left out of the account. Indeed, the entire church is the poorer for losing the richness of women's experience and gifts, a poverty it can ill afford. Thus, while this work focuses attention on one of the significant renewal processes in the history of Christian spirituality, the implications of our work extend beyond the reinterpretation of this text to its underlying dynamic. This book is not primarily a textual criticism or a manual for giving the Spiritual Exercises. It springs from a desire to help redress an ancient imbalance and to open new perspectives on what it means to come "to the measure of the full stature of Christ" (Eph 4:13).

Three realities, then, continually interact in the work that follows: (1) the text of the *Spiritual Exercises* as we have received it, along with its history of interpretation; (2) our attempts to reconstruct the dynamic process evoked by the text, then and now, with all the challenges, frustrations and "aha" experiences entailed in this hermeneutical endeavor; and (3) contemporary women's experience—that dynamic, ever-changing and vast, yet largely untapped, reality. Contemporary women's experience provides the privileged perspective upon which we base our treatment of the text, but the text itself and its classical understanding ground and set limits on our interpretations. Fortunately, as we struggle to hold all these realities together, the text itself often opens up its meaning in surprising ways.

## Organization and Conventions Employed in This Work

The discussion unfolds as follows. Chapter 1 lifts up the problems and possibilities that we find in the Spiritual Exercises and sets out the major interpretive perspectives we bring to the material. Some readers may wish to skip this section and move directly to the next chapter or to part 2.

Chapter 2 centers on the women surrounding Ignatius and the Spiritual Exercises during their early days. Here we attempt to address the problem expressed by so many women: "The Spiritual Exercises are so masculine in their origins and images." In fact women have been present from the beginning, a perspective the standard histories have obscured. Because they were influential in the formulation of the Exercises, they can also influence contemporary interpretations.

Part 2 moves to the text of the *Spiritual Exercises,* but focuses on the all-important processes by which one enters into them. Chapter 3 deals with the "who" of the Spiritual Exercises, the relationship of the persons involved and how they interact as the process unfolds. Scattered throughout the *Spiritual Exercises* we find various explanations, notes and additional directives. Together these directives and explanations contain Ignatius's assumptions about the dispositions and conduct of both the person making the Exercises and the person guiding them. These process directions form the heart of the Spiritual Exercises. Chapter 4 deals with the "where," the Principle and Foundation. Here we examine the implications for interpreting the Spiritual Exercises from within a new cosmological paradigm, offering a liberating gesture to women. Chapter 5 lifts up the "how," the central activity of the Spiritual Exercises, prayer. It discusses the various forms of prayer that Ignatius recommends, some of which are embedded within the Exercises themselves and comprise an integral part of the experience (examen, meditation, contemplation and application of the senses), as well as others Ignatius suggests as adaptations for various persons or situations (the three methods of prayer and additional suggestions for prayer on the mysteries of the life of Christ).

With part 3, we shift the figure and ground, allowing the processes to recede to the background as we turn our attention to the content of the Spiritual Exercises. Chapters 6–9 treat material raised by each of the "Weeks," or dynamic movements of the Exercises. Each one builds upon the Week preceding it; in turn it is subsumed into the subsequent Week, forming an integrated process.

But the *Spiritual Exercises* is about more than inner conversion and personal holiness. Fruitfully entered into, the Spiritual Exercises issue in a spirituality actively engaged in the world. Part 4 treats those aspects of the Spiritual Exercises that undergird and enhance this outward direction toward mission. Chapter 10 addresses the wisdom Ignatius sets out for learning to distinguish the subtle inner clues about what leads to God and what does not; discernment of spirits provides us a "grammar" of personal and communal choices. Our choices intensify and focus our ordinary life in God, and chapter 11 explores Ignatius's method for carefully and prayerfully choosing in harmony with one's essential call. But Christian life is lived in community, and particularly in that community called church. Chapter 12 addresses the often painful issues raised by Ignatius's Rules for Thinking with the Church. Nothing less than a revisioned ecclesiology allows us to reclaim this final section of the Spiritual Exercises.

In the spirit of Ignatius's "repetition" and "application of the senses," we conclude by imaginatively reconstructing the dynamics of the Spiritual Exercises. The form, a contemporary morality play, *AnyWoman,* invites deeper reappropriation of the journey through the Spiritual Exercises and this book. It is best performed aloud by persons already immersed in the Exercises, utilizing the sensory images and objects elicited in the text. In our experience of exploring the possibilities in the Spiritual Exercises, this play has evoked new and creative ways of understanding and embodying them. Some readers may wish to begin with the drama as an imaginative introduction to the rest of the book. *AnyWoman* represents our constructive reimagining of the Spiritual Exercises.

The *Spiritual Exercises* comprise the center of gravity of this work. Occasionally, when it helps us to illumine a point in the *Exercises,* we will range into other parts of Ignatius's corpus, usually his *Autobiography* and letters.[2] Ignatius wrote the text of *Spiritual Exercises* over a nineteen-year period. It was first published in Latin in 1548, twenty-six years after its inception.[3] We will generally follow George Ganss's translation (1991, 113–214, 387–432) based largely on the Autograph, the text Ignatius marked in his own hand.[4] It follows the paragraph numbering first employed by Marietti in the Spanish-Latin version of 1928; these citations will appear in square brackets. Thus, the reader may use any contemporary translation in tandem with this work.

Since the phrase "Spiritual Exercises" can refer both to a printed text and also to a process taking place over thirty days, more or less, some confusion may arise in differentiating the two. *Spiritual Exercises* will denote the text, "Spiritual Exercises" will denote the process or major dynamics within it, and "spiritual exercises" will denote a particular set of directions given by Ignatius. The distinctions, especially between the text and the process, frequently blur, making this convention somewhat arbitrary. When we mean to refer to both the text and the process at the same time we will use the non-italicized capitalized form, reserving the italicized form for references to Ignatius's book itself. Since we believe that the transformative process lies embedded within the text, but is not simply coterminous with the content of the exercises, we generally refer to both the process and content with the term "Spiritual Exercises."

We employ two levels of citations throughout the volume. Those sources upon which we rely directly as we develop the discussion appear in parentheses within the text itself in the author-date-page style. The full bibliographical information for these citations appears in the works cited. Occasional digressions, elaborations, nuances or caveats and further bibliographic resources appear in notes at the conclusion of the chapter. When these notes refer to sources that do not otherwise appear in the body of our text (and therefore not in the works cited at the conclusion of the book), we include full reference information in the note. These notes, therefore, serve as a kind of bibliographic essay that, together with the works cited, points to the various literatures undergirding this book.

The Spiritual Exercises are a rich and multilayered interpenetration of content and process. It proved impossible to treat all the options that opened up to us as we reflected, consulted and discussed this spiritual classic. We have attempted to address those most salient to North American women. Our organization may appear somewhat arbitrary, but it emerged as we worked and prayed with the implications of the material. Therefore, we encourage you, our readers, to work systematically through the text with a copy of the *Exercises* in hand. We hope that at the conclusion of the volume you will have thought about the Spiritual Exercises in a new way and have posed many other questions to yourself and to the text.

# Notes

1. The text of the *Spiritual Exercises* and the process it sets out live deeply in the experience of the members of the Society of Jesus (Jesuits). The conversations about legitimate interpretations, appropriate adaptations and implications of the *Spiritual Exercises* have been carried on under the auspices of and largely within Jesuit contexts. Yet the experience of women making the Spiritual Exercises rarely appears in this scholarship.

An examination of the recent English-language bibliography on the *Spiritual Exercises* by Paul Begheyn and Kenneth Bogart, *Studies in the Spirituality of Jesuits* 23 (May 1991), reveals this lack. Only thirty-six of the 750 entries or slightly under 5 percent (some works are listed in more than one section of the bibliography) were unambiguously authored or coauthored by women. These include one major biography by Mary Purcell, one translation of the *Spiritual Exercises* by Elisabeth Tetlow, one coauthored "handbook" on giving the Exercises by Marian Cowan and John Futrell, one five-volume series of retreat exercises based on the *Spiritual Exercises* by Jacqueline Bergan and Marie Schwan, one dissertation and twenty-five articles. The vast majority of the 714 remaining works are authored by Jesuits. The bibliography contains no section on Ignatius and women or women and the *Spiritual Exercises,* presumably because the number of works devoted specifically to this focus does not merit its own section; only three titles specifically refer to women.

The literature about the *Spiritual Exercises* authored by women has increased in recent years. Two-thirds of the woman-authored works in the Begheyn/Bogart bibliography have appeared since 1980. In addition, the summer 1992 edition of *The Way Supplement* and volume 66 of *Manresa* were devoted to women and the Spiritual Exercises, and Anne Carr's *Women Religious and Ignatius Loyola* (Chicago: The Jesuit Community Corporation at Loyola University, 1992) has appeared. Lisa Fullam authored an issue of *Studies in the Spirituality of Jesuits* 31 (November 1999) entitled "Juana, S.J.: The Past (and Future?) Status of Women in the Society of Jesus." But the impact and influence of women on the contemporary interpretation of the *Spiritual Exercises* far exceeds this meager published output.

2. Ignatius's autobiography will follow the translation of Parmananda Divarkar contained in *Ignatius of Loyola: Spiritual Exercises and Selected Works,* ed. George E. Ganss, Classics of Western Spirituality (New York: Paulist, 1991), pp. 68–111. Citations will be noted in the text as [*Autobiog, #* ], following the section numbers used in this edition. Ignatius's correspondence will be cited from *Letters of Ignatius of Loyola,* ed. and trans., William J. Young (Chicago: Loyola University Press, 1959) and Hugo Rahner, *Saint Ignatius Loyola: Letters to Women,* trans. Kathleen Pond and S. A. H. Weetman (Freiburg: Herder KG, 1956; second impression, New York: Herder and Herder, 1960).

3. Of the early versions, the three most important are the Autograph text in Spanish, Ignatius's own copy containing some thirty-two handwritten notations; the early Latin translation of 1534, probably translated by Ignatius himself; and a more stylistic classical Latin translation prepared for Pope Paul III's approval. Both the Latin texts were also used by Ignatius.

4. Ganss's translation employs functional equivalence that allows the reader to grasp the thought accurately and with reasonable ease. It is gender-inclusive in reference to human beings but does employ the masculine pronoun in references to God.

# PART I:

 **Context**

# Chapter 1

# Reinterpreting the Spiritual Exercises: Problems and Possibilities

The *Spiritual Exercises* have surprisingly liberating possibilities for contemporary women. This belief, however, does not erase the difficulties many women have found and continue to find in Ignatian spirituality and the Exercises. The Spiritual Exercises have presented serious obstacles, either in their content or in the way they have been interpreted and presented. Ignatius was a person steeped in the culture of his time with its deep-seated patriarchy.

Some are put off by the symbolism embedded in the text of the *Spiritual Exercises,* finding it at least uncongenial if not almost deadly to their spirits. Still others question Ignatius's unswerving obedience to the church, an institution that has been singularly destructive of women's full personhood at times in its history. The centrality of Christ in the *Spiritual Exercises* raises for others another cluster of reservations centered around the issue of a male savior. These women wonder how they can ever become autonomous spiritual persons if they "access" God exclusively through a male savior.[1] How can the pivotal place of Christ in the Spiritual Exercises lead, not to further oppression of women, but to their liberation?

## Possibilities for Women Today

Despite these significant difficulties, beneath the sometimes repugnant symbolism, Ignatius's embeddedness in his culture, and women's struggles with an oppressive church structure, there lies a core of liberating possibilities for women in the *Spiritual Exercises* and in the spirituality flowing from them. Our experience suggests that spirituality based in the *Spiritual Exercises* can offer contemporary women numerous important values: (1) the value of the human experience of God shared with another; (2) the value of a spirituality of the whole person; (3) the value of a spirituality grounded in Scripture; (4) the value of prayer in life, of contemplation in action; and (5) the value of adaptability and flexibility as signs of authentic spirituality.

### The Experience of God Shared with Another

Each phrase, "experience of God" as well as "shared with another," is important. Experience, says theologian Thomas Clarke, has to do with the *perception* of reality, with *receptiveness* toward the real in all its dimensions. Building up an authentic spiritual consciousness in any individual or community requires paying attention. Since spiritual consciousness comprises the raw material of spirituality, the first and most basic moment of spiritual accompaniment happens in the act of attending to the experience of God (Clarke 1983, 20, 22).

Yet women's unique spiritual experience has remained largely invisible, both to men and, more significantly, to women themselves. This invisibility has critical repercussions, as author Carol Christ notes:

> Women's stories have not been told. And without stories there is
> no articulation of experience. Without stories a woman is lost
> when she comes to make the important decisions of her life. She
> does not learn to value her struggles, to celebrate her strengths,

to comprehend her pain. Without stories she cannot understand herself. Without stories she is alienated from those deeper experiences of self and world that have been called spiritual or religious. She is closed in silence. The expression of women's spiritual quest is integrally related to the telling of women's stories. If women's stories are not told, the depth of women's souls will not be known. (1980, 1)

Carol Christ uses the word *story* to include all articulations of experience that have a narrative element, including fiction, poetry, song, autobiography, biography and even simple talk between friends. In this extended sense, story implicates *all* women to some degree. Stories shape lives. Without authentic stories, women lack imaginative possibilities to try out in their own lives. Certain religious stories provide orientation to sources of ultimate meaning, and many other seemingly mundane stories also have a sacred meaning that grounds one's existence in ultimates. Distancing women from their own experiences and from their history as women essentially denies them authentic spiritual consciousness. Thus, the basis for all spiritual care of women lies in effectively attending to women's experience (Christ 1980, 1–4).

Such attending forms the substance of the relationship between the one guiding the Spiritual Exercises and the one making them. In the context of the Spiritual Exercises, each person *listens* to her own experience in all its aspects, not just in areas she would name as religious. Attentive listening to one's experience is by no means automatic; many women must learn this skill. Next, she *names* these experiences and gives them life outside herself. Simultaneously, she receives validation that her experiences are not idiosyncratic, but that she belongs to a community of shared experience and articulates one unique aspect of it.

This attending to experience applies both to the one giving the Exercises and the one making them. Both need to ground themselves in their own experience so as to grow in authentic spiritual consciousness. The companion has the additional task of attending to the seeker's experience; indeed the very quality of the companion's attending facilitates the seeker's attending. This mutual honoring of experience underlies the dynamic of the Spiritual Exercises. When it does occur, women's spiritual lives can flourish.

The Spiritual Exercises also provide a context where each person experiences and deals directly with God. If the one giving the Exercises is skilled enough to follow Ignatius's directives [2, 6, 15 and 18, for example], she or he will not dilute or distract from the relationship between God and the one making the Exercises. On the contrary, the one giving the Exercises will provide a safe and welcoming context in which the seeker can notice, name, clarify, appropriate and act upon these direct experiences of God. This context and process can be extremely beneficial to women, estranged as many have been from their own spiritual experience.

## A Spirituality of the Whole Person

The Spiritual Exercises focus spiritual experiences and themes central to a Christian spiritual quest, allowing the seeker to find a way forward.[2] These themes are also basic to the *human* spiritual quest, pointing to issues that all spiritual seekers must address in some fashion. The Spiritual Exercises, except when overly reified (and they have been, in many women's experience), provide wide latitude for individual women to come to grips with these issues in their own time and style. Furthermore, many women struggle with taking responsibility for their own lives;[3] the Spiritual Exercises encourage them to seek the healing and maturity they need to act as responsible agents in their dealings with God, others and themselves. The Spiritual Exercises and the spirituality flowing from them provide one means to spiritual maturity, a means readily accessible to many women.

Although many commonly assume that the Spiritual Exercises are highly rational and "left brain," they actually evoke a far more holistic range of competencies. "Ignatian contemplation" involves rich use of the imagination, and a wide range of affects plays a crucial part in the experience of the Exercises. Memory undergirds the examen, a prayer form Ignatius thought so significant in the development of a continually discerning spirit that he never speaks of omitting it in favor of a greater good (Aschenbrenner 1972, 21). Data gleaned through the senses grounds the repetitions Ignatius encourages, simplifying, focusing and embodying material generated in meditations and contemplations. Repeated prayers, formal and spontaneous vocal prayer, spiritual reading and reflections on the essentials of the Christian faith all find their place on the palette of spiritual exercises. Any and all may be used, their selection and timing based upon the needs of the individual. Ignatius states his goal explicitly: that persons "may become better able to profit from the exercises and to find their prayer a pleasing experience" [238]. Insisting on a single prayer style for all is definitely not Ignatian.

Furthermore, Ignatius directs the one giving the Exercises to pay great attention to the physical context in which they are received. Light and dark, eating and drinking, praying and sleeping, conversing and silence, standing, sitting, kneeling, lying down, the press of business or family affairs—all these should be adapted to the person's situation and the content of the exercises. The Spiritual Exercises takes embodiment with great seriousness.

## A Spirituality Grounded in Scripture

The Christian scriptures grew out of the spiritualities of the earliest Christian communities. Christians believe the Bible stands in a privileged position as a source of Christian spirituality. It contains the essential record of God's revelation to humankind and nourishes a rich variety of spiritualities. In turn, the continuous work of biblical interpretation occurs within a variety of spiritual contexts. Spirituality and biblical text, then, exist in a complex interrelationship.

Unfortunately, the Bible as it has been interpreted has not proven an altogether liberating text for women.[4] However, a growing body of feminist biblical interpretation has laid the groundwork for a biblical appropriation more friendly to women than that offered them throughout most of the Church's history. Such woman-sensitive appropriation of Scripture opens to women the full power of this privileged avenue of God's revelation.

The genius of the Spiritual Exercises lies in bringing persons face to face with the biblical story, trusting that the Holy Spirit will reveal God through the contemplation of the biblical mysteries, primarily the person and work of Jesus Christ. The resulting encounters may not be particularly easy, yet the process respects each woman's attempt to live out of an authentic and liberating spirituality.

## Prayer in Life, Contemplation in Action

In contrast to the notion that holiness requires a life of solitude, silence and withdrawal from the world, Ignatian spirituality offers the possibility of experiencing God *in* one's daily life. Because of the complexity of modern life, women's situation today, regardless of lifestyle, differs radically from the sixteenth century. Many act as the sole caregivers for spouse, children and parents. An increasing number find themselves working double shifts, one at their paid work outside the home and another attending to a never-ending round of domestic duties. Many of these women feel like second-class Christians, with "real Christianity" reserved for professional religious persons who have a special call and the leisure to pursue holiness.

In fact, the spirituality that flows from the *Spiritual Exercises* suits Christians of any lifestyle, for it invites them to understand the call in the midst of their own lives. Indeed, Ignatius conceived the *Spiritual Exercises* and completed most of the revisions as a layperson, prior to his ordination and the founding of the Society of Jesus. Ignatian spirituality can offer a viable spiritual path to contemporary women immersed in even the most repetitious or secular-appearing activities by encouraging each person to determine the pattern of life realistically possible given her actual circumstances.

## Adaptability and Flexibility as Signs of Authentic Spirituality

Indispensable to the Spiritual Exercises is the principle of adaptability. Individual persons and circumstances dictate a range of decisions about giving the Exercises. In the Eighteenth Preliminary Consideration, Ignatius suggests choosing the basic form, length and set of exercises to respect the "disposition of the persons who desire to make them, that is, to their age, education and ability." This preliminary consideration, together with the nineteenth and twentieth, spawned numerous versions of the Spiritual Exercises in the years following Ignatius. After studying the early Directories, or sets of directions on giving the Spiritual Exercises, Michael Ivens (1983, 4) concludes that virtually no age group, no social or religious category, no level of spiritual or educational attainment seems excluded on principle from the classifications in the Directories.

In addition to these large-scale adaptations, Ignatius sprinkles directions throughout the text for the one giving the Exercises to adjust the various exercises to particular situations and needs. For example, Ignatius instructs the Exercises guide to "adapt to the needs of the person," to do so "in accord with the person's greater or lesser progress," and that "the norm is the help found by the exercitant" [72]. When those giving the Exercises adapt them to each individual, women will find their unique personalities, desires and competencies informing their experience of the Exercises. Such personal adaptation encourages women to take their own unique needs and desires seriously. The Spiritual Exercises can enable women to come home to themselves.

The Spiritual Exercises have always been adapted both to the persons making them and to the changes in the sociocultural context in which they were presented. For example, versions of the Exercises have taken root in inner-city Glasgow among persons with little formal education, as well as with Protestants, Jews, Buddhists, Confucians and Taoists.[5] The rising self-consciousness of contemporary women comprises an entirely new cultural context, which, in turn, requires a fresh appropriation of the Spiritual Exercises.

So, what does contemporary women's experience tell us about the usefulness of the Spiritual Exercises? About helpful ways to understand and interpret the Exercises? These are important questions, both for the women themselves and for those who direct others through the Spiritual Exercises.

## Meaning-Making: Principles of Interpretation

Several interpretive strategies undergird our approach. We rely on a particular hermeneutical perspective in dealing with the text of the *Spiritual Exercises,* on feminist interpretation with respect to the seriousness with which we wish to take women's experience, and on certain epistemological perspectives in defining the nature of the questions asked and the possibility of arriving at some answers.

## The Interpretation of the Text

An approach to a classic text[6] from the Christian spiritual tradition necessarily involves several levels of interpretation: the exegetical, the critical and the hermeneutical. The most basic involves the exegetical task of determining the language, thought patterns and intended meaning of the author within the culture of the time. The task of extensive reconstruction of the language patterns and thought world of Ignatius lies outside the scope of this work. Instead, this book relies on contemporary translations and extensive reconstructions of Ignatian thought published and critiqued in recent years. It is not merely expediency that determines this strategy, however. This body of "received interpretation" informs the experience of the Spiritual Exercises as contemporary women meet them—the text comes to most women already translated.

The second level, the critical, involves the process of selecting a method for analyzing the text and assessing the quality of that analysis (Schneiders 1991b, 124).[7] This work falls within the class of criticism called ideology criticism; it lifts up liberating possibilities in the text and insists that these possibilities coexist with or supersede oppressive interpretations (Schneiders 1991b, 120). If such be the case, contemporary women may experience the *Spiritual Exercises* as a freeing and enlivening text. That some contemporary women do find freeing dynamics in the *Spiritual Exercises* encourages this kind of ideology criticism.

The interpretive task also includes the reappropriation of an "old" text by successive generations of readers who bring new questions to it. Four aspects of Paul Ricouer's hermeneutical perspective (Capps

1984, 42–47) allow contemporary persons to interpret a classic text through categories and experiences unavailable to its author: (1) Texts are partly the effect of an author's intentions, yet they also have meanings that the author did not envision. (2) The original readers do not have privileged status with respect to understanding or interpreting the text. (3) Texts have meaning both in the author's and original readers' life setting but also have meanings that transcend the immediate situation. (4) The hermeneutical process begins when the reader enters into the task of understanding the text. Thus, the *Spiritual Exercises* may legitimately extend beyond either the meaning Ignatius intended or the meanings expounded in the history of interpretation of this text. One can read it anew from women's perspective.

Not every possible interpretation, however, validly explicates a particular text. Valid interpretation must preserve the integrity of both the text and the context. In other words, the work itself determines the parameters of interpretation.

## Feminism as a Hermeneutical Perspective

A work dealing extensively with women and their experience must take seriously the perspective of others who have focused on women; many of these works are self-consciously feminist in their orientation. Feminism refers to a movement to overcome the oppression of and discrimination against women deeply embedded in our social and cultural institutions. Feminism seeks, through imaginative immersion and active engagement, to develop and refine a critical consciousness based on women's experience of the asymmetries of power and opportunity and to develop alternative ways of living in which individuals of both sexes can flourish in diverse ways (King 1993, 4, 10, 19). Theologically, the Gospels challenge us to align ourselves with the "reign of God." In this ideal social order all persons and nature itself can flourish. To the extent that women, children, disabled or dependent adults and persons of color have been excluded from this vision, they must be given priority.

Feminism does not seek to replace men's exclusive privilege with women's, but seeks a vision giving advantage to both. Within a Christian theological context, it gives a lens with which to focus experience and sharpen attention to the ways the Spiritual Exercises function for women.[8]

Jesuits themselves have consciously moved in this direction. In March 1995, for example, the 34th General Congregation issued a document, "Jesuits and the Situation of Women," inviting all Jesuits to align themselves in solidarity with women and to take concrete steps to enhance the situation of women, not only in their individual relationships, but also in their institutions and in the cultures in which they live. They specifically note their appreciation for the contributions women have made to the Spiritual Exercises historically and currently: "…they have enriched the Ignatian tradition and our own understanding of ourselves and of our ministry" (741).

## Contributions from Feminist Epistemology

Epistemology, the study of how knowledge is possible and of the origins, limits and sources of knowing, can provide valuable benchmarks in searching for an interpretation that honors women's experience. Epistemology's first expression, says author Ellyn Kaschak, is not in the answers, but in the questions it generates. Beginning in the diverse experiences of women, feminist epistemology poses two basic questions: (1) How fully can the ordinary experience of this woman and of women in this society be understood? and (2) What are the *multiple* meanings of these experiences (1992, 10, 19, 32)?

Feminist epistemology asserts that knowing cannot be absolute. On the contrary, knowing is relative, contextual and complex. One's understanding of truth, therefore, is not independent of its location, nor does it function without a social context (Farganis 1986, 24). Thus, feminist epistemology allows for interrelated and embedded aspects of the same experience and for the intersection of complex influences.

Women's experience provides the starting point for analysis of women's spirituality. Women share certain experience by virtue of being women (for example, the effects of a normative violence against women and economic disparity in earning power compared to men of the same education, job preparation and race). At the same time, each woman is a unique individual, formed in a matrix of race, class, sexual orientation, family background, economic opportunity, age and personal choices. Hunches about women as a group may arise from careful listening to many women recount their experiences, but these generalizations must not overshadow the particularities of each woman's spirituality. No woman speaks for all women.

Feminist epistemology also claims that no aspect of our experience escapes being engendered. Ellyn Kaschak (1992, 21) speaks of "woman" as a metaphor. As such, it is neither "real" nor independent, but a function of the viewer, the definer, the organizer of categories. In the case of "woman," or "the wife of a man,"[9] the organizer is male, and the category "woman" derives from his values, his needs, his experience. The very subject of discourse is a function of epistemology, one's manner of knowing, and what is defined as worth being known. It is inescapably gendered.

Finally, feminist epistemology underscores the reality that culture, defined as a framework of values and beliefs and a means of organizing experience (Kaschak 1992, 30), dictates what is foreground and what is background, what is conscious and what must remain unconscious. Incest, an issue that has enormous implications for giving the Exercises, provides a clear example of culture defining our awareness. Until feminist consciousness provided a context for naming it, incest seemed a strange and horrible but relatively infrequent deviation from parental love. Indeed, many women who suffer incest "forget" about it; it becomes unconscious even to themselves. Culture, then, has defined the very nature of repression in women. Similarly, the determination of what constitutes "context" is an epistemological act, one of drawing boundaries. Whoever draws the line between the subject of focus and the background "context" controls the boundaries of the discussion.[10]

These insights of feminist epistemology have implications for a classic text such as the *Spiritual Exercises.* The Exercises have formed countless women and men in a way of holiness. They comprise an epistemology, that is, a way of knowing and intimacy with God, with all things in God, and with self in relation to God. But the model of holiness assumed in the interpretation of the *Spiritual Exercises* has been gender-marked and at points assumes a male norm for holiness. Both the *Spiritual Exercises* and its interpretation thereby merit a "negative hermeneutic" to uncover any complicity with a patriarchal ideology as well as a "positive hermeneutic" to uncover any liberating possibilities for women.

In line with feminist epistemology, then, this book employs both an "obedient" and a "disobedient" reading. As obedient readers, we try to grasp what Ignatius worked to communicate; as disobedient readers we look for the ways he reinforces social arrangements. Such an approach uncovers the values and loyalties with respect to women embedded in the *Spiritual Exercises*, not only what the text says explicitly about women (which is little enough), but how the process affects women, both positively and negatively (Miles 1992, 11). We will read the *Spiritual Exercises* as *women,* yet also as white, middle-aged, educated, Roman Catholic, celibate members of a religious congregation. Our social location inevitably influences our perspectives on the situation of women and the interpretation of the *Spiritual Exercises.*

### Contributions from Feminist Biblical Interpretation

Scripture, scriptural allusions and biblically based prayer permeate the Spiritual Exercises. The approach to Scripture matters deeply. Feminist biblical interpretation has uncovered the androcentric bias of the canonical Scriptures, critiqued received interpretations institutionalizing women's marginal status in family, church and society and lifted up for fresh consideration the women who do appear in the pages of Scripture. Without a critical feminist hermeneutic, the Scriptures themselves reinforce much that has crippled women.

Therefore, selecting and interpreting biblical texts—and extrabiblical texts as well—must flow from four hermeneutical moves: (1) a hermeneutics of suspicion (In what ways is this text an instrument of invisibility or domination for some groups of people or of this woman?); (2) a hermeneutics of proclamation (What portions of Scripture open toward greater interior and exterior freedom for this woman and for all women?); (3) a hermeneutics of historical reconstruction (How can we imagine women's presence in the biblical and historical record?) and (4) a hermeneutics of creative actualization (How will our lives be different now?) (Schüssler Fiorenza 1984, 15–22). Since biblical material comprises such a significant aspect of the Spiritual Exercises, those who give the Exercises must alert those making them to how biblical texts function, both in their individual circumstances and in the psyche, as well as within the social situation of women in general.

These same feminist principles of biblical interpretation can apply to other texts, including the *Spiritual Exercises* themselves. This text faces the same four questions feminists apply to biblical texts: In what ways is this text an instrument of invisibility or domination for women? What portions of the *Exercises* facilitate greater interior and exterior freedom for all women and for this woman? Where are the

women who influenced Ignatius and had an impact on the beginnings
of the Exercises? How can we imagine the presence and influence of
these women in the absence of a full record of their participation?
One additional question is critical: what difference does this text
make for contemporary women?

## Contributions from Feminist Theology

Feminist theology, including its Christian forms, occurs within
the praxis of life experience and is particularly grounded in women's
experience of the Divine, themselves, community, world and all of
creation in an interacting dialectic (Ruether 1983, 12). A feminist perspective insists that theology is fundamentally relational and that
speaking about God with integrity is inseparable from solicitude for
all creatures, including—but not limited to—other human beings.
This solicitude appears in the rightness of personal, interpersonal,
social and ecological relations (Johnson 1992, 21).

Christian feminist theology bears witness to the dynamic changing character of religion and hence of theology itself. Those holding
this perspective seek to correlate the central and liberating themes of
biblical and Christian tradition with the experience of contemporary
women. First they critique the past, then recover the lost history of
women in the Christian tradition and, finally, re-vision Christian categories in ways that take the integrity, equality and experience of
women seriously (Carr 1988, 7–9).

Feminist theological anthropology insists that women as well as
men image Christ, not through replicating sexual features, but through
participating in the life of Christ. Both women and men image God
through their creativity, sociality, generativity, stewardship of the earth,
intelligence, freedom, bodiliness and destiny (Johnson 1993, 62, 70–75).

Finally, Christian feminist theologians share common commitments
to shared theological reflection. They take issues of accountability

seriously, asking whose interests the theology serves, to whom theology is accountable, and for whom the theologians speak. They work dialogically, asking with whom theological work converses, what truths emerge from it and how various realities relate to one another. They proceed collaboratively, developing common purpose and processes.

## Contributions from Feminist Historical Studies

Traditional research on the *Spiritual Exercises* often begins by documenting the four-hundred-year history of the Society of Jesus, chronicled in numerous languages, expertly interpreted from various cultural perspectives. The rich resources of church historians and Renaissance and Reformation scholars expand the data. The additional lens of the specialist in Ignatian spirituality refines and focuses the bounty. Yet even the combined fruit of these sources leaves much unsaid, particularly about the women present during this sweep of history. Because the experience of women has not been a major concern or emphasis in these historical studies, women have been largely excluded as subjects, authors and interpreters of this history. A footnote, a few pages or an exceptional chapter occasionally surfaces. Even these sources view women as objects of male study, not subjects of their own.[11]

The *Spiritual Exercises* face the same critique as spiritual classics in general; the elite and powerful dominate the subjects and sources of spiritual writing as in other historical writing. The "underside" of the history of spirituality, both theory and practice, reveals that persons on the margin of society are often ignored or trivialized. Men speak for and about women. Male biographers or chroniclers interpret women in terms of male perspectives and norms. When women are present in the history of spirituality, it is usually through the viewpoint of a male writer.[12]

Feminist theory provides the basic method for pursuing women's historical reality on its own terms. This perspective presumes that the interpretation of history involves a threefold movement: critiquing the patriarchal culture and androcentric mindset of the times; reclaiming women's participation and contributions according to their experience and perspective; and revisioning new and creative interpretations expanding the horizon of understanding. Allowing women's presence at the genesis of the Spiritual Exercises to emerge from the mists obscuring them requires that the tools for recovering women's history be applied to both the origin and also to the contemporary reinterpretation of the Spiritual Exercises. This analysis frees women to claim their rightful place not only at the origins of the Spiritual Exercises, but also in their current reinterpretation.

## Contributions from Feminist Psychology

Although Ignatius of Loyola lived prior to the rise of the modern discipline of psychology, he still employed a psychology implicit within the reigning worldview of the time. Indeed, his attention to inner states and motions and to human processes such as thinking, feeling and choosing is remarkably sharp given the absence of a contemporary psychological mindset.

Three constructive contributions from feminist psychology are particularly illuminating for this project: relationality, embodiment and particularity.

Women's primary experience of self is relational. In this culture, a woman, more so than a man, organizes herself in the context of interpersonal relationships. The researchers at the Stone Center describe women as "self-in-relation" (Jordan and others, 1991),[13] underlining the conclusion that connection with others comprises a key component in women's psychological growth. But this relationality, judged from the perspective of men's development of self, appears diffuse, weak and dependent. Only when theorist Carol Gilligan (1982) challenged the immense epistemological oversimplification that men's experience can be generalized to human experience was this judgment about women's development modified. The resulting conceptions of development recognize women's strength in affiliation as a human strength, something "good" for humankind, and not just some kind of "default setting" for women.

Second, women's psychological self is grounded in their bodies. Women's bodies impinge regularly upon their lives; their endocrine systems can profoundly color their perception of reality; the rhythms of menstruation, gestation, birth and lactation punctuate not only their biological but also their psychological reality, and the effects of menopause appear in their physical aging in overt and undeniable ways. Many women have experienced the indisputable connection between their bodies and their spirituality as a source of restriction within a system that tends to identify the body and nature with evil. But valuing the body-nature connection can contribute richly to healing the dualisms of body versus spirit and nature versus technology.

Third, women's development of self, voice and mind, their ways of knowing and learning, do not match norms established exclusively with male subjects. Thus, what women need for their optimal intellectual development often varies from what men need (Belenky and others, 1986). Women's circles of storytelling, which serve to overcome the isolation that gendered, familial and work relationships impose on them, offer many women a lifeline out of psychological stagnation.

Despite the theoretical advances in allowing women a psychology of their own, however, the political, cultural and economic structures within which the vast majority of the world's women live do not yet legitimate their development in ways that count, namely in the power arrangements between women and men. When women live in psychologically, physically or sexually abusive situations, when exploitative images of their bodies bombard them, when their bodies and selves are bought and sold or taken as spoils of war, when professional and academic arrangements conspire to render them invisible, when economic structures enforce a perpetual economic dependence, women become psychologically constricted, if not deeply wounded. Such constriction or actual wounding of women's self-in-relation results in all manner of havoc in the psychological lives of women, including depression, loss of self-esteem, misplaced and destructive anger, inappropriate and paralyzing fear, inability to speak on one's own behalf, self-deprecation and a high need for external validation.[14] These obstacles to women's full development as persons inevitably color their experience of the Spiritual Exercises.

## Conclusion

Thus, again and again women's experience grounds this exploration of the Spiritual Exercises. A person who enters into the dynamic of the Spiritual Exercises and comes to understand and live out their fruit will manifest integrity in the interpersonal, social and ecological relations. The Spiritual Exercises bear an examination according to the norms of feminist epistemology, biblical interpretation, theology and psychology. The process of reinterpretation is precisely—and properly–the task of women.

This work, then, makes visible certain aspects of women's experience of the *Spiritual Exercises*. In so doing, it does not claim to describe the experience of all women, still less a normative experience that women "ought to have." But many women over the course of the past four hundred years have experienced through the Spiritual Exercises a way of liberating intimacy with God. It is to these women, both historical and imaginative, that we now turn.

# Notes

1. For a discussion of various aspects of this problem, see Elisabeth Schüssler Fiorenza, "Toward a Feminist Biblical Hermeneutic," in *The Challenge of Liberation Theology,* ed. Brian Mahan and L. Dale Richesin (Maryknoll, N.Y.: Orbis Books, 1981), Anne Carr (1988), especially chapter 8, "Feminism and Christology," and Elizabeth Johnson (1992), especially chapter 8, "Jesus-Sophia."

2. This value was also reported by women in our consultations. One person, however, felt that the Spiritual Exercises would be constraining to persons in the habit of "contemplative prayer," presumably meaning quiet, free-flowing, imageless prayer. See also Jacqueline Hawkins, "Foreword," *The Way Supplement* 74 (Summer 1992): 3–6.

3. See, for example, Jean Baker Miller, "Toward a New Psychology of Women," in *Women's Spirituality: Resources for Christian Development,* ed. Joann Wolski Conn (New York: Paulist, 1986), p. 116. Baker's analysis reveals the underlying systemic oppression that contributes to women's collusion in their own oppression in this fashion. She does not intend to "blame" women for this state of affairs, nor do we.

4. For an accessible overview of the effect of biblical interpretation on women, see Sharon H. Ringe, "When Women Interpret the Bible," in *The Women's Bible Commentary,* pp. 1–9, ed. Carol A. Newsom and Sharon H. Ringe (Louisville, Ky.: Westminster/John Knox, 1992).

5. For working with lower socioeconomic background, see Martha Skinnider, "Who Is the Nineteenth Annotation For?" *The Way Supplement* 49 (Spring 1984): 59–69. On adaptations with Protestants and Jews, see Michael Ivens, "The Eighteenth Annotation and the Early Directories," *The Way Supplement* 46 (Spring 1983): 3–10; Susan Anderson, "Reflections on the Experience of Making and Giving the Exercises," *The Way Supplement* 68 (Summer 1990): 13–21; Linda Mary Evans, "Catholic and Protestant Approaches to the First Week," *The Way Supplement* 68 (Summer 1990): 5–12; Joyce Hugget, "Why Ignatian Spirituality Hooks Protestants," *The Way Supplement* 68 (Summer 1990): 22–33; and Graham Chadwick, "Giving

the Exercises and Training Directors in an Ecumenical Context," *The Way Supplement* 68 (Summer 1990): 35–41. On adapting for Buddhists, Confucians and Taoists, see Aloysius Pieris, "Ignatian Exercises Against a Buddhist Background," *The Way Supplement* 68 (Summer 1990): 98–111 and Lily Quintos, R.C., "Experiences of the Heart: The Spiritual Exercises across Cultures," in *Common Journey, Different Paths: Spiritual Direction in Cross-Cultural Perspective,* ed. Susan Rakoczy, I.H.M. (Maryknoll, N.Y.: Orbis Books, 1992), pp. 89–96.

6. Sandra Schneiders (1991b, 150), describes a classic text as "one whose subject matter is somehow universal, whose composition is singularly effective, and whose style is beautiful to such an extent that the work is relevant to the human situation as such."

7. Elsewhere in *The Revelatory Text* (1991b, 164–67), Schneiders articulates other principles of valid interpretation to which we subscribe. First, the interpretation meets the standard, "that which cannot be done or must not be left undone." Some interpretive processes cannot be applied to some texts without destroying the obvious sense of the text; others must not be omitted at the risk of deforming the text's meaning. Second, the interpretation is fruitful. An interpretation that "makes the text speak" without violating the canons of good exegesis ought to be taken seriously. Third, valid interpretation is consistent with itself, free from internal contradictions. Fourth, it successfully (or as successfully as its competitors) explains anomalies within the text. Fifth, it is compatible with what is known from other sources. Finally, a valid interpretation should have used responsibly all the methods appropriate within the framework of interpretation chosen.

8. Feminist thought can also function as a decisive critical category for spirituality in general because, as Ursula King (1993, 15) claims, "...it challenges and examines the foundations of our language, thought and institutions, our social and political power structures and their hierarchical divisions. In its most radical form, feminism asks what, if anything, in the past and present experience of religion and spirituality remains usable for women today. Reformist feminism, on the other hand, holds that aspects of religion and spirituality may be life-giving, and seeks a new approach to symbols, myths and

rites capable of better expressing the richness of women's experience of God, self, world and cosmos." Clearly, our work follows this reformist feminism.

9. Webster's *New Collegiate Dictionary,* 8th ed. (Springfield, Mass.: G. C. Merriam, 1973). *Female* carries its own inherited problems with meaning; besides referring to the sex that produces eggs and produces young, *female* also connotes a hollow into which a corresponding (male) part fits and the unstressed endings in poetry or in music—females are passive, receptive, gentle, unstressed, weak.

10. Susan Faludi, *Backlash: The Undeclared War Against American Women* (New York: Crown Publishers, Inc, 1991) describes in vivid detail how the process of naming the contours of the discussion forms and unforms the understanding of "woman" and literally changes women's consciousness of themselves.

11. See the following chapters in two recent books: "No Women Need Apply" in Jean Lacouture's *Jesuits: A Multibiography* (Washington, D.C.: Counterpoint, 1995), and "Women" in Meissner (1992), 238–71. Also see our earlier analysis of the citations in a commonly accessible Ignatian bibliography in the preface, n. 1.a.

12. See, for example, Jerome's account of Paula and Eustocium, Gregory of Nyssa's life of his sister Macrina, Raymond of Capua's life of Catherine of Siena, Thomas of Celano's legend of Saint Clare, Rudolfe's life of Leoba, Joseph Dirvin's life of Elizabeth Seton, Robert Coles's life of Dorothy Day and Pope John Paul II's "On the Dignity of Women."

13. Several papers in this collection are particularly illuminating on women's relational development, especially: "The Development of Women's Sense of Self" (11–26) by Jean Baker Miller, "The Self in Relation: A Theory of Women's Development" (51–66) by Janet L. Surrey and "The Meaning of Mutuality" (81–96) by Judith Jordan.

14. For further discussion on these dynamics, see Dana Crowley Jack (1991) and Christie Cozad Neuger, "Women's Depression: Lives at Risk," in Maxine Glaz and Jeanne Stevenson Moessner, eds. (1991), 146–61.

# Chapter 2

# Remembering and Imagining: Wise Women Then and Now

*At that time there was at Manresa a woman of great age with a long record also as a servant of God, and known as such in many parts of Spain, so much so that the Catholic King had summoned her once to communicate something. One day this woman, speaking to the new soldier of Christ [Ignatius], said to him, "Oh! May [sic] my Lord Jesus Christ deign to appear to you someday." But he was startled at this, taking the matter quite literally, "How would Jesus Christ appear to me?"*

—Autobiography, #21

*While he was still in Barcelona before embarking, he sought out, as was his practice, all spiritual persons to converse with them, even though they lived in hermitages far from the city. But neither in Barcelona nor in Manresa during the whole time he was there did he find persons who could help him as much as he wished. He found in Manresa only that woman mentioned above, who told him she prayed God that Jesus Christ might appear to him. She alone seemed to him to enter more deeply into spiritual matters.*

—Autobiography, #37

## Remembering

Who is this woman? Why is she nameless? The *Autobiography* singles her out for her significant spiritual influence on Ignatius. Today this prophetic yet nameless woman hovers on the edge of our contemporary consciousness as a symbol of invisible and forgotten women. When the history and interpretation of the *Spiritual Exercises* includes women's perspective, a whole new story emerges from the "underside" of the Ignatian tradition.

Although women were indeed present during the formation, reception and transmission of the Spiritual Exercises, most people have heard little about their role in Ignatius's life or their impact on the theory and practice of the Spiritual Exercises in its early stages. Not acknowledging the presence of women during this foundational time, however, both denies women their history and gives many the sense that the Exercises are "too masculine" in source and substance. Both situations create problems for women's full appropriation of the Spiritual Exercises. This chapter aims to revive the memory of the women significant to Ignatius, highlighting their participation in and contributions toward the development of the Spiritual Exercises. In doing so, it invites contemporary women to see themselves as included in the dynamic development of the Spiritual Exercises and to claim with new energy the legacy left by Ignatius's female contemporaries.

Before discussing the women in the life of Ignatius, we need to recall the highlights of his own story. The life of Ignatius of Loyola provides ample material for writers be they historians, devoted Jesuits or storytellers searching for saints who make sense. Scholars from every century since Ignatius's birth have interpreted his life with a perspective drawn from their own historical and cultural realities.[1] Yet certain events stand out no matter what the interpretive lens. Ignatius was a man who crossed the boundaries of the Middle Ages into the Renaissance. A Basque by heritage, Ignatius eventually received a classical education. Travels took him from Spain to the Holy Land, France and finally to Italy, where he remained as founder and leader of a new order called the Company of Jesus.

Ignatius was probably born in 1491 just before the European "discovery" of America. He was baptized Íñigo Lopez de Loyola and changed his name to Ignatius later in life. The youngest of thirteen children, his family network placed him in the house of the chief treasurer of Castile in his early teens. As a youthful soldier defending Pamplona against a French attack in 1521, his leg was shattered by a cannonball. He almost died during the long period of convalescence at the Loyola castle. His recovery at Loyola marks one of the most famous conversion stories in the Christian tradition. As he was healing he requested romance novels but received instead the only books available, the lives of Christ and the saints. He records in his autobiography that this turning point transformed him into a man who wanted to do great things for God.

Ignatius the soldier became Ignatius the pilgrim (as he called himself). In 1522 his spiritual journey took him first to Montserrat and then Manresa. These places provided the environment for the experience of God, and this year-long sojourn gave him the time to reflect and formulate what would become his spiritual classic: the *Spiritual Exercises*. In 1523, he followed his heart's desire to go to the Holy Land as a pilgrim. The religious authorities there refused him permission to remain, so he returned to Spain and continued to teach and preach the essentials of the *Spiritual Exercises*. At the same time, he became a student in Barcelona, Alcalá and Salamanca. Under pressure from the Inquisition, he decided to pursue more serious studies in Paris from 1528 to 1534. At this time Ignatius met his companions, grounded them in the Spiritual Exercises and together they discerned their call to place themselves at the service of the pope and live by a common rule of life. Ignatius was ordained a priest in 1537, oversaw the approval of the Society of Jesus by Pope Paul III in 1540 and was elected first general superior in April 1541. In the years that followed, Ignatius provided the leadership that insured the approval of the *Spiritual Exercises* and the Society and completed the *Constitutions of the Society.* He died on July 31, 1556.

The life experiences of Ignatius mediate the charism of the Spiritual Exercises. Consider the familiar images of his life: convalescing at Loyola, praying at Manresa, preaching at Alcalá and Barcelona, establishing apostolic projects in Rome. The multifaceted Ignatius—soldier, penitent, pilgrim, student, priest and spiritual and religious leader—is frequently portrayed as a solitary figure, occasionally surrounded with like-minded men (popes, princes and fellow Jesuits), and sometimes as a mystic absorbed in God or in conversation with the Virgin Mary and the saints. These powerful visual images form our sense of him: strong, singular and often solitary.

Yet, Ignatius did not receive his spiritual enlightenment as an isolated individual somehow set apart from history and culture. Rather he was a man of his times—and his times included women. Women were part of his world as he was part of theirs, and history records women exerting significant influence on his physical, psychological, spiritual and apostolic life. Women, present in his childhood and youth, his convalescence, his conversion, his pilgrim travels, his formulation of the Spiritual Exercises, often supplied the human resources necessary for his personal, spiritual and apostolic success. They also practiced in their daily lives the principles of his Spiritual Exercises.

A more accurate picture reveals Ignatius not as a solitary figure but as a relational one; these relationships included specific women. Two groups of women stand out: influential women in Ignatius's early life and women who were spiritual seekers, served by his ministry and who, in turn, desired to share in his mission. Some even requested to become Jesuits. Their desire for spiritual growth converged with Ignatius's spiritual vision and leadership, although history does not record how much these women influenced Ignatius or the formulation of his vision and practice. But their presence cannot be denied. Not just individuals, but a whole *company* of women emerge. God's transforming work in Ignatius the pilgrim, communicated to the women of his time, continues to be embodied in contemporary women searching for God and following a similar spiritual path. This company of women gather as a "cloud of witnesses." They express the wisdom and power the Spiritual Exercises offer to contemporary women.

## Early Years

Although Ignatius says nothing about his early years, three women provided him with life, sustenance and healing. First comes Doña Marina Sanchez de Licona, Ignatius's mother. No records remain of her birth or death, but it is known that her father was a man of court and provided a valuable dowry for her marriage. Her memory is kept alive as visitors tour the restored Loyola house tower and walk through the room where Ignatius, the youngest of thirteen, was born. Various paintings of Mary and the infant Jesus on the walls evoke a sense of the holy associated with motherhood in that era.

Down the road from Loyola stands the house of the blacksmith. Here Ignatius spent many hours of his early years in the care of Maria Garin, the blacksmith's wife. As Ignatius's wet nurse, she is remembered for her physiological role, "but no one ever speaks of the nurturing psychological role that she must have played in his early life" (Tellechea Idígoras 1994, 44).

When Ignatius was about seven years old, Magdalena de Araoz, the wife of Ignatius's second oldest brother, Martín García, who received the Loyola inheritance, became the lady of the house. Before her marriage she served as a lady-in-waiting to Queen Isabella, who gave her as a wedding present the picture of the annunciation that still hangs in the Loyola chapel, another example of the prevailing Marian devotion of the times. Magdalena introduced Ignatius to Ludolph's *Life of Christ* and de Voragine's *Legends of the Saints* while he recuperated from wounds received at the battle of Pamplona and played significant roles for Ignatius: sister-in-law, mother figure, healer and educator. Historians describe her as one "who won his undying affection" (H. Rahner 1960, 115)[2] and who was "ever sensitive to the marvels of God" (Tellechea Idígoras 1994, 143).

After Ignatius's conversion and recovery at Loyola, he set out on his new life direction and encountered many women whose presence would influence the Ignatian story. They leave a valuable legacy for contemporary conversation. The first clues to the identity and behavior of these women appear in his *Autobiography*. Some women are specifically mentioned by name: Isabel Roser [*Autobiog,* #54], Doña Teresa de Cárdenas [*Autobiog,* #60], and Doña Leonor de Mascarenhas [*Autobiog,* #80]. More frequently we encounter nameless women with generic titles: a woman of great age, a sister, prominent ladies, a mother and her daughter dressed in boys' clothing, a married woman of rank, the lady of the place, a woman well versed, a mother and daughter, both widowed. Even more intriguing is the discovery that hidden behind group references and impersonal pronouns ("the rest of the household," "they took care of him," "those who gave him alms," "many people came to visit him in jail," and "certain souls") stood significant women with identities and lives of their own who influenced Ignatius and the early Society. For example, the simple words, "…with the help of the pilgrim and his companions some pious works were begun in Rome" [*Autobiog,* #98], refer to the House of St. Martha, an apostolic project of great importance built on the support and labor of specific and well-known women of the time.

Political, social, economic, legal, educational and religious structures influenced women and men of Renaissance Spain and Italy.[3] Women associated with Ignatius and influenced by his spiritual teaching came from every class: royal, noble, middle, peasant and lower. Many heard him preach and teach. Others had more individual and personal contact, giving financial and political support. In return they expected access to the spiritual resources Ignatius and his Society offered.

Personal conversion, spiritual growth and freedom were and continue to be the primary goal of the Exercises. Women learned forms of prayer included in the Spiritual Exercises, although it is not always clear what Ignatius meant when he used the term "Spiritual Exercises." Yet the fruit in the lives of women is clear: They desired a deeper attachment to Christ expressed in deeds more than words. Women who associated with the Jesuits certainly found themselves filled with spiritual confidence and motivated by apostolic zeal. Ignatius's "objectified recording of his own religious journey for the help of others" and his desire "to induce in others a conversion and religious experience similar to his own during the early years of his religious quest" (O'Malley 1991, 3–4) characterized his ministry with women.

## Ladies of Manresa

Women sensitive to the ways of God appeared regularly in Ignatius's life after his conversion. Particularly prominent are the women of Manresa, the most familiar one being the unnamed woman of the *Autobiography* described at the beginning of this chapter. Others are noted in general terms: "…he still conversed occasionally with spiritual persons…" [*Autobiog,* #21], "…helping in spiritual matters certain souls…" [*Autobiog,* #26], "…some ladies who had come there to visit him…" [*Autobiog,* #32]. These ladies of Manresa received his spiritual counsel while he received food, shelter, nursing care and financial support for his studies and for the projects of the early Society.

Testimonies for Ignatius's canonization process actually reveal more about the ladies of Manresa than his *Autobiography*.[4] Known for their laudable lives of prayer and service to the poor even before they met Ignatius, they welcomed him as he shared with them the fruit of his own spiritual experience. The chroniclers describe them as "very honorable women, good Christians, virtuous, and of good reputation" (Segarra Pijuan 1992, 96). One of the most influential was Inéz Pascual who, with her friend Jerònima Calver, initially met a limping Ignatius on the way from Montserrat to Manresa. They first directed him to the hospice Jerònima ran and continued to provide him with food and shelter as needed. Later, Ignatius stayed at the homes of these and other women.

One of the more dramatic accounts of the life-saving interventions of these women occurred at the chapel of Our Lady of Viladordis just outside of Manresa. On that particular day the women had discovered Ignatius missing from the Hospital of Santa Lucía and began searching for him. They found him in the chapel

> …almost unconscious on the floor, so weakened by his prayers and abstinence that he could barely sample any of the things they had brought in their basket. Gradually he began recovering and when they saw that he was not strong enough to return to the city two of them decided to remain with him in the church while the others went back to Manresa in search of a steed, and they took him to the Amigant house as best they could and there he was well cared for. (Segarra Pijuan 1992, 96)

The women's care contributed to his recovery and in turn, accounts tell how the people of Manresa profited from the pilgrim's Spiritual Exercises. Ignatius improved their lives by giving them a greater knowledge and desire for God.

## *Inéz Pascual*

Inéz Pascual, one of the most significant of the Manresan women, emerged as a leader. The widow of a Barcelona merchant, she owned a house in Manresa and a "modest house and shop in Barcelona" (H. Rahner 1960, 174): she often went back and forth attending to her properties. She met Ignatius in Manresa, but on several occasions he stayed with her and her son, Juan, with whom he shared a room. She sent funds to help support his studies in Paris and often collected money for him from friends in Manresa and Barcelona. According to later accounts, Inéz accompanied Ignatius on his begging tours to homes of people of rank (Tellechea Idígoras 1994, 229).

Inéz received the earliest extant letter of Ignatius, dated 1524, encouraging her to practice virtue in the midst of criticism and gossip about her and other women associated with him (Ganss 1991, 326). This type of controversy occurred in both Manresa and Barcelona when women gathered around the pilgrim.

## Women of Alcalá

Class differences and their implications showed up clearly in Alcalá, a town central to the formation of the Spiritual Exercises. In 1526, Ignatius arrived there as a pilgrim and layman. He intended to take up studies, but as he began sharing his spiritual exercises and teaching catechism, he became more focused on apostolic activities than on studies. People assembled to listen to him at dawn, midday and late afternoon: the baker and his wife, the wine maker, caretakers of the hospice, married and unmarried persons and widows appeared at the hospice where Ignatius had a room. Women gathered wherever he preached or taught, often giving him food, clothing and necessary supplies. Theologian Hugo Rahner describes twenty women of Alcalá as "widows, artisans' wives, servant-maids, so-called 'praying women' or *beatas,* women too of dubious occupation, a student's wench, young apprentice-girls—in short, life itself, ordinary, every-day, sinful and devout" (H. Rahner 1960, 11). However, the constant goings and comings of the women seeking Ignatius aroused suspicion, and the authorities brought him in for questioning.

Depositions taken during the subsequent investigation by the inquisitors suggest what went on at these various meetings:

> Ignatius taught his followers about "the commandments, capital sins, and the five senses and powers of the soul, and did so very well. He explained these by using the Gospels, the writings of Saint Paul, and the examples of other saints. And he told them that they should make an examination of conscience twice a day by calling to mind how they have sinned, and that they should perform this exercise before some religious image. He advised them further to confess every eighth day and to receive the Eucharist with the same frequency." (Tellechea Idígoras 1994, 251)

It is possible that Ignatius was giving the Spiritual Exercises he later described in his eighteenth Annotation to these hearers, many of whom were women.

The *Autobiography* mentions several of these women, including one whose class, but not her name, was known: "…a married woman of rank came at dawn wearing a veil to his room" [*Autobiog,* #59]. Her visit provoked an investigation of Ignatius and his activities. He also mentions a "mother and her daughter, both widowed. They had made great spiritual progress, especially the daughter." The unidentified women actually were María del Vado and her daughter, Luisa Velásquez, along with their maid Catalina.

These women had spoken to Ignatius on many prior occasions, listened to his lectures on the commandments and lives of the saints, and followed his recommendation for weekly communion.

> …these two pious women had told Íñigo that they were determined to travel about the world, going from hospice to hospice in the service of the poor. He had always dissuaded them from such an undertaking because the daughter was so "young and so attractive." Íñigo said that he told them that they could visit the sick and poor without leaving Alcalá and they could even accompany the priest when he brought Viaticum to the dying. (Tellechea Idígoras 1994, 261)

The *Autobiography* [#60] also mentions Doña Teresa de Cárdenas, who visited Ignatius in jail in Alcalá. She took a great interest in him and worked hard to have him released. She was called "the fool of the blessed Sacrament" because of her great devotion (de Dalmases 1985, 99–100).

Another woman who played an important part in the Alcalá drama is María de la Flor, Mary of the Flower. She represents lower-class women whose lives were changed by Ignatius but who nevertheless caused suspicion and gossip among the townspeople. In her deposition for Ignatius's canonization, she describes herself as a "woman of ill repute, who went around with many of the enrolled students, and who was lost" (Tellechea Idígoras 1994, 253). She became intrigued with Ignatius as she observed him conversing with her aunt and friends. She gathered her courage and asked him to speak with her about serving God. Ignatius responded positively and told her she must meet with him "continuously for a whole month," to expect that she would experience joy and profound sadness and that her advancement and "cure" would be found through this means. Ignatius, probably the first man who did not treat her as a sex object, introduced her to methods of prayer. In the enthusiasm of her conversion, she wanted to go to the desert and live like Mary of Egypt.[5]

## Women Desiring Jesuit Affiliation

As the impact of the Spiritual Exercises on women expanded through Spain and Italy, and women experienced the spiritual and apostolic orientation and charism of early Jesuit leaders, many women desired a closer affiliation with the Jesuits. Some wanted to start a group of female Jesuits while others wished to be incorporated into the existing Society. Women in the convents undergoing reform also experienced a greater sense of spiritual conversion and developed apostolic desires similar to the early Jesuits. "Indeed, much of the appeal of the Jesuits for women was the opportunity to live a religious life in the world" (Blaisdell 1988, 238). Several women actually took vows. The Jesuit movement also appealed to women involved in the reform movement, who used their financial and personal resources to further the cause of reform. As we shall see, Ignatius eventually resisted all forms of permanent affiliation with women although some Jesuits in Spain and women themselves did support the cause of female Jesuits.

### *Isabel Roser*

One woman, Isabel Roser, actually did take vows in the Society. She belonged to the Catalonian nobility and was married to a wealthy merchant, situating her among the most influential families in Barcelona. Her relationship to Ignatius, a poor beggar desirous of traveling to Jerusalem, began when she encountered him teaching catechism to children in the street below her house. She and her husband invited him to dinner. "From that day on, Isabel became so fond of the pilgrim that she became his greatest benefactor in Barcelona, Paris and Venice" (de Dalmases 1985, 72). In an early letter from Ignatius to Isabel dated November 1532, he describes his gratitude to her: "…for to you I owe more than to anyone I know in this life. As I am conscious of this, I hope in God our Lord that he will help me to cancel the debt of my gratitude to you." At the end of the letter he closes with "…and to me may [God] grant no more than that which I desire for you" (H. Rahner 1960, 265–67).

After the death of Isabel's husband in 1541, she contemplated joining a convent but instead went to Rome to join Ignatius in his work. She and her companions, all friends of Ignatius, assisted in the finance, organization and management of the House of St. Martha. In 1544, the ladies from Barcelona led by Isabel and including Vittoria Colonna (friend of Michelangelo) helped furnish the House of St. Martha.

While in Rome, Isabel applied to the pope for permission to take vows before Ignatius (H. Rahner 1960, 285). She and her two companions, Lucrezia di Bradine and Francisca Cruyllas, pronounced vows in the Society of Jesus before Ignatius on Christmas Day 1545, before the altar in the church of Santa Maria della Strada.

> I Isabel Roser, widow,…promise and solemnly vow before God
> Our Almighty Lord, in the presence of the Holy Virgin Mary
> my mistress, St. Jerome and the heavenly court of Paradise and
> before all who are present—and before you most Reverend
> Father Ignatius, General of the Society of Jesus, our Lord, as
> the representative of God: perpetual poverty, according to the
> limits which are laid upon me by your Reverence, chastity, and

obedience to the rule of life laid before me by your Reverence. (H. Rahner 1960, 286–87)

Rahner comments that this event laid out at least in principle the foundation of an order of female Jesuits, "…a far from welcome Christmas present for Ignatius" (H. Rahner 1960, 287). This relationship proved stormy from the beginning and, in April 1546, due to a variety of economic, political and personal reasons, Ignatius sought and received from Pope Paul III release from their vows for these women. Ignatius wrote a letter to his spiritual daughter renouncing her vows. After a complicated period of estrangement, Ignatius and Isabel eventually reconciled personally. Before returning to Spain, she made her confession to Ignatius and they parted in peace. Upon her return to Barcelona, she adapted a small house as an orphanage and looked after children. Evidently, Ignatius later advised her to enter a convent that pleased him by its faithfulness to the rule (H. Rahner 1960, 288–91).[6]

## Juana of Spain

Another vowed woman member of the Society of Jesus was Juana, regent of Spain, the only known female who died a Jesuit.[7] Jesuit documents refer to her by her alias, Mateo Sánchez. She secretly took Jesuit vows as a scholastic although she remained active in the world.

Juana (1535–73) was the daughter of Charles V, king of Spain and Holy Roman Emperor, sister of Philip II of Spain, wife and later widow of the king of Portugal, and mother of Sebastian. In 1554, during the time her brother was married to Mary Tudor, her father appointed her regent of Spain for five years.

In 1554…Juana of Austria, the talented and willful daughter of Charles V, sister of Philip II, and sometimes regent of Spain,

managed to bring such strong pressure to bear that Ignatius took
counsel with Nadal, Polanco, and several other Jesuits in Rome.
This committee recommended the acceptance into the Society
under certain carefully stated stipulations of "Mateo Sánchez,"
the code name for the Infanta. Juana therefore became a Jesuit
and remained one until her death in 1573—a secret known only
to herself and a few members of the Society. The discomfort those
Jesuits, including Ignatius, felt with this anomalous situation and
with the possibility of the recriminations it might provoke from
Juana's brother should he learn the secret was balanced by the
hope that she might provide the Society with help and protection.
She in fact threw her support behind the Jesuits in some important matters, but she also caused them much anxiety. The exper-
iment was never repeated. (O'Malley 1993, 75–76)

We know that after her mother died, Juana was brought up by
Leonor de Mascarenhas, who knew Ignatius. Juana was educated in
Latin and music and promised in an arranged matrimonial pact to the
sickly heir to the throne of Portugal. Juana, a young widow at nineteen, emerges from the pens of those who wrote about her as a complex woman, but understandably so, as she was of royal linage and by
her nature involved herself in the familial and monarchical regime
and intrigues of the day. Some have described her as one of the most
beautiful women at the Spanish court and, more than that, as displaying "masculine intelligence" and strength of will. But we also
know she lived a kind of monastic life and conversed with Francis
Borgia, her director, "concerning the manner of ruling without forgetting to attend to the spiritual life" and the daily practice of the rosary
of the Holy Name (H. Rahner 1960, 54–55). One of the Jesuits writing
to Ignatius described her as edifying the entire kingdom by her good
example in her leadership position. "Besides dedicating herself to

works of mercy and leading a secluded life in the privacy of her home, she dedicated herself with so much energy to the affairs of state that 'neither her age nor her sex seems to be a hindrance'" (de Dalmases 1991, 102–3). A great defender of the Society in controversies, she also supported the Roman College and others, and supported the reform of the Spanish convents (Meissner 1992, 250).

### Teresa Rejadell

Teresa Rejadell was a noblewoman who belonged to the convent of Santa Clara in Barcelona. Teresa probably first met Ignatius during his student days in Barcelona while he was still searching for persons with whom to share his zeal for God. They sustained their relationship through correspondence. Their letters back and forth echo their earlier conversations and provide a "classic example of Ignatius's basic spiritual teaching, for [their correspondence] is like a commentary on the book of the Spiritual Exercises" (H. Rahner 1960, 330). Jesuit scholar de Dalmases (1985, 90) also recognizes the significance of their correspondence when he describes Teresa as "…this fervent religious, rightly considered to be the best example of St. Ignatius's spiritual direction in the area of discernment of spirits." He recognized and confirmed her religious experience, her desire for God and to work for God's service: "Once more I confirm that you should chiefly dwell on God's love for you which is certain and think only of repaying him love for love" (H. Rahner 1960, 337). Ignatius's confirmation gave Teresa confidence in her experience and insights. The quality of empathy in these letters easily reveals the correspondence between Teresa's struggles, desires and doubts and Ignatius's own, particularly in the areas of prayer and discernment.

Unfortunately, the passionate desire of Teresa and this small group of nuns wanting a deeper spiritual and religious life repeatedly met obstacles. Eventually Ignatius decided to step back from any involvement in the ongoing direction of reform convents. Although Ignatius had earlier encouraged Teresa and her sisters in their desires, he declined when they wanted to place themselves under obedience to him and put these desires into concrete action. During the painful correspondence back and forth between Barcelona and Rome, the women indicated they had support from the Jesuit provincial of Spain, Father Aroz, and had acquired the property on which to build a convent and funding from supportive family and friends. But Ignatius was immovable; he resisted providing any practical assistance for this foundation. Perhaps he could only see the disadvantages. Today, in retrospect, we can imagine the alternative had Ignatius seen in Teresa the potential for their partnership in establishing a place for women to live his vision, even in the manner allowed at that time. Teresa Rejadell represents a moment of sadness, a failure for the fulfillment of the Ignatian vision, a loss for all.[8]

## Leonor de Mascarenhas

Leonor de Mascarenhas (1503–84) also expressed a desire to be a Jesuit. Her letter of February 1542 to Peter Faber states:

> I would with readiness choose the life of perfection, that is, follow you and Ignatius, if I were a man. But I am only a woman, a sinner making no progress in virtue, and so I may not join you in meditating and speaking about holy things, much less those that concern the Company of Ignatius. (H. Rahner 1960, 418–19)

This request culminates many years of contact with Ignatius and the Society.

Leonor was a noblewoman who served as the governess for the children of Charles V after their mother's death. She decided not to marry and lived a life of prayer and service to the poor. A close friend of Francis Borgia, she is called one of the most influential protectors of the Society. Ignatian scholar Tellechea Idígoras describes her as a "Portuguese Renaissance scholar and one of the most important ladies-in-waiting to Charles V's wife, the Empress Isabella and nurse to her newborn son Prince Philip" (1994, 299). Hugo Rahner refers to her as "the Mother of the Society of Jesus," for "she did all in her power to assist Ignatius in the founding of the Society of Jesus" (1960, 417).

### Sebastiana Exarch

Sebastiana Exarch, wife of a rich citizen of Valencia, wanted to make a vow of obedience to her confessor and thus, in her mind, be admitted to the Society. After making the Spiritual Exercises, her desire to give herself wholly to God led her to write this imploring letter to Ignatius:

> Therefore, prostrate before God and Your Reverence, with all the reverence and humility I can, I beg you to grant me this permission for my Father so that he may be able to receive this poor offering which I make to God from my unworthy soul. For the love of our Lord I ask you not to consider the wretchedness of my state in being a woman but rather the mercy the Lord has shown me in willing to place desires for him in a vessel so wretched and of so little worth as mine. Consider that as the Lord makes no exception of persons, so he leads all, both single and married, straight to him. I hope, then, in God, my Lord and Father, that a soul so much God's servant as is that of Your Reverence, will not refuse this charity to mine, in which the Lord has placed so great a desire of serving him. (H. Rahner 1960, 302)

Because Ignatius continued to be adamant in his refusal, women never received a permanent place in the structure of the Society. In

May 1547, Ignatius petitioned Pope Paul III "to free the Jesuits for all time from the spiritual direction of women who, living together as a community, wished to place themselves under the obedience of the priests of the Society of Jesus" (H. Rahner 1960, 290). Ignatius formulated his strong resistance to a women's branch of the Society on seeing the Franciscans and Dominicans "burdened and troubled by the constant complaints of their houses of nuns" (H. Rahner 1960, 308). "As far as we can judge in our Lord, what really matters is to keep the Society free to move unhampered in order to meet essential demands, and we must not tie ourselves down to unessential things. Moreover, we must, if we wish to progress along the way of the Lord, think first of ourselves and look after ourselves" (H. Rahner 1960, 308). This attitude appears in his letter to Isabel Roser releasing her from her vows: "…since according to my conscience, it is not fitting for this little Society to have special charge of women bound to us by vows of obedience" (H. Rahner 1960, 289).

## Implications for Today

Expanding the horizon of the Spiritual Exercises to include women's experience reveals the participation and influence of a company of women imbued with an Ignatian vision, lived out through the world of women and influencing the larger milieu. Women provided for Ignatius's material well-being, food, shelter and clothing, particularly during the critical time at Manresa. Women provided funds for Ignatius's theological education. Women attentive to his preaching of the Exercises allowed themselves to be formed by what they heard and thus deepened their prayer and service. Often this led them to activities not "suitable" for women at this time—missionary activities, radical convent reform, desire for equal membership in the new emerging society. The presence and participation of strong, intelligent and passionate women from various classes, nations and lifestyles, with names and identities, who influenced their culture through a variety of gifts appear throughout Ignatius's life. This network of women often knew one another and worked together in solidarity and service in Manresa, Barcelona, Alcalá and Rome. Women were transformed by the Spiritual Exercises and inspired to live beyond words into deeds of service. These women fed the hungry, gave drink to the thirsty, comforted the sorrowful, healed the sick, visited those in prison, sheltered the homeless and provided a safe haven for women and children fleeing violence and abuse. They shared personal and financial resources for the works of the church and society. They were faithful witnesses to the church in turbulent times. They comprehended the significance of personal spiritual conversion and renewal as preliminary to institutional reform. They were present to the preaching and practice of the Spiritual Exercises and, similar to the men drawn to the early Society, claimed spiritual equality culminating in apostolic zeal. Yet they were also constrained by a culture that limited women's potential, and at times they even internalized these limitations.

When we acknowledge the women influenced by Ignatius and his spiritual vision by walking in their shoes, listening to their voices, trying to capture at least a glimpse of their lives, hopes and struggles, we must confront history's most formidable challenge for the future: to welcome knowledge, insight and opportunity and to creatively adapt the Spiritual Exercises to include women's perspective.

Four significant conclusions for the present emerge from this reflection on the past. First, the history of the Spiritual Exercises reveals the world of women as a place of revelation, further enabling us to discover God in all things. God is at work, now as then, in towns and cities, where women live in their homes with their families, or in convents and churches. Likewise, conversations of women with spiritual directors or confessors about their concerns centered on husband and children, family property and finances, faith development, service with the poor and spiritual renewal become revelatory. Women carried on correspondence, searching for spiritual grounding amid the controversies in politics and church. Women desired more participation than allowed by culture, church and the Society of Jesus, deeply sensing a call to "more." Nonetheless, women's relationships with Ignatius and the early members of the Society vividly revealed the presence and power of God laboring in the worlds of women through their spiritual conversation and apostolic action.

A second conclusion follows from the first. Since God's revelation can occur in the gendered experiences of women, inclusive discernment becomes essential in the inevitable struggle to make choices that lead to spiritual freedom. A scan through history reveals the enormous formative influence of social structures and the barriers created among people and between classes, races, genders and religions. Such barriers create pockets of power and powerlessness, models of domination and subordination, situations of inclusion and exclusion that must be eradicated. No longer can women's desires and actions be ignored in any movement toward social transformation for the reign of God.

Third, class is inevitably intertwined with power, and power partially determines the degree to which the fruits of the Spiritual Exercises can be actualized in the world. Women of various classes participated in differing ways in the ministry of the Spiritual Exercises and early apostolates of the Jesuits. Class influenced the degree to which women participated in apostolic ministries, but it also influenced the mode of reception of certain texts and images of the Spiritual Exercises. Definite class assumptions occur in the imagery of the Exercises that addressed, perhaps unconsciously, upper-class women and men. For example, early in the Exercises Ignatius notes:

"I ought not to seek…wealth rather than poverty, honor rather than dishonor…" [23]. Obviously, one cannot be indifferent to such things unless one has access to riches and honor in the first place.

But while contemporary persons may be tempted to dismiss class distinctions as irrelevant, we still encounter ranking systems by ethnicity and race, education, professional expertise, gender and socioeconomic status—the new and hidden "class" structure. The contemporary challenge facing the Spiritual Exercises might be stated: Can the current practice of the Spiritual Exercises accommodate and even welcome diversity in these areas? The Spiritual Exercises continue to have the potential to reinforce the status quo or to liberate for new possibilities.

Finally, this remembering raises the need for right relationships for mission. The tendency to limit women's potential by consciously or unconsciously accepting the cultural stereotypes for women is clearly visible in Ignatius's dealing with women. Ignatius and often even the women themselves are caught in assumptions about women's subordinate status and role. Women in relationship with Ignatius constantly grappled with the impact of his message in the reality of their lives; it caused conflict, challenge, ambiguity, struggle, liberation, desire for God, conversion and suffering. How could women live out their spiritual vision, so identified with the context of their lives? The religious-cultural expectations restricting women to traditional roles in family and society prevented a free apostolic response to the Spiritual Exercises.

Yet historical data also provides examples of women helping Ignatius and Ignatius facilitating the gifts of women for the common mission where all contribute as equals respecting the diversity of gifts. Nonetheless, it remains a mystery of history why, out of this pool of talented women, exceptional in their gifts of mind and heart—Inéz Pascual the businesswoman and fund raiser, Isabel Roser the activist,

Isabel de Josa the philosopher, Vittoria Colonna the poet, Leonor de Mascarenhas the pastoral leader, Juana the politician, Teresa Rejadell the reformer and Juana de Cardona the missionary—no one emerged as a leader comparable to Ignatius. None developed a partnership with Ignatius paralleling other great apostolic partnerships such as Jeanne de Chantal and Francis de Sales, Louise de Marrillac and Vincent de Paul, Teresa of Avila and John of the Cross. The loss of the energy and resources of these women who shared the passion of Ignatius and possessed the gifts to actualize this vision must confront us and cause us to reconsider how to form right relationships for mission today.

What are the implications of the Spiritual Exercises for the mission of women today? Now, as then, women desire, receive and benefit from the Spiritual Exercises, and they expect greater freedom and responsibility to pursue their own spiritual and apostolic desires. Conversion and readiness of heart continue to characterize those inspired and empowered by the Spiritual Exercises. When responding to the graces of the Spiritual Exercises, neither the culture nor the Society nor even the church can contain where or to what the Spirit is calling women—and chances are it encompasses more than the current reality.

# Notes

1. Recent English-language biographies of Ignatius include de Dalmases (1985), Tellechea Idígoras (1994), Egan (1987), Meissner (1992) and H. Rahner (1968). See also James Broderick, *St. Ignatius Loyola: The Pilgrim Years* (London: Burns and Oates, 1956); Mary Purcell, *The First Jesuit: St. Ignatius Loyola* (Loyola University Press, 1981); and Philip Caraman, *Ignatius Loyola: A Biography of the Founder of the Jesuits* (San Francisco: Harper and Row, 1990). The historical novel by Louis De Wohl, *The Golden Thread* (New York: Lippincott, 1952) imaginatively captures the spirit of Ignatius and his times.

2. *St Ignatius Loyola: Letters to Women,* edited by Hugo Rahner, who collected, translated and wrote commentary throughout, provides a rich historical resource for knowledge about the women associated with Ignatius, their individual personalities and the events that drew them together. Not only do the letters contribute to a greater understanding of the role of women of sixteenth-century Europe, they also reveal more of the nuances of Ignatius's relationships with women and his corresponding concern for the mission of the Society. The commentary provides the context for the letters, but also reflects the bias of the author, who makes unquestioned assumptions that perpetuate stereotypes of women. Nevertheless, the book provides valuable information and insights into the world of women and Ignatius and the early Society.

3. Historian Joan Kelly suggests that women's experience of the Renaissance was not the liberating and humanizing event that their male counterparts experienced. Kelly examines the quality of women's historical experience during this time by comparing several aspects of life: the regulation of female sexuality with male sexuality; women's economic and political roles, such as the kind of work they performed as compared with men, and their access to and education for property and political power; the cultural roles of women in shaping the outlook of their society; and ideology about women in the sex-role system displayed or advocated in the symbolic products of the society. See Joan Kelly, "Did Women Have a Renaissance?" in *Women,*

*History and Theory* (Chicago: University of Chicago Press, 1984), 20. See also the following for further development of feminist historical theory: Gerda Lerner, *The Majority Finds Its Past: Placing Women in History* (New York: Oxford University Press, 1979); Berenice Carroll, ed. *Liberating Women's History: Theoretical and Critical Essays* (Urbana: University of Illinois Press, 1976); Joan Wallach Scott, *Gender and the Politics of History* (New York: Columbia University Press, 1988); Mary Margaret Fonow and Judith Cook, *Beyond Methodology: Feminist Scholarship as Lived Research* (Bloomington: Indiana University Press, 1991); and Joan Kelly, *Women, History and Theory: The Essays of Joan Kelly* (Chicago: University of Chicago Press, 1984).

4. Joan Segarra Pijuan, S.J., (1992) lists these "esteemed and respected" ladies of Manresa as Angela Sequi Amigant, Joana Ferrer, Jeronima Claver, Mrs. Canyelles, Catarina Molins (29). He further describes them as "married women who lived honorably with their husbands, and were very devout and charitable, admiring of holy persons and the poor and engaged in works of charity and mercy" (16). An additional group listed as followers of Ignatius and as "women who performed many exercises" included Brianda de Paguera, Eufrosina Roviralta, Agnes Claver, Agnes Vinyes, Jeronima Sala, Joana Dalmau, Agnes Roca and "others who were well known in the city" (149).

5. Tellechea Idígoras (1994, 253–57) devotes an enlightening chapter to Maria de la Flor. He describes her testimony for Ignatius's canonization with insight and compassion into a woman's spiritual journey of conversion; he does not stereotype her words as those of a prostitute.

6. Several authors develop this chronology and the details of the financial conflict that erupted among Isabel, her relatives and the Society. They also include the deliberations and decisions of the political and religious leaders concerning her case. See de Dalmases (1985, 253–55); Meissner (1992, 260–70); and Jean Lacouture, *The Jesuits: A Multibiography* (Washington, D.C.: Counterpoint, 1995, 150–54).

7. See Lisa Fullam, "Juana, S.J.: The Past (and Future?) Status of Women in the Society of Jesus," in *Studies in the Spirituality of Jesuits*. 31 (November 1999).

8. One cannot help but compare the experience of Teresa of Avila and the affirmation of her spirituality and vision received from Jesuits, particularly Francis Borgia. What if Teresa Rejadell had the same level of support from Ignatius and his influential friends as Teresa of Avila for her reform and spiritual renewal?

# PART II:

# Movement

# Chapter 3

# Coming Together in Love: Processes and Relationships

*The one giving the Exercises should not urge the one receiving them toward poverty or any other promise more than toward their opposites, or to one state or way of life more than to another.... [D]uring these Spiritual Exercises when a person is seeking God's will, it is more appropriate and far better that the Creator and Lord himself should communicate himself to the devout soul, embracing it with love, inciting it to praise of himself, and disposing it for the way which will most enable the soul to serve him in the future. Accordingly, the one giving the Exercises ought not to lean or incline in either direction but rather, while standing by like the pointer of a scale in equilibrium, to allow the Creator to deal immediately with the creature and the creature with its Creator and Lord.*

—Spiritual Exercises [15]

*My retreat this year was so interesting, and I use that waffle-word deliberately. I went to [center with long experience in directed retreats] because retreat is such an important time to deepen my relationship with God, to give it full attention. The grounds were lovely, the meals superb, the liturgies actually helpful. But meeting with my director was very strange. It's like he never heard me. I'd describe my prayer, he'd latch onto a word, and treat it as if it were a code word for some universal experience. In would go the word and out would come the suggestion for prayer. Just in case there was something there for me, I'd dutifully begin my next day's prayer at that point, but soon be off to where my own experience took me. God was surely there in the retreat—I have no doubt about that—but I've always wondered what would have happened if the director had really listened to me and what was going on in my retreat. The whole experience was just a bit surreal.*

—A Contemporary Woman

Important aspects of the Spiritual Exercises take place prior to the first meeting of the companion and guide. The guide has already internalized the dynamic of the Spiritual Exercises at a deeply personal level and has listened carefully to the seeker, discerning the degree to which she manifests the gifts of character, generosity and readiness to embark on the Spiritual Exercises. The guide has also checked the external realities of setting, time and context, recognizing that the final experience will be both freed and limited by these realities. Against this backdrop, specific suggestions aid the movement of the Exercises.

## Annotations and Directions

The *Spiritual Exercises* is actually a book of directions, which Ignatius wrote for the guide rather than for the one making the Exercises. His recommendations occur in their most focused form in the first twenty points of the text, often called the preliminary annotations, and then periodically throughout the text of the *Spiritual Exercises*.[1] This material affects every aspect of the Spiritual Exercises. Thus, they truly begin at this level.

This chapter addresses virtually all the process notes internal to the *Spiritual Exercises,* treating them in several groups: overview and general notations, characteristics of the one making the Exercises, characteristics of the one who accompanies and the role of the body in the Spiritual Exercises.

## General Notations

Imagine trying to put down on paper the essential guidelines that will enable others to lead a retreat dynamic you yourself discovered through experience. Although no easy task, this is precisely Ignatius's challenge in composing the *Spiritual Exercises*.

He begins his text with some general considerations. Spiritual exercises, Ignatius observes, consist of any activities, including prayer, that assist in ordering one's life around God's priorities. Gradually one moves with greater and greater consistency and integrity toward the fulfillment of life, letting go of any obstacles to one's wholehearted response to God [1]. In its entirety, the Spiritual Exercises is an intense experience of discipleship and God's service in ever deeper spiritual freedom. Ignatius's suggestions for the exercises do not exhaust the possibilities. Both the seeker and the guide remain free to search for the spiritual exercises that best facilitate movement toward God, adapting to the pace and needs of each individual seeker [4].

### Ignatius's Specialized Terminology

Ignatius uses terms in the introductory notes that he does not carefully define, including "motions," "affections," "disordered affections" and "desires." This technical language merits some discussion.

The term "motions" refers to interior experiences such as thoughts, reasonings, choices, moods, urges—any change in a person's inner climate (Ganss 1991, 338, n. 4). The stimulus for this movement may be exterior, for example, one may be moved to tears by a film. Or they may be interior, as when one is moved to tears by the memory of her mother's dying. Ignatius finds both inner and outer stimuli significant. For this reason he directs the one making the Exercises to reason, remember and imagine, but also to arrange the external environment so that it reflects the grace being sought [78–81, 213, 217, 229, etc.]. Ideally, both exterior and interior stimuli come together to foster a rich, internalized, direct, dynamic and personal relationship with God.

Movement is the stuff of the Exercises; it indicates direction, marks progression or regression and reveals true preferences. Since the Spiritual Exercises aim to promote movement, Ignatius encourages the guide to examine the experience and quality of the individual's participation [6] if it is absent. Movement, in fact, forms the primary matter for discernment.

Consistent with the anthropology of his time, Ignatius believed that interior movements are caused by personal beings. They may result from one's own activity, from God's action either directly or through an intermediary, or from malevolent beings intent on deflecting or destroying one's Godward direction. Interestingly, the phenomenon of interior movements and Ignatius's wisdom about how to notice and discriminate among them transcends his anthropology. A contemporary perspective that locates the origin of many interior movements in the dynamic unconscious, for example, can still employ the wisdom Ignatius discovered, though it will obviously sacrifice his theological interpretation. Ignatius's wisdom about discernment transcends his time and place and can be employed by those of widely differing perspectives.

The term "affections" also begs explication. "Feelings," or the subjective sensations in response to internal or external stimuli, and "affections" are often used interchangeably. Here "affections" will function as a more inclusive term. Affections include, beside subjective sensations arising from stimuli, reflecting about these sensations and choosing to follow some but not others. Affections indicate the direction of one's heart in a way that feelings, as subjective response to stimuli, cannot. Affections both move one and result from movement, which explains why Ignatius says affections lead to greater reverence than merely thinking [3].

Affections can be in harmony or disharmony with one's personal integrity. "Disordered affections" conflict with one's deepest humanity, unfolding spirituality and growth in spiritual freedom. Ignatius uses the term to designate a tendency or attachment lying outside the scope of the Principle and Foundation [23], the "plumb line" anchoring the Spiritual Exercises (Ganss 1991, 388, n. 2).

The term "desire" surfaces in the preliminary notes [for example, 5, 16, 20, 89] and reappears with refrainlike regularity throughout the Exercises: "…ask for what you desire; here it will be…." What does Ignatius understand by desire? Why is it so important to the dynamic of the Exercises?

Desire stands at the heart of the person, the source of all one's striving (McGrath 1993, 27). It refers to an interior movement toward what one perceives as good. A superficial reading of the text suggests that the one making the Exercises controls his or her own desires; however, a closer reading reveals that Ignatius clearly understands that God both implants our Godward desires and brings them to completion [5, 15, 16, 20].

As many have noted, the Holy Spirit rarely appears in the Spiritual Exercises. Perhaps Ignatius simply mirrored the general paucity of systematic treatments of pneumatology in his time (Dreyer 1996, 49, 88). But perhaps desires express the role of the Holy Spirit in the Exercises.[2] That the Holy Spirit works directly through desires was not a novel teaching, even in Ignatius's day.[3] One cannot even *desire* God, or any good, without the Holy Spirit first igniting that desire. The Holy Spirit reveals the true condition of the heart by allowing one to see desires for what they really are and what they really move one toward. If desires do express the role of the Holy Spirit in the Spiritual Exercises, the centrality of desire within the Spiritual Exercises is then rooted directly in a trinitarian spirituality.

### Those Who Will Profit from the Exercises

According to Ignatius, a particular disposition should characterize the one who embarks on the Spiritual Exercises, namely, a spirit of generosity and self-donation [5]. Ignatius willingly spent considerable time and effort developing this disposition in persons he was preparing for the complete Spiritual Exercises, especially when he sensed that they had great potential for influencing the renewal of the church (Clancy 1978).[4]

Who will profit from the Exercises also has to do with other internal developmental criteria and external circumstances. Additional Directives eighteen through twenty address these various circumstances. Ignatius clearly believed that some persons were not suitable candidates for the fullest form of the Exercises as described in the twentieth Annotation. His general principle—that the Exercises must be adapted to each person's circumstances—led him to judge carefully the seeker's ability to bear the exercises and profit from them without fatigue. When he found the necessary developmental prerequisites for the fullest form of the Exercises lacking, Ignatius offered an adaptation suited to their present desires, circumstances and abilities.[5] Ignatius constantly encouraged a shorter, foundational form for the vast majority of persons as more suitable to their present spiritual condition and abilities. For those whose circumstances prevented them from withdrawing from daily life for the entire thirty days, Ignatius suggests spreading the Exercises over some months, and provides in the nineteenth Annotation one example of how to do this.[6] Many women today encounter the Spiritual Exercises in this form.

Ignatius's insistence on adapting the Exercises to the person receiving them reveals a positive pedagogical principle as useful now as then: Give those making the Exercises as much as they are willing to receive or as much as their circumstances will allow; give them, likewise, whatever will provide them greater help and progress.

The third criterion for determining who should make the Exercises is pastorally pragmatic. As the fruit of the Spiritual Exercises became evident, Ignatius received numerous requests to lead others in the Exercises or to send one of the Company to do so. Such requests poured in from the monied, titled, the politically influential and those interested in church and convent reform so crucial at the time. He had to set priorities in this evangelical explosion. His solution: Offer the intensive labor of companioning the full Exercises to those who will achieve greater results as "time is insufficient to do everything [18]." This pragmatic turn has led some to charge that the Spiritual Exercises are elitist.

## The One Making the Exercises

The most developed treatment in Ignatius's introductory notes addresses the dispositions and actions of the one making the Exercises. She should relish a few points deeply rather than try to cover many points [2], enter the Exercises with a spirit of generosity [5], work diligently at the exercise at hand rather than desiring to know the exercises farther along the process [11, 127], spend a full hour on each of the exercises [12], work actively against any temptation to cut short difficult or apparently unprofitable exercises [13], strive to develop the virtue opposing any disordered affection [16] and share the various movements during the Exercises with the one giving them [17]. As the

Exercises progress, she should focus her whole day, not just the times explicitly set aside for formal prayer, on her purpose [74]. She should use her whole body in prayer [75–76], arrange her exterior environment to match the feeling tone of the exercise [78–79, 130, 229], and bring her whole demeanor into harmony with the tenor of the exercise in which she is engaged [80, 81, 82–87, 89, 210–17]. She should use penances to dispose her to receive the graces she desires [82–87, 130, 229]. Whatever reading she might do should enrich her contemplation [100]. These dispositions and characteristics, which encourage considerable self-assertion and autonomy, are good news for the many women making the full Spiritual Exercises today.

## The One Giving the Exercises

The third cluster of material in the preliminary notes centers around the qualities, attitudes and actions of the one giving the Exercises. Ignatius presumes that the person entrusted with giving the Exercises should himself or herself have made the Exercises. Once that experiential foundation has been established, he expects the guide to adapt the length of the Weeks, the length and placement of prayer, the particular exercises given and the amount and kind of penance suggested to fit the needs of the one receiving the Exercises [4, 8–9, 18, as well as 72, 89 and others].

The one guiding the Exercises must have an extraordinary self-knowledge and the self-discipline to refrain from inserting himself or herself into the relationship between God and the one making the Exercises. Such insertions may be quite subtle or even unconscious: telling the one making the Exercises more than her current experience indicates is necessary [8, 10], preaching or lecturing at length about the subjects for the seeker's prayer [2] and expressing undue curiosity about the seeker's thoughts or sins [17].

Ignatius also urges the giver of the Exercises to act with either gentleness or assertiveness according to the needs of the seeker [7], to adapt the dynamics of the Exercises according to the needs of each one [4, 6, 8, 9, 10, 18–20] and to refrain from any overt or covert persuasion toward particular vocational choices on the part of the seeker, even if the object of choice is desirable in itself [14, 15]. For Ignatius, the guide occupies a crucial role in the dynamic, but a role always in service and subject to the relationship between God and the seeker and to the needs of the seeker in fostering this relationship.

## Mutuality and Generosity between Seeker and Companion

Following the explanatory notes and just prior to the beginning of the Spiritual Exercises themselves, Ignatius speaks of how the guide and seeker—indeed "every good Christian"—should relate:

> ...it should be presupposed that every good Christian ought to be more eager to put a good interpretation on a neighbor's statement than to condemn it. Further, if one cannot interpret it favorably, one should ask how the other means it. If that meaning is wrong, one should correct the person with love; and if this is not enough, one should search out every appropriate means through which, by understanding the statement in a good way, it may be saved. [22]

The mutuality of this admonition is striking. Ignatius asks of each party this respect and willingness to put as generous an interpretation on another's words as possible, and, if necessary, to expend considerable energy searching out possible mutually acceptable positions. This admonition does not apply more strongly to the one making the Exercises, nor is the assumption of correctness limited to the one giving the Exercises.

Contemporary feminist epistemology corroborates Ignatius's insight by recognizing the relativity of all knowledge. It therefore implies that there may be multiple valid interpretations depending upon the unique and varied horizons of the interpreters (Farganis 1986, 30). Thus all parties in the discussion need to "search out every appropriate means through which, by understanding the statement in a good way, it may be saved." Even similarly situated women will not necessarily hold the same views.

Ignatius's presupposition will have particular relevance for those who accompany women in the Spiritual Exercises. These companions, especially if they are male, need to convey implicitly and explicitly their willingness both to learn from and be corrected by these women. The primary interpreters of the Spiritual Exercises, then, are those persons in the midst of them. This experience forms the basis for any generalizations about women's experience of the Spiritual Exercises. Furthermore, this presupposition calls into question any notion of an elite director and a subservient directee.[7]

Ignatius's presupposition asks, then, for a deep and sincere attempt to struggle with both sides of a question. At times this will mean entertaining uncomfortable perspectives, but at other times, it will call for reliance on another's generosity to hear out our cherished point of view.

This presupposition taken to its logical extreme, however, seems to legitimate the conclusion that all interpretations are equally good and that, finally, one has no way to judge between them—a position Ignatius definitely did not hold. He insisted on two "external" criteria with which to adjudicate truth claims: the orthodoxy of the position as determined by the hierarchical church and "the greater glory of God." Each of these norms causes some problem for contemporary persons, who tend to have more suspicions about orthodoxy as a basis for assessing the truth of an assertion than Ignatius did. Contemporary persons believe that orthodoxy is itself inescapably a social construction bound by the same constraints as other shared social realities. The uncovering of discriminatory treatment women have received at the hands of the hierarchical church only heightens suspicion.

The "greater glory of God" as a criterion presupposes that one knows what the greater glory of God might be, and therein lies the difficulty. The possibility of arriving at a consensus about God's desires in any fine detail is not self-evident to contemporary persons. Whatever violates or diminishes human beings also diminishes God's glory (Johnson 1992, 14). That, at least, can be said.

Ignatius also proposed a process for assessing the validity of certain choices, enshrined in the *Spiritual Exercises* as the Election and as the Rules for Discernment of Spirits. They provide women with powerful tools for assessing their inner data respecting the decisions facing them.

## The Role of the Body

Contrary to the frequent perception of the Spiritual Exercises as overly heady and superrational, they actually contain many encouragements toward an embodied spirituality. Because of the important implications for women, this discussion includes not only the Annotations and Directives but other body references within the Exercises. Some references are overt, as when Ignatius suggests bodily preparation before entering into each spiritual exercise [75, 239, 244, 246], during it [76] and upon its conclusion [77]; or when he discusses how physical arrangements form an important backdrop to the Exercises and should be focused toward the particular mysteries the seeker is engaging [79, 130, 229]; or indicates that the timing, frequency and intensity of individual exercises be adjusted to the age, physical condition and disposition of each person making the Exercises [72, 129, 205].

Encouragements toward embodied spirituality also occur indirectly, but they are nonetheless significant in their subtlety. For example, Ignatius directs the guide to observe whether the seeker experiences any interior motions, and, if not, to investigate how the seeker enters into the exercise, including the way the body is used [6]. He expects that adding or changing the embodied expressions of a spiritual exercise will prompt deeper engagement and, conversely, that disembodied prayer may prevent or hinder engagement with the mystery. He urges the seeker to enter into various exercises with the whole self, understood as a composite of body and soul [47]. Finally, Ignatius suggests forms of prayer grounded in embodiment, a topic treated in the following chapter.

Clearly, Ignatius thinks of the body as an important part of any spiritual exercise. Its use is to be governed by a "right mean" [84, 213], that is, the body becomes a rightfully proportioned facet of the whole person. He develops this latter point extensively in the additional Directives dealing with penances [82–90] and in the Rules for Taking Food [210–17]. In sum, positive aspects of Ignatius's treatment of embodiment harmonize with the Principle and Foundation, which encourages the use and enjoyment of any aspect of creation insofar as it assists one's divine vocation. Such relationship to creatures, including the body, is "ordered" in Ignatian terminology.[8]

Yet Ignatius's treatment of the body evokes ambiguity today. For example, in the First Week, he asks the seeker to contemplate her soul imprisoned in her corruptible body [47] and the corruption and foulness of her body [58].[9] Such suggestions, when used today, seem to objectify the body, splitting it off from other aspects of personality. Contemporary seekers find the objectification untenable. Such images, even when contextualized within the overall direction of the particular exercise and understood as a product of Ignatius's time, must today be reappropriated within a more unified conception of the human subject. Ignatius's positive sense of the body emerges when he assumes that the seeker is an embodied and unified subject.

Ignatius intended his treatment of penance [82–90] to reinforce a balanced relationship to one's body, but it too appears ambiguous to many contemporary persons. To the extent that penance is perceived or actually interpreted as yet another form of hating the body, it reinforces the worst in women's relationship to their bodies. By closely examining what Ignatius does say, one can explore the possibility of reclaiming this aspect of the Exercises for contemporary women.

He begins by distinguishing between "interior" penance, the fruit of the grace of God acting within to bring forth contrition and sorrow for sins, and "exterior" penance, self-inflicted responses to our sinful condition. Ignatius assumes that exterior penance is the *effect* of interior penance and not the other way around. In other words, without God first acting to bring one to a new freedom, one's self-chosen actions are as liable to reinforce an inordinate attachment as to liberate. Without recognizing this priority of God's freeing grace, a point so easily unnoticed, one misinterprets Ignatius's comments on penance.

Ignatius next devotes two points to distinguishing between temperance and penance, with temperance being the moderate use of eating and sleeping, and penance being the deprivation of even that which is deemed essential. Interestingly, what Ignatius calls "temperance" in bodily matters has been elevated to such importance today that it can actually border on a new intemperance. In pursuit of the healthy lifestyle some will go to inordinate lengths to achieve a toned body, buy and prepare food devoid of pesticides and additives, protect their skin and take preventive health measures of all kinds. Simultaneously, they avoid "penance" as Ignatius defines it at all costs. A toned and healthy body is a "good"; even so, one can become addicted to a "good." This example highlights the need to discern an appropriate asceticism for today.

Ignatius divides exterior penance into three kinds: eating, sleeping and chastising the body—with the last [85] being the one contemporary persons most resoundingly reject. Ignatius is actually more moderate here than might be expected in his culture. He permits rather than promotes penance, and for a specific reason: to help persons find the right mean with their own bodies [84]. He sets clear parameters about the limits of penance. Finally, Ignatius suggests three reasons for doing penance: to satisfy for sins, to obtain a new kind of freedom that includes the body with the spirit, and to obtain a particular grace. Notice that all the examples that he lists are graces of inner conversion and freedom.

## Problems and Possibilities for Women

The preliminary Annotations and Directives sprinkled throughout the text of the *Spiritual Exercises* offer a vision of relationship, a whole way of being that undergirds the culture of the Spiritual Exercises.[10] They set forth a rich variety of material significant to women, both negatively and positively. Seven aspects of the material emerge as significant: the potential elitism of the Exercises, overrigid or overliteral application of the text, and issues around gender arrangements, embodiment, penance and desire. When these issues are understood in a context of right relationship, the positive potential of the Exercises for contemporary women emerges.

### Are the Exercises Elitist?

Many experience the Spiritual Exercises as thoroughly elitist. This charge arises from a perceived preference for men over women and for educated, leisured and monied classes over common persons, for those who can withdraw for an enclosed experience of the Spiritual Exercises over those who must continue to carry on their ordinary life in the world, and for "professional religious" over laypersons.

While Ignatius and the first members of the Company did give the Spiritual Exercises to women in all the forms sketched out in Annotations eighteen, nineteen and twenty (O'Malley 1993: 75, 132–33), access to the Exercises increasingly favored men over women. While a wide variety of men, women and children drawn from all classes experienced some form of the Exercises through the preaching and catechesis of the early Companions, propriety around gender arrangements eventually resulted in increasingly stricter separation between the Jesuits giving the Exercises and the women desiring to receive them. Author John O'Malley (1993, 129) tellingly observes that women made up the only group of persons whose participation in the Exercises decreased after Ignatius's lifetime.

One of the characteristics of contemporary spiritual culture, however, is its feminization. Anecdotal evidence suggests that far more women than men seriously explore their relationship with God, engage in retreats or approach a serious vocational choice through discernment. Anecdotal evidence also indicates that currently more women than men make the Spiritual Exercises[11] and that increasing numbers of women give the Exercises to both women and men.

What implications will this have for the Spiritual Exercises? Surely, the culture of the Exercises will become increasingly influenced by the presence of women as both receivers and givers of the Exercises. Ways of relating and of ordering the environment and schedule, ways of praying and the range of symbols and images evoked will become more compatible to women. As the number of women involved in the Spiritual Exercises increases, men will have to choose the Exercises within this gendered context. It remains to be seen if men will abdicate the Exercises to women, as so frequently happens when women become present in higher ratios.

But what about the charges of elitism centering around privilege, money, leisure and education as doorways to the Exercises? These issues continue to plague contemporary persons as they did persons of Ignatius's time. It takes considerable money to free oneself and to compensate a director for thirty days. Unless they belong to religious congregations that offer or require the Spiritual Exercises, women's lives scarcely ever allow such disengagement. The nineteenth Annotation may well emerge as the premier form of the Spiritual Exercises simply because it allows access by a greater number of persons.

Two questions underlie the issue of elitism in its various forms: What are the "real" Exercises, and what are the second-best or "watered down" Exercises? We maintain that Ignatius considered all forms of the Exercises "real" Exercises and challenge a bias that favors first the twentieth Annotation form, then the nineteenth and only grudgingly includes the eighteenth Annotation form as legitimate expressions of the Exercises. The appropriate form of the Exercises is the one possible for and desired by the seeker and tested by its fruits.[12]

## Overliteral Experience of Ignatius's Text

The second problem area centers around the danger of overrigid or overliteral application of Ignatius's directives. Should the one making the Exercises *always* remain for a full hour in each of the prescribed Exercises [15]? *Ought* women look at the corruption and foulness of their bodies, and upon themselves as a sore or abscess from which has issued great sins [58]? Should one *always* act against a temptation; might not a less direct approach sometimes lessen the power of a compulsion? That most women find such images less than helpful and that more helpful symbols should replace them raises little controversy within the community of practitioners.

More significantly, should the one giving the Exercises follow Ignatius's text precisely, or should he or she introduce the dynamic of the Exercises by moving freely from within the seeker's needs, images, language and desires? Working with this tension requires adapting to the seeker's needs and experience, as well as the way God works with the person. The Exercises should never be imposed upon the seeker (Gray 1993, 75–77); if the dynamic of the Exercises somehow does violence to the one making the Exercises, it must be sacrificed to the needs of the seeker's relationship with God. At the same time, inviting an individual seeker to try new forms of prayer, bodily postures, arrangements for eating or ascetical practices invites her to find her own "right mean" [84, 213]. All external aspects of the Exercises, that is, all the dynamics suggested by another and therefore coming from "without," exist in a delicate relationship with internal call and relationship with God.

The one facilitating the Exercises has the primary responsibility for adapting them. This person assumes the responsibility to reverence the culture of the Exercises from deep personal experience and love, to reverence the reality of the one desiring to make the Exercises and to bring these two "cultures" together in a way that respects both. The rest of the task basically requires that they stay out of the way of the direct relationship between God and the seeker.

## Gendered Communications

The third problem area clusters around gendered communications and arrangements between the guide and the seeker. The hierarchical arrangement of power connoted in the long-standing language of director-directee symbolizes these relationships, especially when the one giving the Exercises is a man and the one making them is a woman. A male director may unconsciously express his expert status, and a female directee just as unconsciously receive his expert advice. Women may more easily abdicate their personal autonomy in spiritual matters and succumb to overdependence on a guru, especially if male and even more so if a cleric. All these forms of hierarchical power must yield to a new and deeper understanding of the integrity, autonomy and subjectivity of the seeker. Coming to this stance may require radical conversion in worldview, attitude and actions in both the giver and maker of the Exercises.

Even the arrangement that one person "gives" the Exercises and one person "receives" them, Ignatius's language, suggests an imbalance of expertise. This imbalance must be understood as strictly functional and temporary. Just as God, the only "director" of the Exercises, accommodates to the needs of humankind and individual seekers, so too the guide accommodates the seeker's needs. When the guide cannot fulfill this commitment, he or she must withdraw from the role.

The role of gender in communication also raises the issue of matching guides and seekers. How does one handle the situation where one party adamantly insists on working with a person of a given sex? Persons may express such strong sentiments—for or against—that they refuse to consider the alternative. Whether such rigid gender preferences stem from unconscious resistance or from consciously chosen ideology, a predetermined decision about the gender mix can foreclose surprising graces. In line with the presupposition [22] that both parties presume a generous interpretation of the words and motives of the other, we propose an openness in principle to working with a person of either sex, discerning in each circumstance if the guide and seeker are helpfully matched.

## Embodiment in the Exercises

Ignatius encourages the use of the body in the Spiritual Exercises in several ways. This support is helpful to women, who tend to have negative issues about body. Thus, ironically, women may find authentic embodiment as difficult as men, though women's path to integration may differ significantly from men's. Studies show that a surprisingly high percentage of women hate or feel dissatisfaction with some aspect of their bodies. Dieting has now become endemic in preteen girls, for example, and eating disorders have reached epidemic proportions among North American women. The cultural overvaluation of youth leads women to expend inordinate time and expense delaying or covering over the natural effects of aging on their bodies. Since images of body subtly but profoundly influence self-perception, this body loathing negatively impacts women's health. Clearly, in this area all is not well for women.

The body comprises a primary locus of differentiation; one's body makes one always and irretrievably oneself. The surrounding world, be it nature, interpersonal relationships or culture, is mediated through this body and no other. The store of data to which memory returns, which imagination recombines and creates and which intellect ponders all comes to oneself through this body. The body stores and remembers every experience. In the body-self each person is, therefore, totally unique. And God loves and personally relates to this unrepeatable body-self. Therefore body becomes, in a very real sense, a sacrament of God. From this perspective, embodiment becomes a precious gift, never to be numbed, squandered or denigrated. Instead, embodiment is to be relished, honored, enjoyed and celebrated for its wisdom and revelation.

As the silence around gender arrangements breaks down, the pervasive reality of the physical and sexual abuse of women, children and dependent adults appears in all its ugliness. Women who have suffered these forms of abuse will need particularly sensitive accompaniment to experience their embodied selves as loved by God and as a healed, positive, sacramental aspect of their persons. Here the gender of the one giving the Exercises may prove crucial, and women's desires in this regard must be honored scrupulously. Women who have survived abuse may react strongly to aspects of the Exercises, including the centrality of Christ; the relationship to church as hierarchical and clerical, issues of sin, guilt and penance in the First Week, and even to God, whose "laboring for me" did not protect her from such deep wounding. Issues of the physical arrangement of space, inclusive language and touch will, at minimum, need careful attention—and may sometimes require delicate negotiation—to establish a climate of trust and healing. But at a far more significant level, the one who gives the Exercises must offer a safe space for the appearance of *any* feeling at *any time* the woman decides to share it. Any unconscious censorship from the one who gives the Exercises can profoundly derail the work of God with the seeker in this area.[13]

Sexuality makes up an intrinsic aspect of embodiment and is thus inherent in all human responses. Understood as the gendered response of the human being moving toward generativity, sexuality includes but extends far beyond genital activity. Because of its centrality to personhood, issues of sexuality often emerge within the context of the Spiritual Exercises, indeed the absence of any allusions to sexuality might profitably be noted. An individual woman may need to reclaim her sexuality as a gift from God. Another may need to experience healing from using her sexuality to manipulate others, another from denying her sexuality. Yet another may need to move toward a new freedom in relating to one or other sex.

Issues of sexuality also hold importance for the one giving the Exercises. His or her sexual integration comprises perhaps the single most significant factor in establishing right relationship between the guide and the companion and in preventing sexual acting out in the relationship. Furthermore, the one giving the Exercises must exercise caution about sexual stereotypes and avoid value judgments about diverse lifestyles. In short, the giver of the Exercises provides the safe relational space that will enable the seeker to bring such sensitive material before God.

The body is too significant a facet of the human person to denigrate it, ignore it or allow it to "rule the roost" like a spoiled child. Denigrating the body has been the legacy of too much of the spirituality inherited from the past. Ignoring or numbing the body—through illness, trauma or simply through internalizing the skewed understanding of body endemic in contemporary culture—is the legacy of the body's betrayal. Indulging the body remains perhaps the particular problem of the affluent, who not only have everything their bodies need, but far in excess of what is necessary. Ignatius's comments on penance, as strange as they may sound to contemporary ears, have relevance here.

## Penances and Contemporary Women

Ignatius's treatment of penance has a focused and limited purpose. He simply sets out a series of practices that aim to help the individual become at home in her body. He wants it to receive neither too little nor too much attention, so that the body may become part of the ordered response of the whole person within the structure of the Exercises and beyond.[14] Because the issue of penance is difficult for the entire culture, not only for many women, this topic merits a somewhat more extended treatment.

Author Kathleen Norris (1993, 23) helps contemporary women begin to reconstruct penance. Asceticism, she notes, can offer a radical way of knowing exactly who one is in the face of the powerful societal forces that aim to make us forget. The antidotes she suggests include awareness, intentionality and moderation. An evening without television can become an invitation to nourish the inner world through a novel or poetry; an understanding of the body's use of antigens can remind us to diversify our foods naturally before the body must do so through allergic reactions. The possibilities are endless, the freedom welcome.

Historian Margaret Miles (1981, 149–54) provides a context in which to place a contemporary asceticism. She begins where Ignatius did—with the approach that changes in the condition of the body can open the soul to greater insight. This belief also makes sense within an anthropology that understands that body and soul together comprise one person. Today's seeker, just as in Ignatius's time, often comes to the Spiritual Exercises inattentive to habits of food, sleep and practical daily concerns. Various exercises and directives, including penances, help focus attention on these aspects of self and facilitate a reintegration marked by conscious awareness and a more productive synthesis in service of others. The discernment question follows: To what am I attached and therefore unconsciously substitute for the source of life?

Three more points complement a contemporary approach to penances (Miles 1981, 160). First, an asceticism for today must consist of practices as fully good for the body as for the soul. The body is an essential element of our humanness and must be cared for and honored *as spiritual practice*. Second, ascetic practices must be temporary and individually designed to locate and correct a particular debilitating addiction. They must confront those aspects of contemporary life that destroy both body and soul. Third, some ascetic practices remain perennially useful because they address essential human needs. Fasts, not only from food, but also from frantic activity, stimulants, deadening amusements, superfluous possessions and dominating others can have a deeply liberating effect. Disciplines of prayer, silence and solitude address the contemporary situation just as surely as in earlier times.

Ignatius himself provides a last point. Paying close attention to his insight about inner conversion leading to outer asceticism can help keep penances in their rightful place as useful means to a significant goal: assuming one's rightful freedom as called, graced and missioned.

Ignatius's treatment of penance centers on the individual person. Expanding his perspective to include cultural and social systems and the natural environment within which each individual dwells as an interdependent member uncovers new possibilities for reclaiming asceticism. For example, the rising and falling prices of produce at the grocers can become an invitation to bioregional food consumption, that is, eating only those seasonal fruits and vegetables produced locally. Such a practice discourages devastating cash crop economies in developing countries and saves the expensive fossil fuels involved in transporting perishables huge distances to affluent markets. One's body, its needs and how one satisfies them become, quite literally, an embodiment of one's place in the community of creatures.

At their deepest, then, the Spiritual Exercises invite women to use every aspect of their embodied selves to foster their openness to God. This embodiment is not simply offered for the duration of the Exercises, but as habitual practice.[15] As they come to love, comfort and responsibly use their bodies, women will take immense steps toward becoming most deeply their unique body-selves. Any subsequent action on behalf of others will flow from this unified, healed, transformed self.

## Desires and Contemporary Women

Finally, what implications does the treatment of desires in the Spiritual Exercises have for women?

Desires can be freighted with meaning for women. Women may often feel that paying attention to their desires is somehow selfish and that they should not honor their desires if they are being truly generous with God. Or they may experience a pervasive hopelessness with respect to their own desires: "I can't have it anyhow, so what is the purpose in saying what I desire?" Or, they may well be able to articulate their desires but may be unsure about trusting them at all or distinguishing which they can safely trust to lead them toward God. In these situations, it would not serve women well to dictate to them—or have Ignatius dictate to them—what they should desire. This procedure, while faithful to the text of the *Exercises,* would distance women from their own sense of themselves as expressed through their desires. The primary goal here remains helping each woman get in touch with her desires and feel free to place them before God without first having to compare them with those Ignatius suggests. Only after women have noticed and named these desires can they be discerned in dialogue with the desires Ignatius names. The woman who resists paying attention to her desires may require some encouragement to ask for what she desires, albeit tentatively, by understanding that the Holy Spirit works precisely through her desiring.

Relationship provides the interpretive frame. Desires initiate relationship because they move one toward that which is desired. Ignatius certainly understood that the heart is often "plagued by a plurality of desires," as author Thomas McGrath (1993, 30) puts it, but for Ignatius the issue centers around the most fundamental and appropriate desire, which in turn orients other desires. Assuming, as

Ignatius did, that desires indicate the state of our heart and that all desires are not benign and growthful, how might one discern desires?

Once women have the ability to notice, name and own their desires, they can begin to look at the fruit of their desires. "Is what I desire an object to be possessed or a subject with which to be in communion?" The desiring "feels different" in each case. "Do my desires close me in on myself or open me out to others?" These questions pointedly raise issues of "selfishness" and appropriate care of self. "Do my desires activate my deep generosity toward all God might reveal?" This last question can serve as a principle with which to "test" desires. Desires may activate an anxious striving or nonproductive self-castigation. Or they could issue in a peaceful sense that one cannot move oneself toward God, but that God can and does hold oneself lovingly no matter what. These very different outcomes suggest different responses, yet all of them illustrate the significance of desires as an aspect of women's personhood.

What if a woman's desire at a point in the Exercises doesn't match Ignatius's? The woman can go with her own desire and see where it leads her, or she might "try on" Ignatius's suggestion and see where that takes her. What happens interiorly in each case? Perhaps each avenue might be appropriate at various times, or even within various repetitions on the same exercise.

## Wisdom for the One Giving the Exercises

Exploring the processes and relationships within the Spiritual Exercises, highlights the person and preparation of the guide. As women swell the ranks of those guiding the Exercises, what preparation is considered ideal for this ministry?

Certain basic knowledge characterizes these competent spiritual guides. They know Scripture. They need not be professional biblical scholars, but they do need the facility to adapt the biblical material in the Spiritual Exercises appropriately: simultaneously faithful to the Scriptures, to the dynamic of the Spiritual Exercises and to those they guide. They also need to know the large themes of Ignatian spirituality so that they can faithfully adapt the Spiritual Exercises to the time and place and the present circumstances of those making the Exercises today. In addition, they have a basic grasp of contemporary theology and contemporary psychology, two disciplines that explore the inner life of human beings and their relationship to God.

Psychologically, spiritual guides serve as important affective mentors for those they accompany. The more they themselves live a rich affective life, the more readily they will help those they accompany to develop their own affectivity in their relationship with God. The personal maturity of these guides is essential to forming and maintaining an appropriate, trustworthy and helpful relationship. They understand and maintain appropriate ethical boundaries at all times,[16] meeting their own needs for intimacy and support outside the spiritual guidance relationship.

Spiritual guides also take their own continual growth in the spiritual life seriously, and they employ appropriate means such as prayer, spiritual direction, retreat, study and supervision. They will themselves have made the Spiritual Exercises before they agree to guide another. Knowing that the issues of those they accompany will inevitably raise their own unrecognized or undealt-with issues, they will regularly deal with these upwellings in their own spiritual direction and supervision.

There are many routes to such preparation, formal and informal, but no shortcuts. Women, who have until recently been excluded from theological and pastoral formation, will need effective programs, mentoring and even financial support in order to insure their access to such preparation. Paradoxically, women's presence in programs to prepare for guiding the Spiritual Exercises has proven an instrument of profound renewal not only of the women themselves, but of the very way of guiding the Exercises.

## Conclusion

Ignatius's introductory and process material sets up the psychological space and the interpretive world in which the Spiritual Exercises occur. So central are these processes and relationships that from them emerge some provisional conclusions about the Spiritual Exercises.

First, movement is a central reality in the dynamic nature of the Spiritual Exercises. Desires function both as indicator and activator of movement and are discerned within each individual's human development and motivation and God's free action of grace. Rather than any externally determined priority of "higher and lesser," internal and contextual parameters determined by the individual herself should be used to judge desires. Desires can be "read" through affections, the "tracks" inner movements leave in the psyche. While an individual does not totally control these inner movements, one's participation in her own movement does matter. She collaborates through her attitude of generosity toward God; through her openness to movement, change, transformation; through her active hope for God's action in her life, personally, corporately, structurally; and through her willingness to discern the direction of her inner movements, even when they uncover disappointing or destructive tendencies.

This perspective leads to a stress on adaptability. Nothing in the Spiritual Exercises is so sacred that it must be done in one and only one way. The particular needs of each seeker guide adaptation. All persons should be met where they are and encouraged to move where they can, as far as they can, in the style that most suits them. The Spiritual Exercises are a means, not an end.

In light of the preceding, this reading of the Spiritual Exercises is nonhierarchical, dynamic, cyclic, fluid and process-oriented. It makes room for many persons—while still acknowledging the Spiritual Exercises may not be for all. It also acknowledges the complexity of both the Spiritual Exercises and the relationships between the persons giving and making the Exercises, the relationship between the Exercises and the many cultures into which it is received, including the gendered culture of contemporary women. It is impossible to generalize for any group, including women. Thus, conclusions and suggestions must remain provisional and tentative. At the same time, and perhaps because of this process-oriented and tentative stance, the Spiritual Exercises contain a freshness that continually invites one to probe their depth.

# Notes

1. The first twenty points include the nature and purpose of the Spiritual Exercises [1], the general procedure [2, 3], the division and duration [4], the disposition required of the one making the Exercises [5], directions to the one leading the Exercises concerning the one making them [6–17] and adaptations for various constituencies [18–20]. Some of the notes deal with the disposition of the one making the Exercises [3, 5, 11–13, 16, 20], while others deal with the giver himself or herself [2, 4, 6–10, 12, 14–15, 17, 18–19]; see Ganss (1991, 387–88). Sprinkled throughout the text are further explanations and directions: a "Presupposition" [22], which we treated in chapter 2, various examinations [24–44], additional directives and notes [73–82, 99–100, 127–34, 148, 159–64, 174, 188, 199, 204–9 and 226–29]. We will also consider here the "Rules to Order Oneself Henceforth in the Taking of Food" [210–17].

2. See Peters (1967, 79). Peters insists that the Exercises from the Second Week on are Trinitarian, recognizes that the Holy Spirit is nowhere mentioned and points out that the so-called triple colloquies [147, 156, 199] are always addressed to Our Lady, the Son and the Father. This association suggests that Mary does the work of the Holy Spirit in the Second and subsequent Weeks. However, the triple colloquies follow the *meditations* introduced in the Second Week, not the contemplations. The first colloquy of the Second Week contemplations [109], the model for the remaining contemplations, mentions prayer to "the Three Divine Persons, or to the eternal Word made flesh, or to our Mother and Lady."

3. Elizabeth Dreyer (1996, 77) asserts that the most moving expressions of Augustine's treatment of the Holy Spirit are those in which he links the Holy Spirit with desire. Philip Sheldrake, in "Befriending our Desires," *The Way* 35 (April 1995): 92–93, points out the role of desires in Catherine of Siena, Meister Eckhart and Thomas Cranmer; Sheldrake concludes: "The fact that we frequently do not allow ourselves such risks and lack a lively spirituality has close connections with the historical absence of a serious and healthy theology of the Holy Spirit in western Christianity."

4. For a contemporary perspective on eliciting readiness for the Spiritual Exercises, see Joseph Veale, "The First Week: Practical Questions," in *The Way of Ignatius of Loyola: Contemporary Approaches to the Spiritual Exercises,* ed. Philip Sheldrake (St. Louis: Institute of Jesuit Sources, 1991), 53–65.

5. For a fuller discussion of the developmental perspective on readiness for the Spiritual Exercises, see Elizabeth Liebert, "The Eighteenth Annotation in the Spiritual Exercises of St Ignatius" in *Symposium: Ignatian Spirituality: Summary of Proceedings* (Guelph, Ontario: Loyola House, 1993), 10–31.

6. Evidence exists for versions of the Spiritual Exercises of various lengths (8, 8–10, 10–12 and 15 or more days) and for various groups of people. The whole spectrum of devotional activity was included. Closed and open forms were recommended. The time given to prayer varied from a period or two of about thirty minutes to three hours per day, to leaving the amount entirely to the retreatant. Instruction was included when necessary, suitably adapted to the needs of the retreatant. See Martin Palmer (1996): 42–45, 87–100, 105–10, 120–22, 154–55 and elsewhere.

7. Based on this presupposition and the burden it places on each party to try to understand the other, we have chosen not to use the language of director and directee or exercitant in this book, substituting instead "the one who gives the exercises" and the "one who receives or makes them," or, alternatively and more concisely, "companion" and "seeker." With this language shift, we intend to follow Ignatius's lead and assert that the difference between the giver of the Spiritual Exercises and the receiver of them is only functional and does not imply any special holiness or privilege. Furthermore, this difference is strictly temporary, confined to the Exercises alone, and even in that context is constantly mitigated by the revelation and enrichment *both* parties receive as the one making the Exercises narrates her religious experience.

8. Ignatius's positive treatment of the body also spilled over into his pastoral practice as suggested in the earliest of his extant letters, to Inéz Pascual, in 1522: "All the more so since the Lord does not require you to do anything exhausting or harmful to your person. He wants you to live taking joy in him and granting the body whatever it needs. Let all your words, thoughts and behavior be in him and attend to your bodily necessities for his sake,

always placing the observance of God's commandments first..." (Ganss 1991, 327).

9. This negative view of the body occurs when Ignatius asks the seeker to stand outside her body and reflect on it from within the theological anthropology and rhetoric of his time. See Alison Weber, *Teresa of Avila and the Rhetoric of Femininity* (Princeton, N.J.: Princeton University Press, 1990). This strategy's positive goal, according to Margaret Miles, *Fullness of Life: Historical Foundations for a New Asceticism* (Philadelphia: Westminster, 1981), p. 154, is subverting the unconscious balance of pain and joy ordinarily constructed in daily existence for the purpose of reconstructing a life in which all aspects are consciously chosen to foster loving service.

10. For the concept of the culture of the Exercises see Howard Gray (1993): 72–84. Gray defines culture as "a total composite of religious values designed to reorient how men and women choose to live their lives," and he names three constitutive elements of the Ignatian Exercises as "a *context* for discovering God's leadership in life, a statement of *priority* in God's leadership and the establishment of *criteria* for discerning whether the leadership attributed to God is authentic" (73).

11. For example, in the years between 1983 and 1996, of the nearly 600 persons who made the Spiritual Exercises in daily life in the Seattle area, 69 percent were women, 31 percent were men, according to Celia Chappell, SP., Core Team, Spiritual Exercises in Everyday Life, Seattle, Washington, private communication.

12. The terse wording of the Exercises may not make Ignatius's thought clear on this point. But his letter to Francis Borgia of 20 September 1548 sheds light on the issue: "God sees and knows what is best for each one and, as he knows all, he shows each the road to take. On our part we can with his grace seek and test the way forward in many different fashions, so that a person goes forward by that way which for them is the clearest and happiest and most blessed in this life" (*Letters,* tr. Young, 1959, 181).

13. An increasing body of literature treats the effects of physical and sexual abuse, the healing process and the role of various helping professionals. See, for example, Marie Fortune, *Sexual Violence: The Unmentionable Sin* (New

York: Pilgrim Press, 1983); Pamela Cooper-White, *The Cry of Tamar: Violence Against Women and the Church's Response* (Philadelphia: Fortress, 1995); Mary D. Pellauer, Barbara Chester and Jane Boyajian, eds., *Sexual Assault and Abuse: A Handbook for Clergy and Religious Professionals* (San Francisco: Harper and Row, 1987); Anne L. Horton and Judith A. Williamson, eds. *Abuse and Religion: When Praying Isn't Enough* (Lexington, Mass.: D. C. Heath and Company, 1988); and James Leehan, *Pastoral Care for Survivors of Family Abuse* (Louisville: Westminster/John Knox, 1989).

14. Ignatius's mature thinking on the place of penances can be seen in his letter to Francis Borgia of 20 September 1548 (Ganss 1991, 346–49).

15. The placement of the rules for eating has been a source of some discussion. Various suggestions have been offered: this kind of awareness ties in well as an embodiment Third Week prayer; the one receiving the Exercises is learning to carry the Exercises into daily life by becoming reflective even about so ordinary an occupation as eating, and even that there were so many directions and things to internalize earlier in the Exercises that this position is merely a "clear space" for this new practice of intentionality. See Peters (1967), 13–14, 139–41.

16. Two examples of ethical guidelines are "Spiritual Directors International Guidelines for Ethical Conduct" (San Francisco: SDI Coordinating Council, 1999) and Thomas Hedberg and Betsy Caprio, *A Code of Ethics for Spiritual Directors* rev. ed. (Pecos, N. Mex.: Dove Publications, 1992).

# Chapter 4

# Grounding in Truth: Principle and Foundation

*Human beings are created to praise, reverence, and serve God our Lord, and by means of this to save their souls.*

*The other things on the face of the earth are created for the human beings, to help them in working toward the end for which they are created.*

*From this it follows that I should use these things to the extent that they help me toward my end, and rid myself of them to the extent that they hinder me.*

—Spiritual Exercises [23]

*I am drawn outside any time the weather permits. Here I come alive in an unaccountable way. Energy rises gently inside me even as I become still.*

*A student has just given me a book on chaos theory. I am strangely moved and excited by the photographs. Suddenly unlikely things are related: an aerial view of the coast line of Great Britain and a mushrooming cumulus cloud. An oak tree reproduces the same pattern as the cloud—down to the smallest vein in the smallest leaf. Fractals, they call them. Invisible to us until computers could graph the countless points of non-linear equations. Funny, what finally lets us see what has been there all along. Hmmm.*

*My eyes range over the salt-water marsh at my feet and up the side of the forested mountain which the Native peoples believed to be a sleeping princess. I can see her hair streaming out behind her. Where I am now sitting is just about in her ear. Today she is clothed in muted grey-green velvet, trimmed in browns around her neck. She has straw hair at her crown. The colors of the marsh upon which she lies are likewise muted. The morning fog lingers over the damp turf. Two brilliant white egrets move in and out of my line of sight as they fish in the waterways. A gull wheels. My attention is caught by a hummingbird in the oak just over my shoulder. For a while, my eye traces the delicate angular etching of the oak tree against the sky.*

*The marsh edge is also a people place, a space caught between hills, where animals and humans alike share the corridor. Once I saw a fox in the yard, napping. School sounds waft out over the marsh from the playground next door.*

*I sigh deeply, exhaling all the air out of my lungs. Again. The air smells damp and cool and clean.*

*Suddenly everything comes together. I know why I am here. I know the purpose of human life. There are moments when we—and I—manipulate, destroy, create, cure. But our true place in all this is so simple. To notice. To appreciate. That's all.*

—A Contemporary Woman

Juxtaposing Ignatius's seemingly didactic statement and one woman's narration of her religious experience raises the question of appropriate starting points for the Spiritual Exercises. Both are human responses to the meaning of life.

Human beings are formed within a matrix of stories of family, culture, religion. One's very life is story. Every human person tells and lives within many stories throughout a lifetime. One periodically needs to ask: Who am I? Who is God? How do I fit in this world? What is my heart's desire? Is God leading? Am I? Or are we walking together?

Entering into the Spiritual Exercises joins one more deeply with individual and cosmic senses of story. The *Exercises* concern personal stories as well as the stories of faith communities, the community of the universe and ultimately God's story-in-Jesus.

This chapter will explore the Principle and Foundation both for its distillation of Ignatius's story and for its invitation to consider one's own relationship to others, the world and God. Considering both the problems and possibilities inherent in its articulation will involve contrasting sixteenth- and twenty-first-century worldviews or stories and their implications for women, as well as for theology and spirituality. In light of women's ever expanding consciousness and experience, a contemporary reframing of the Principle and Foundation will conclude the specific suggestions for persons giving the Exercises

## Different Ways of Telling the Story

The Principle and Foundation tightly articulates the basic principles of Ignatian spirituality (Ganss 1991, 393, n. 18) and expresses the prevailing sixteenth-century European worldview. A worldview situates humans with respect to earth and its events, other persons and companion creatures, and God. As a document of the sixteenth century read in the twenty-first, however, the Principle and Foundation often raises strong resistances. The history of interpretation also reveals a certain hesitation and ambiguity about the real purpose of the Principle and Foundation and how the one making the Exercises can best deal with it.

Contemporary persons can easily be offended by the anachronistic and privatized notion of "saving their souls," the objectification of nature and the preoccupation with the well-being of humans. The very language of "using" or "ridding" self of things in working toward one's end sounds more like either Pelagianism or an outgrowth of an individualistic consumer society than a lofty ideal toward which to strive. To make oneself "indifferent" to all created things could suggest a coolly detached, almost antiseptic stance toward creation, in contrast to the positive view of creation that figures so prominently in the Contemplation to Attain Love at the close of the Exercises. The admonition not to seek certain life situations rather than others in a dualistic hierarchy seems presumptuous, especially in light of desires one "ought" to have. It is startling to confront the possibility that health, wealth and good reputation may not be the "goods" that one supposes.

For women, probably the most offensive portion in the original text has usually been translated, "...man is to use [other things on the face of the earth] as much as they help him on to his end." Although "man" presumably refers to humankind, as Ganss renders it, women's current consciousness that for thousands of years they and nature have been used as a means to an end triggers a painful reaction.

## Principle and Foundation in the Structure of the Exercises

Structurally, the Principle and Foundation [23] and the Contemplation to Attain Love [230–37] represent bookends to the four weeks of the Spiritual Exercises (Cusson 1988, 52, n. 21; Tetlow 1989, 13). The Principle and Foundation distills the fruit of Ignatius's mystical experiences in the period from his recuperation at Loyola to his most treasured experience along the river Cardoner at Manresa about two years later, when he received an intellectual vision of great depth and intensity. Yet it reads much like a rational philosophical statement. The Contemplation to Attain Love, on the other hand, is an impassioned outpouring of gratitude and mutuality of love by and for a God who lavishes gifts of all kinds, seeks to assure every form of presence and labors in and with humans in all of creation. The Contemplation to Attain Love may well be, like the Song of Songs, a reciprocal pledge of love and deeds between God and the person.

The Spiritual Exercises can be likened to a symphony in which the opening movement (the Principle and Foundation) presents various themes. Subsequent movements then develop them through repetition and variation, with everything culminating in a final grand movement that unites all in a sweep of sound and passion. In essence, the Principle and Foundation establishes the basis and contains, in highly compressed form, the themes and dynamics of the entire Exercises.

## History of the Principle and Foundation

Ignatius's early mystical experience moved him to begin composing the *Spiritual Exercises,* originally known only as "the book." His profound awareness of being loved and taught by God set free his desire for the Holy Mystery. His subsequent education in classical theism, which stressed the transcendence of God, was balanced by his own mystical experiences, which gifted him with a heart-knowledge no book could impart. Regardless of how he phrased the Principle and Foundation, this mystical experience reoriented his life. While the theologically proper terminology of the Principle and Foundation could not adequately express his subjective experience, it could and did withstand the inquiring probe of the Inquisition.

Historically, Ignatius began giving a simpler version of the Exercises to pious persons of good will, especially women, at Manresa, Barcelona and Alcalá (Cusson 1988, 46). These first Exercises lasted about a month and included a number of instructions that presumably incorporated the material of the later Principle and Foundation. In Paris, he further modified his presentation, allowing a preparatory stage to create the necessary dispositions.

Ignatius's purpose for the Principle and Foundation seems to have been twofold. He wanted to situate the one making the Exercises within God's plan of creation but he also hoped that reflecting on the wonder of creation might elicit a deeper affectivity, a great desire for this God who so desires each person.

Like any good director, he "felt out" each person's religious depth and only if the individual evinced a certain maturity of experience did he speak of his own awareness or move the person into the full Exercises. In this sense, the experience of the Principle and Foundation served as a kind of screening process.

Apparently, from the time Ignatius wrote the eighteenth, nineteenth and twentieth Annotations until the publication of the *Official Directory* in 1599, the Principle and Foundation was considered part of the matter connected with the Election and consequently not utilized with persons making the Exercises according to the eighteenth Annotation. In other words, Ignatius connected the Principle with making the whole of the Exercises according to the twentieth Annotation (Tetlow 1989, 19).

At least two recent commentators seem to have touched the core of the Principle and Foundation. Joseph Tetlow (1989) employs the Latin term *Fundamentum* for Principle and Foundation, a term found in all the sixteenth-century directories of the Exercises. William Barry (1994, 9) speaks of the *affective* Principle and Foundation. Both understand the essence of the Principle and Foundation as a profound felt awareness of "being created *momently* by our God and Lord in all concrete particulars" (Tetlow 1989, 7). Tetlow's choice of the word "momently" conveys the radical awareness that creation of each person consists of a continual outpouring of gifts and a luring by God through the individual's deepest desires. This luring leads to transformation and to the service of others, including the universe. To paraphrase John's Gospel, "The Father/Mother goes on working and so do I" (John 5:18). Placing that insight within the context of an emerging scientific paradigm gives an expansiveness and awesomeness to Ignatius's inspired genius that has hitherto been unavailable.

Humans have always struggled to find meaning, to locate their place in relation to others, the world and God in light of their understandings or perceptions of the world. The recognition that God creates humans moment by moment expands to include the sense that God creates everything moment by moment—suffuses the very evolutionary process—and that humans can and indeed must collaborate in that process.

The Exercises provide symbols that mediate a dynamic deeper than antiquated terminology or images. The Principle and Foundation evokes a religious experience in the one making the Exercises, a sense of awe and wonder at this God-in-Christ who cherishes and creates each one momently through the different eras of our lives. Such a relationship fosters liberation and a growing desire to become God's word for others.

## Cosmology and Worldview

A brief survey of the cosmology and general worldview of the sixteenth century will provide significant clues to the formulation of Ignatius's Principle and Foundation.

A woman's worldview is like a pattern emerging in her individual life, a thread that draws apparently disparate pieces together and joins them into a coherent whole, a tapestry of her story. Her personal, functional worldview, the background myth within which she lives, has been radically shaped by the totality of life experiences: location

and situation of birth, family of origin, illnesses, religious background, opportunities for travel and education, interrelationships,
physical makeup and condition, as well as cultural circumstances.
The effectiveness of her personal worldview, or the birth of a new one
where the old has failed, rests ultimately with the individual and the
extent to which she is in touch with her experience, deepest intuitions
and longings as part of a larger moment in time (Zohar 1990, 232–33).
Ignatius described his worldview; each woman needs to bring her
own to consciousness.

Cosmology, or the story of the universe at large, including its origins, development and destiny, as well as humans' place in the
dynamics of the solar system, has an enormous impact on one's worldview even though one may be unconscious of it. Traditional cosmology operated as a kind of wisdom tradition, drawing upon
philosophy, religion, art and natural science. In the last three centuries, cosmology has become increasingly mathematical, seeking
concrete answers to physical facts of the universe, its size, composition, age, structure and so on. Social and political structures, philosophy, theology, as well as anthropology, ecclesiology and spirituality—
literally every aspect of life—mirror one's perception of the universe.[1]

## Ptolemaic Cosmology

Ignatius lived between 1491 and 1556, at the cusp of the late
Middle Ages and the European Renaissance, and just before the
Scientific Revolution—an enormously unsettling process that began
with the publication of Copernicus's theory of astronomy, "On the
Revolutions of the Celestial Spheres," in 1543. Prior to Copernicus
(1473–1543), Western scholarly thought about the universe had been
largely dominated by the work of Plato and Aristotle and the ensuing
cosmology of Ptolemy (2nd c. A.D.)." Thomas Aquinas (1224–74)

embraced the thought of Aristotle, assuming the inferiority and subordination of woman, along with a Ptolemaic and Aristotelian geocentric or earth-centered cosmology. Christendom subsequently came
to accept this cosmology because it seemed compatible with Christian
Scripture and provided a perfectly balanced whole.

Ptolemy envisioned the planets as a series of nested or concentric
spheres in which lower layers were moved by the next higher ones.
Each layer was embedded in a single ethereal sphere or "shell" and carried around by it. The sphere of the stars, which did not move but
remained fixed to spheres and carried about by them, surrounded all.
Ptolemy adopted Aristotle's notion of the four elements—earth, water,
air and fire, which extended as far as the moon in an area of change,
generation and corruption. During patristic and medieval times,
including the period in which Ignatius lived, people thought the airy
realm between earth and the moon was filled with demonic spirits,
with the devil ruling over the nonhuman and non-Christian world
(Ruether 1983, 81). In contrast, the supralunar world of Ptolemy's cosmology, a magic region composed of ether reaching from the moon's
orb outward to the stars, was changeless and imperishable. Later theology saw this as the dwelling place of God and the angels and saints.

A metaphor, the "Great Chain of Being," referred to a hierarchy
of existences beneath this incorruptible substance of the heavenly
world, each imparting form and change to the one below it. The farther one was from the pinnacle, the Unmoved Mover, the more inferior the being. Women ranked toward the bottom of the chain, but
above animals and lifeless matter. The hierarchical dualism of mind
over body was duplicated in the hierarchy of male over female and
human over animals and nature.

Patriarchy, a system of oppression of women that has existed in
Western civilization for the past five thousand years, also affects
social structures as well as cosmological, scriptural and theological

formulations. In patriarchal cultures, domination of women provides a social and symbolic link to the domination of the earth, which is seen as feminine.[2]

As one commentator explains, "Medieval theology as a whole can be characterized as an all-embracing Christian interpretation of the world, but at the same time, as an interpretation of Christianity from a geocentric cosmology" (Wildiers 1982, 77). This total enmeshment of physics and religion reflected a cosmological worldview that was static, ordered, hierarchical, dualistic and anthropocentric or human-centered (McFague, 1993, 136). It was also clearly androcentric or male-centered. As historian and philosopher Carolyn Merchant points out, any potential advantage women might have accrued from their association with earth as the center of the universe in a geocentric Ptolemaic cosmology was obliterated in the next scientific shift (1983, 128) when the sun, associated with man, became the center.

In 1543 Copernicus published his thesis postulating a heliocentric or sun-centered universe. This threatened not only the Ptolemaic model of the universe, which Christians had adopted, but also the status of theology and women. Challenging the reigning cosmology's claims about the physical universe repudiated the preceding religious outlook as well as the antiquated science.

While the medieval cosmology of Ignatius's time was flawed, the mechanistic worldview that ultimately followed proved even more harmful to nature and to women. While the birth of Newtonian physics did away with the Great Chain of Being, the popular association of women with earth persisted. The living cosmos of Greek and medieval times was now understood as a nonliving machine. The rational mind was seen as the essential self, while matter, nature and the universe became objects for exploration and mastery. With the universe now mere matter, lifeless and dead, nature could rightly be probed, subjugated and manipulated (Johnson 1993, 14). Women, still identified literally and symbolically with the natural world, could be probed, subjugated and manipulated as well. Both were identified as objects.

This analysis does not imply that Ignatius himself intended to disparage women or that he demeaned the beauty of the earth; persons of the Middle Ages reverenced nature as a reflection of God. Rather, it attempts to make clear that cultural consciousness and prevailing scientific paradigms affect the way one articulates human experience and responds to questions of human meaning. Ignatius reflected his times in his views of heaven and earth, the human person, the origins of evil, even images of God.

## Toward a Paradigm Shift

Science is often perceived as objective "hard" data that unambiguously defines reality. The way the universe has been investigated and interpreted for the past four hundred years has gained its credibility from this understanding of science. But philosophers of science recognize that, by itself, science cannot resolve the questions of meaning and purpose that lie behind the increasing mass of data and the theories developed to account for it. Science provides but one story among many elucidating the meaning of the universe.

Over the last century and a half, changes in science, especially quantum and information physics, thermodynamics and the physics of chaos have turned upside down and inside out not only medieval cosmology in the West but also the mechanistic determinism that succeeded it. The rise of women's liberation and ecological movements also highlight the fact that divergent perspectives have replaced the worldview of Bacon, Descartes and Newton.

Humans are latecomers on the scene of an evolutionary process that began some fifteen billion years ago with the birth of the universe in the Big Bang.[3] An unfolding cosmology reveals an expanding universe that

- God is not distant from the universe but a sustaining presence in all of creation. God's presence is not inseparable from creatures (pantheistic) but present and involved with the universe while still being independent of it (panentheistic) (O'Murchu 1997, 50). The universe is pregnant with the presence of God whose creative action is at the heart of the evolutionary process. God acts as compassionate partner, as lure toward the future and as cocreator. Indeed, God labors on humans' behalf [236].

- A human-centered norm of progress must give way to a biocentric focus. Humans are within the cosmos, not apart from or above it. The earth can flourish in the absence of humans, but humans cannot flourish in the absence of the earth. Humankind is dependent on earth, its larger body (McFague 1993), for existence. The poet Wendell Berry somewhere reflects that humans rely on creatures and survive by their deaths. In sustaining life, humans break the body and shed the blood of creation. When done respectfully and reverently, it is sacrament; when done destructively or greedily, it is desecration. The arrogance of human beings is destroying plant and animal species, each taking millions of years to evolve and each necessary for planetary ecology.[5]

- Cultivating a renewed sacramental vision is the richest way of recovering both a sense of reverence for and companionship with all of creation. *Sacrament* has a much broader context than usually imagined.[6] An earlier genius of humankind saw nature as the primary source of revelation. The work of poets, artists and mystics has always drawn attention to the numinous quality of the ordinary, calling us to poet Gerard Manley Hopkins's realization that "the world is charged with the grandeur of God."[7]

- Salvation is planetary and global as well as personal. A shift from other-worldly to this-worldly redemptive hope flows from this new paradigm. Persons no longer seek simply their own redemption but that of all creation, including the earth itself. The life and death of Jesus must be lived out salvifically by all Christians. The universe, the sacred body of God, also needs salvation (Rom 8:18–23).[8]

- Humans are called not to dominate nature, but to be cocreators within the evolutionary process. Humankind is not the center by means of which all is dominated, but the center through which all enter into kinship and communion. Women and men are called to become partners in mutuality and respectful companions of all creation.

The current paradigm shift invites us to recapitulate the wisdom of the previous epistemological shift from Ptolemaic to Copernican cosmology even as another takes place. The task calls for a return to nature with a second naiveté, reimagining and reparticipating in the mythical, poetic and religious, even as the struggle with the political, ecological, economic and technological realities continues.

Many persons' worldview remains largely unexamined, an unconscious frame of reference for living and relating to God, self and creation. Each person making the Spiritual Exercises needs to answer the implicit questions in the Principle and Foundation: How would you describe your world and how it influences you? How do you imagine God? What is your relationship to others and all of God's creation? What is your part in creation? What are the dominant influences on your sense of God, humans, heaven and earth? What does it mean to exist in this vast unfolding universe?

In Ignatius's era people in the West making the Exercises operated out of a universally accepted cosmology. Today the cosmology of the one guiding the Exercises can conflict with the one making them, or both can be operating out of an irreconcilable hybrid. It is incumbent on those giving the Exercises to ascertain what cultural, philosophical, theological and scientific assumptions they bring to the text. These presuppositions will affect how guides "hear into speech," the one making the Exercises, to borrow author Nelle Morton's (1985, 74) felicitous phrase.

## Reframing the Principle and Foundation

In its essence, the opening line of the Principle and Foundation, "Human beings are created to praise, reverence, and serve God our Lord," seeks to uncover both who God is and our relationship to this Creative One. Paradoxically, many women may feel called to pay more attention to self as a prelude to paying attention to God, to discover for the first time—or all over again—the God present within the mystery of one's self. To turn away from self is to turn away from God, despite inner voices chanting "Don't be selfish." As one woman said, "It was easier to use my gifts in an outward way, to share what I could with family and faith community than to try to look inside myself and cherish, nurture and enjoy my self as a gift from God to me." Seeing oneself and all of creation as continually loved and desired into being by a passionate and solicitous God prompts an awe and still deeper reverence for God, self and the sacrament of creation. Such was the case with Ignatius at the river Cardoner. A sense of the diaphanous presence of God in everything undergirds the awareness of gift.

The second part of that goal, "by means of this to save their souls," has been well discussed by Ganss (1991, 392) and others. Ignatius understood *soul* as the Hebrew equivalent of the "total self." But the new cosmology puts a different spin on soteriology, for now salvation includes the universe. Furthermore, feminist theologians stress the relational, communitarian nature of salvation, seeing salvation as not only a single past event, but an ongoing reality in which humans participate. Like Jesus, women must call for responsibility—for themselves, for the powerless, for the earth, the greater body of God. It makes a great deal of difference if the one making the Exercises seeks life for self and others "beyond this world" or precisely in the messiness and beauty of ordinary experience.[9]

The traditional "means" of the Principle and Foundation, "...other things on the face of the earth created for human beings...use these things to the extent that they help," seems singularly anthropocentric in light of our dependence on the earth and the need for a compassionate relationship with it. As interdependent companions of all that exists, we must place much more focus on the welfare of all species, not just the human.

A closely related issue concerns the objectification and dismissal of other human beings as "means," particularly women and children. Statistics fluctuate, but the continuing reality of a very small percentage of people using a vast amount of the world's resources while millions die from starvation, water pollution or the loss of arable farm land is morally reprehensible. The U.S. bishops' pastoral on the economy, "Economic Justice for All" (1986), admonishes all to reflect on how purchases affect the poor. The "poor" must also include the earth itself.

*Nonuse* may have as much importance as *use*. One can ignore gifts of nature, of the arts and sciences or of the person, such as self-expression through poetry, dance, journaling or potting. Everyone should have access to these gifts of God, not just the affluent. All things beautiful comprise important resources for spirituality and should be treasured as such.

The convoluted issue around "making myself indifferent to all created things" cannot be dealt with as simply a question of will power.

Indifference presumes passion. Women cannot act with indifference in any positive sense until they have identified their desires and passions. Indifference demands liberation. Detachment follows from attachment to Someone whose love empowers with blessed freedom.

Ignatius seems to suggest moving toward whatever gives fullness of life in the service of the world, while avoiding whatever ties down the spirit. Indifference does not so much seek this rather than that—health rather than sickness, wealth rather than poverty—but rather, entails a more receptive looking for, with and in God at whatever life circumstances are present, precisely because of a grounding relationship with God. Indifference means finding God who sustains, supports and lures toward the future in the process of life. While few people truly enjoy this degree of freedom, the *desire* for it remains essential.

After the named things one "ought not to seek," (health, wealth, honor) comes a fascinating phrase, "and so on in other matters." What might the "and so ons" be for women in contemporary society? Cultural myths, certainly, including beauty, body shape, youthful appearance, dependence on external validation—especially from men—stylish dress, security and doing it "right." Having the one making the Exercises list her own "and so ons" could prove helpful.

Desires also intimately relate to the Principle and Foundation because desires flow from a worldview and reveal how one wishes to be in relationship. Those guiding the Exercises do important work when they assist those making them to discover what they really want—their functional Principle and Foundation. Some women have little sense of the choices or options existing even within impossible situations. The difficulty might stem from a lack of imagination, but also, perhaps, from fear. "It's risky to discover my own needs and desires because it leads me on a path away from the crowd and into the unknown," said one woman. "I will have to take responsibility for my actions, and I may fail."

Women may listen to exterior voices saying they are inferior, not "good enough," or "different," rather than listen to the God-self and their own deepest desires. Culture and church so program women to see themselves as inferior or "not enough" that they may not allow themselves the luxury of desires for fear of yet another disappointment. Women generally put the needs and desires of families, parents and coworkers first, leaving little room for self. In not a few cases, they face enormous conflict from spouses or partners when seeking to fulfill their God-given desires.[10] Internalizing the core of the Principle and Foundation will give a sense of their dignity and uniqueness and elicit authentic desires and genuine indifference. One woman imaged the movement into healthy autonomy as "coming out of a coma."

Psychological and sociological studies of women have indicated that many lack "voice," a metaphor for growth in autonomy and maturity. Even a community of two, the one guiding and the one making the Exercises, can facilitate and encourage a woman's movement toward greater freedom and delight in self and a healthy desire to serve others when affirmed or lovingly challenged. Those giving the Exercises cannot presume capacity for self-reflection, for tapping into and articulating one's experience, feelings, desires and thoughts.

Strong and powerful women can also get caught in desires evoked by their very success, such as the desire to make more money, to associate oneself with what one earns, to look down on those less powerful or successful, to "do it myself." Feminism itself can set up conflicting desires. For those women who have "found their voice," how do they choose to use it?

The Principle and Foundation is intended to evoke a present or remembered experience, an awareness of how God continues to create and to cherish each individual moment by moment throughout life. This realization must precede any consideration of sin, or else the First Week becomes painfully introspective. The Principle and Foundation "grounds" a person in graced self-awareness and God-awareness, which is food for the journey of life and ministry. The God of the Principle and Foundation loves women compassionately and asks them to trust themselves and act out of this deep, true sense of who they really are.

## Wisdom for the One Giving the Exercises

An inductive, intuitive approach to the Principle and Foundation enables the guide to feel out where each woman enters the process in terms of cosmology and worldview. Moving from a macro to a micro level, a new paradigm generates not only cosmic but also personal questions for the one making the Exercises. What is my world? What is the center of my universe? What is my cosmology?

Discussing a faith autobiography or asking a series of informal questions offers clues to a woman's desires and relationship to the Creative One. For example, the one giving the Exercises might ask penetrating questions, such as: Who are you? If you had a photo album of important people and events in your life, what would it look like? Who would be in it? What in your life do you feel most strongly and passionately about? What is the goal of your life? How do you experience God? How do you and God communicate? How do you image Jesus? Why are you choosing to make the Exercises?

Since each woman experiences the call to make the Exercises uniquely, the guide needs to begin with each individual's experience, her story. Each person is, in effect, a living, breathing Principle and Foundation. It is perhaps more important to let the one making the Exercises articulate her own Principle and Foundation rather than reflecting on that of Ignatius. Articulating the end or goal of one's life in relationship to God is a "luxury" some women have not had the opportunity to explore or have resisted because of the responsibility it might entail. Asking a woman what her "passions" are might elicit a variety of responses: "to raise my children to be good Christians," "to seek intimacy with God in Jesus," "to live a good life of service to others," "to be a person of integrity and authenticity," "to use my education," "to satisfy my husband, parent or employer" and so on.

Probing these passions and not simply taking them at face value will yield a variety of rationales for making the Exercises: to meet others' expectations, to be worthy of God, to be a vital contributing member of the faith community or world, to grow in faith, to find one's life direction, to discover and use gifts for leadership or to discern a call to ordained ministry. The guide must listen carefully to the self-expression, worldview and theology of the woman making the Exercises. This dialogue over days, weeks or even months, such as Ignatius encouraged, will also reveal obstacles that need additional work or may prohibit moving beyond the Principle and Foundation at this time.

Humans develop and order experience through images. Granted that no image of God is adequate, it is important to discover how one relates to God. Naming God implies a corresponding self-image. If God is a tyrant, I am oppressed; if God is beneficent, I am gifted.

The two-tiered universe of an earlier cosmology easily lent itself to a theologically dualistic perspective. Western classical theology's understanding of God, almost exclusively shaped by men, presented God as male, as power and might. It experienced God predominantly "as noun, as transcendence, as order, as structure, as law, as rationality" (Nelson 1983, 13). This form of patriarchy physically and emotionally distances women, but also men, from God; it makes God wholly other, above and beyond, and relegates Divine Love to being measured through conformity to law and order—or at least conformity to church and society.

Images of God as judge, tyrant, beyond caring, oppressive and domineering are common among women, particularly those who have experienced psychological, physical or sexual abuse. On the other hand, and equally unhelpful, God can also be experienced only as comforting, allowing a sort of pseudodependent, immature relationship that never challenges one to assume responsibility. Both of these unhelpful and incomplete or even destructive extremes need to be recognized and challenged. The heart of the matter is God-image.

A growing body of work by developmental theorists highlights the fact that many women have been socialized to forget their own needs, desires or passions. One very intelligent woman remarked, "I can see that I arrived at the age of legal adulthood with only the barest acquaintance with my inner being. I knew myself as someone who existed to please, to serve, and especially to accommodate to others." Another woman remarked: "I hide from myself by not listening to what I want and need, but by clinging to my dependencies on others, by blaming my family of origin. I live my fear as I crave things I don't want and need and believe the cravings. I fear that I am not enough. There is anxiety that my not-enoughness will be discovered."

In denying oneself, one denies the very image in which one is made. Failing to love self, one's inmost being expressed in embodied spirit, means failing to love God. The guide can help by asking for clarification. What is it that makes you truly happy, that gives you joy? Who are you when you are most fully alive, most fully your true self? What gives you energy?

Other women find the traditional language of "surrender to God" both offensive and threatening. They equate surrender with obliterating themselves and relinquishing their lifetime of struggle for basic existence, much less for appropriate political power.[11] Many women react to the subliminal message associated with military surrender, realizing the horrible ramifications for them and their children. To surrender to this God would be seen as an act of fear. As one woman declared, "I will have no God, if the only way to God is through the demise of the self that I have worked so hard to form." On the other hand, to surrender the depressed and empty self women so often experience, as well as a false image of God, provides the way forward (Carr 1988, 212).

The most basic image necessary to the process of the Exercises consists of God as loving creator who calls us to full humanity, to identity and to collaboration (Sheldrake 1983, 95). Seeing oneself as a unique and precious creative act of God gives a joy that does not come from success or external validation. Freely and willingly handing oneself over to this God, to a relationship of mutuality that transforms and transcends what one knows about oneself, removes probably the single most difficult psychological obstacle to spiritual growth.

## Conclusion

Ignatius added the Principle and Foundation to the Exercises after his initial work with both women and men. Although we cannot tell from the text of the Principle and Foundation how women influenced its formulation, its impact on women today is of great concern.

Because of the complexity of our era, reflecting on the assumptions inherent in the Principle and Foundation as articulated by Ignatius is as important now as it was for sixteenth-century Christians. At the core of the stated Principle and Foundation exists a way of perceiving reality that needs to resonate with the mystical experience of Ignatius, not by replicating his experience, but in one's affective awareness and life direction. Ignatius's experience of God as loving Creator allowed him to see others and the known world as an expression of that love and worthy of his own. The affective Principle and Foundation or *Fundamentum* constitutes the sine qua non, the lens, the central theme that runs throughout and grounds each movement of the Exercises. This relationship with God both expresses and opens one to the continuing dynamic of the Exercises.

A new scientific paradigm that relocates humans in their relationships to God, others and the cosmos puts the Exercises and all of life into a whole new perspective, providing a liberating movement for women and nature and an expansiveness and numinous quality to all of creation. Theology and spirituality are deeply affected by a new scientific paradigm. A new understanding of cosmology radically shifts meanings of sin, salvation and sanctity from an individualistic soteriology to one of interrelationship, not just with God and others, but also with the planetary systems. Incarnation is no longer seen as an isolated event. The embodiment of God takes place in all of creation as it moves toward greater complexity and communion.

Two contemporary women offer a rendering of the Principle and Foundation that comes close to summarizing these rich insights:

Lord my God, when Your love spilled over
into creation
You thought of me.
I am
from love     of love     for love.

Let my heart, O God, always
recognize,
cherish,
and enjoy Your goodness in all of creation.

Direct all that is me toward Your praise.
Teach me reverence for every person, all things.
Energize me in your service.

Lord God
may nothing ever distract me from Your
love…
neither health nor sickness
wealth nor poverty
honor nor dishonor
long life nor short life.

May I never seek nor choose to be other
than You intend or wish.
Amen
(Bergan and Schwan 1985, 11).

# Notes

1. A non-technical, expansive view of the new cosmologies is given in Brian Swimme (1996). See also B. Bertotti, et al., *Modern Cosmology in Retrospect* (Cambridge: Cambridge University Press, 1990).

2. For an excellent treatment of patriarchy, see Gerda Lerner, *The Creation of Patriarchy* (New York: Oxford University Press, 1986); and Thomas Berry and Brian Swimme, *The Dream of the Earth* (San Francisco: Sierra Club Books, 1988), 138–62.

3. Some helpful books for explaining the evolution of the universe: John Barrow, *The Origin of the Universe* (New York: Basic Books, 1994); Berry and Swimme (1992); Michael Dowd, *Earthspirit: A Handbook for Nurturing an Ecological Christianity* (Mystic, Conn.: Twenty-third Publications, 1991); John Barrow and Joseph Silk, *The Left Hand of Creation: The Origin and Evolution of the Universe,* 2nd ed. (New York: Oxford University Press, 1994); and Beatrice Bruteau, *God's Ecstasy: The Creation of a Self-Creating World* ( New York: Crossroad, 1997).

4. Several books are now beginning to reflect on the new scientific view of the universe and its implications for theology. See, for example, Ivone Gebarra, *Longing for Running Water: Ecofeminism and Liberation* (Minneapolis: Fortress, 1999); Fritjof Capra and David Steindl-Rast, *Belonging to the Universe: Explorations on the Frontiers of Science and Spirituality* (San Francisco: Harper, 1991); Kitty Ferguson, *The Fire in the Equations: Science, Religion and the Search for God* (Grand Rapids, Mich.: Eerdmans, 1994); Paul Davies, *The Mind of God: The Scientific Basis for a Rational World* (New York: Simon and Schuster, 1992); and Charles Birch, et al., eds. *Liberating Life: Contemporary Approaches to Ecological Theology* (Maryknoll N.Y.: Orbis, 1990).

5. On this point, see Larry L. Rasmussen, *Earth Community, Earth Ethics* (Maryknoll, N.Y.: Orbis, 1996).

6. See the comprehensive approach of Michael Himes and Kenneth Himes, "The Sacrament of Creation: Toward an Environmental Theology," *Commonweal* 117 (26 January 1990): 42–49.

7. See, for example, the poems of contemporary Pulitzer Prize winner Mary Oliver and the writings of Anne Dillard.

8. See Rosemary Radford Ruether, *Women and Redemption: A Theological History* (Minneapolis, Fortress, 1998).

9. See Anne Carr (1988, 1996), especially chapter 9; Sallie McFague (1993, 179–82); and Rosemary Radford Ruether, *Gaia and God: An Ecofeminist Theology of Earth Healing* (San Francisco: HarperSanFrancisco, 1992).

10. A fine book on women balancing relationship to self and others is Dana Crowley Jack's *Silencing the Self: Women and Depression* (San Francisco: Harper Collins, 1991). See also her *Behind the Mask* (Cambridge: Harvard University Press, 1999) for a treatment of women and aggression.

11. See the thoughtful book by Carol Lee Flinders, *At the Root of This Longing* (San Francisco: Harper, 1998) for a reconciliation of some aspects of all the great religions (silence, self-naughting, restraint of desire and enclosure) and contemporary feminism.

# Chapter 5

# Knowing Whose I Am: Prayer in the Spiritual Exercises

*God sees and knows what is best for each one and, as he knows all, he shows each the road to take. On our part we can with his grace seek and test the way forward in many different fashions, so that a person goes forward by that way which for them is the clearest and happiest and most blessed in this life.*

—Letter from Ignatius to Francis Borgia, 1548
(Veale, 1995)

*You know, this prayer thing has me stumped. I really do want to pray. But when I sit down, my mind seems to go blank. I talk to God, but God never seems to talk back. After doing this for a while, I get discouraged and quit. But pretty soon, the nagging is back: "You should be praying." So I make a resolution, start again, and pretty soon, I stop. What I really like to do is walk in the wild, so on Sunday afternoon, I give myself a treat and go out to the headlands and hike. Sometimes there I really feel like I am praying. But it doesn't seem to carry over to Monday through Saturday. Anyhow, when my friend told me about the Spiritual Exercises, my heart jumped a little. So here I am.*

—A Contemporary Woman

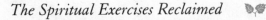 

From the General and Particular Examinations opening the First Week to the Contemplation to Attain Love closing the Fourth Week, prayer permeates the Spiritual Exercises. This rich variety of responses to God may be one of the best-kept secrets of the Spiritual Exercises.[1] Any woman can find here a form of prayer that not only works for her but actually delights her. Yet, how can one choose the richest and most pleasurable [238] if unaware of the possibilities? The following survey describes the feast of prayer forms found in the Exercises as well as raises problems and suggests possibilities for contemporary women.

## Repertoire of Prayer Forms

All manner of techniques for prayer exist, but prayer happens in the graced moment when desire for God brings/initiates an awareness of and response to this One who has first loved us. Desire draws us, but the desire is placed there by the Spirit of God. And where the spirit of the Lord is, there is freedom (2 Cor 3:17) and delight. Not at every moment, of course, for relationship with God, like any other human relationship, has moments of mystery, frustration, emptiness, challenge, dread, boredom and fear. At these times, a technique or structure may help. Yet too much structure or the wrong technique can deflect further from one's desire. Discerning the form, style and timing of prayer is essential.

## Particular and General Examinations

Although Ignatius presents two forms of examination, namely, the daily Particular Examination of Conscience [24–31] and a General Examination of Conscience intended to lead to a general confession [32–44], practice over the years has tended to collapse the two into one process of regular reflection.

The particular examination, often called examen, sets out a regular, structured way of attending to daily life. Upon rising, one recalls the subject of examination and resolves to attend carefully to that issue [24]. After the noon meal comes a formal prayer time [25]. It begins with awareness of one's desires, the indicator of the condition of the heart. Ignatius suggests that appropriate desires for this prayer focus on consciousness of how one has maintained or ruptured the connection with God and on the desire to prevent any future rupture. The body of the prayer consists of an examination of the morning hours. This prayer is repeated after supper, reviewing the afternoon hours [26].

In several additional directives [27–32], Ignatius seems to have three positive strategies in mind. First, one cannot attend to a habit until conscious of it. Second, involving oneself as much as possible will speed the process. Third, the effects of one's attempts to become conscious grow cumulatively over time. Along with these positive strategies, however, comes the risk that the external process, especially because of its regular focus on sinfulness, will remain only an external process or will simply reinforce a sense of habitual failure. As one continues into the Exercises, this examination can become a powerful means of deepening the effects of the other exercises [160].

The goal of the particular examination—refined consciousness of God's presence and action—remains as valid today as in Ignatius's time. But the close attention to faults and failings and the system of keeping account suggested by the text create a huge burden for most contemporary women. The form of the practice clearly needs reclaiming.

Ignatius intended the second or general examination of conscience [32–42] to help persons prepare for confession. Although his points in this section raise many questions today, his comments about the value of confession [44] still have merit, perhaps more so in a contemporary climate in which both Roman Catholics and Protestants have dismissed its worth. Confession or the rite of reconciliation can have beneficial spiritual effects as long as it is entered into freely and arises out of a genuine movement of the Holy Spirit.

In fact, the fivefold method of the general examination lends itself to contemporary adaptation. It deals with thanksgiving, desire, review and assessment, asking pardon, and commitment to renewed growth. This simple progression has generally superseded the particular examination and forms the foundation of most contemporary adaptations, including George Aschenbrenner's now classic adaptation in "Consciousness Examen" (1972).[2] This form takes its name from Ignatius's term *consciencia,* which can mean conscience or consciousness (Ganss 1991, 396, n. 26). The contemporary shift from using "conscience" to using "consciousness" acknowledges a watershed in understanding the role of examination in the spiritual life.[3] It signifies a shift in emphasis from individual acts to the fundamental orientation of one's whole life.

A practice of daily reflection such as that proposed in the reclaimed examination of consciousness both depends on and fosters the skills of noticing, naming and acting on one's awareness of God's presence in daily life. A person will use her ability to notice interior movements all through the Weeks to follow. It is a prerequisite for implementing the Rules for Discernment of Spirits and therefore essential to making carefully discerned decisions. It is truly a foundational spiritual discipline.

## Meditation, with Repetition and Résumé

The next kind of prayer is meditation, which consists primarily in thinking, reasoning and considering, though imagination and affections also play significant supportive roles. The context for meditation, as for all prayer in the Spiritual Exercises, consists in disciplined time, specific place and posture, exterior and interior awareness of the environment and attention to one's desires. Ignatius's structure for meditation [46–49, 54] includes a preparatory prayer, two or three preludes (or considerations framing the experience to follow), several points providing the body of the consideration and colloquy or personal response. He closes each meditation period with one of the vocal prayers that all could recite by heart.

The preparatory prayer can be as simple as a single sentence based on the Principle and Foundation, in which one asks that everything one does be ordered and directed to the service and praise of God. Sometimes two, but usually three, preludes follow. Through them one gathers or "composes" all parts of our mind. Memory is directed to place the topic accurately in its context, the history of God's dealings with humankind. The imagination is invited to create the place. The will is activated through asking for what one desires. The final prelude always concerns desire, and it changes with the focus of the prayer. When Ignatius mentions a specific desire, it signals the most significant grace of the prayer as he understands it. Through the preparatory prayer and preludes, one says to God: "Here I am, every bit of me, ready to pray."

The next part of meditation develops the subject matter. Ignatius breaks the material into "points," usually three, each suggesting a slightly different aspect for consideration.

Then one talks, "as one friend to another," to God, Christ or Mary, as suggested by the particular meditation. This conversation, or colloquy as Ignatius calls it, can happen at any point, but Ignatius specifically recommends it for the end of the prayer. Colloquy is so important that Ignatius sometimes treats it as a new dimension of prayer. The colloquies themselves add to the material for the next pondering and conversation. In effect one says to God, as to a friend, "As I was saying yesterday...now, as I think about it today, I wonder..." Finally,

Ignatius suggests a definite conclusion to the meditation, reciting a familiar prayer such as the Lord's Prayer.

But Ignatius does not stop here. To derive the most from each prayer period, he suggests spending some time after its conclusion noting how it went [77]. Were there consolations and desolations? Where? How did one cooperate with the consolation and work against the desolation? The review brings discernment of spirits into play, exercise by exercise, prayer by prayer, helping bring about greater consciousness of how God works and how one responds.

Then the prayer is repeated. The word Ignatius uses, *discurrir*, means something like "range over" or "wander about," but one does not cast about aimlessly. Instead, Ignatius wants the one making the Exercises to "turn over" the preceding prayer and its review (Peters 1967, 35), to return to both the consolations and the desolations. Repetition [62–63] and résumé [64] serve to distill the prayer into greater focus, allowing one to go progressively deeper into the mystery of God. The prayer may also become simpler and quieter with each repetition. Active prayer may become more passive; the seeker may do less and less and God may do more and more. Repetition and résumé allow these possibilities.

Ignatius has created a process that can be used by anyone. A person quite practiced in prayer and its many manifestations might minimize this structure almost to the vanishing point, but another person will find the structure liberating, allowing her to hear in entirely new ways what God desires to communicate. The structure given by Ignatius encourages freedom, not extinction.

## Imaginative Contemplation

In the Second Week, Ignatius introduces contemplation [101], by which he means attending to persons and events largely by means of imagination. Its form parallels that of meditation: preparatory prayer, preludes, points and colloquy. The contrasts between these two forms of prayer, however, are particularly instructive.

Meditation employs reasoning, supported by memory and imagination, while contemplation employs imagination, supported by memory and reasoning. The preludes to a contemplation ask the seeker to not only recall but actually recreate the event, both by situating oneself imaginatively within it and by desiring interior knowledge of it. Seeking to be so intimately present to the events and persons truly brings a new knowledge of them. Each of the three points entails imagining the event from a somewhat different perspective and to employ a different aspect of the imagination. The colloquy, still "friend to friend," now specifically mentions affections that "I feel in my heart" [109]. Finally, the seeker repeats the contemplations, noting the presence of consolation and desolation. This repetition moves from the surface of events and personalities into the very mystery these persons and events reveal.

The desired outcome of imaginative contemplation—affective knowing—brings about different fruit than does meditation. Engaging the affections ignites prayer, giving it movement, texture, passion. Feeling deeply about someone or something not only moves one to action but also sustains these actions in the face of opposition. Affections form the primary subject matter considered in discernment of spirits. They are so significant to the dynamic of the Spiritual Exercises that when absent, the one giving the Exercises should probe for possible obstacles.

Ignatius introduces contemplation in the Second Week of the Exercises. This Week requires sensibilities and capabilities not necessarily conscious or developed in the First Week. The dispositions and abilities upon which both the Second Week and imaginative contemplation rest include the ability to recognize one's motives, to plan for long-term goals and to "notice key interior facts," as authors William Barry and William Connolly (1982) put it. These same prerequisites make affective prayer and discernment of spirits possible. As one's breadth of prayer experience and degree of self-reflectivity grows, so does one's authority and initiative.

## Application of the Five Senses

The Second Week explicitly introduces the Application of the Five Senses, perhaps Ignatius's finest example of holistic, embodied prayer. His understanding of this form of prayer cuts across the whole array of prayer forms, illustrating the basic truth that faith is as much rooted in one's body as in one's mind.

Even though Ignatius does not specifically use the term "Application of Senses" in the First Week, he utilizes the methodology quite explicitly and graphically in the meditation on hell [65]. Here he asks the one making the Exercises to see the huge fires, hear the wailing and so on. In the fifth contemplation of the Second Week [121] Ignatius finally speaks of the "Application of the Five Senses." From then on, he specifies this method for the final period of prayer each day. The first point highlights seeing, the second, hearing and the fourth, touch. But the third point, stressing fragrance and taste, forms the heart of this experience of prayer: "I will smell the fragrance and taste the infinite sweetness and charm of the Divinity, of the soul, of its virtues, and of everything there, appropriately for each of the persons who is being contemplated. Then I will reflect upon myself and draw profit from this [124]."

Ambiguity abounds in the interpretation of this form of prayer. Ignatius's brevity may indicate either a presumed familiarity with it, at least at one level, or a deliberate vagueness that allows for diversity of God's action without raising a red flag for the Inquisition. At any rate, the debate about what Ignatius meant is far from over.[4]

## Three Methods of Praying

Ignatius introduces this section [238–60] with a surprising assertion: prayer should both be one's own and it should be pleasing. To foster these fruits, he sets out a variety of methods from which to choose.

The first method consists in pondering, after suitable bodily recollection and preparation, a doctrine or an aspect of the person in order to enter more fully and personally into it [238–48]. Ignatius's belief that all prayer is supported by the body appears in his direction [247–48] to pray on each of the five senses.

Most of the Three Ways of Praying have already made an appearance in the eighteenth preliminary Annotation. Yet the *Directory* of 1599 states that these exercises also have value for the spiritual progress of those who have made the Exercises (Palmer 1996, 343), contradicting a common conclusion that relegates these methods to "beginners."

The placement of these points suggests their usefulness in the midst of everyday life, either after completing the Spiritual Exercises in an enclosed situation or as a shortened, eighteenth Annotation form. The three separate yet overlapping methods of prayer are to be used according to circumstances, and, indeed, are to become as natural as breathing itself (Barnes 1989, 270).

## Problems and Possibilities for Women

Each prayer form of the Spiritual Exercises suggests areas of opportunity and concern for women: imagination itself, women's consciousness, using one's mind as prayer, cultivating the imagination, embodiment in prayer, and, once again, what it means to take adaptation seriously, this time in the matter of appropriate prayer forms.

## Imagination

Modern Western culture, in so lauding the intellect, often allows it to overshadow the rational power of imagination that makes knowledge possible. Imagination, so long equated with "the feminine," and therefore irrational, became a burden borne unequally by women. Many still feel burdened by the Cartesian "divorce" of the intellect and imagination, whereas in truth they are intimately connected. Comprehending the complexity of their interaction means understanding imagination as a kind of transformer or scanner that collects images from the outer world. Juxtaposing them with images in one's memories provides raw material for reflection and abstraction. Imagination literally feeds inner reality. Reclaiming imagination's possibilities for prayer is good news for women, who have long been stereotyped and trivialized for being imaginative; women can call on this strength in their prayer.

Philosopher Ray Hart (1968, 242) notes that "in the scale of cognitive acts, imagination remains nearest the event, elaborating its feeling-tone in a universe of non-discursive discourse." The imagination knows things in their concreteness, in their uniqueness within an ambiance of affectivity, while reason takes from reality, drawing deductions and abstractions.[5] For example, one may not be aware of the essence of blue herons, but be thrilled by the beauty and dignity of *this* blue heron on a misty morning. Cognition through the imaginative system complements the conceptual, intellectual approach to truth. Without replacing reason, imagination brings together all the faculties into equilibrium or simultaneity.

Imaging comprises the first level of the imagination. It becomes multivalent as it moves into symbol, suggesting one or more meanings. Those symbols with wide human application are called archetypes (Bryant 1984, 83).

Whatever the level of imagination, its language is indirect, using images, symbol, story, metaphor, myth. These modalities engage the whole person, not just the mind, demanding some kind of response. The language of knowing God is primarily the language of images. In Cardinal Newman's famous analysis, belief begins and grows not through a notion or concept but in the image or symbol. Imagination therefore proves central to both faith and prayer. As the locus of God's initiative, it also ultimately sustains all forms of prayer, preceding even apparently imageless prayer.

Imagination not only discloses the outer world, it also gives glimpses into the inner world of the psyche using the symbolic language of feeling-charged images. Most persons think they control their reality; they fail to see how the unconscious influences them. Only when experiencing unexplained or unusual surges of emotion, feeling out of sorts for no apparent reason or making slips of the tongue does one intuit the presence of an unseen force that contains enormous energy, forms of intelligence and even distinct personalities.

Carl Jung spoke of individuation, a lifelong process of coming to conscious awareness of the totality of one's person—becoming an *imago Dei* in light of who God calls one to become. Individuation, achieved largely by bringing both our conscious and unconscious life into harmony and collaboration, remains much more easily said than done.

The symbols of the unconscious life present themselves to the level of consciousness primarily by two routes, dreams and imagination, but also by prayer when fully entered into. Many women have dream experiences during the Spiritual Exercises every bit as revelatory as conscious prayer or ritual. Assuming that the guide has some skill at helping the one making the Exercises unpack the dream, might not the guide pay attention to these as well? This strategy does not mean that the Spiritual Exercises assume a therapeutic tone, but that the guide chooses to listen to the totality of God's work in the person at both the conscious and unconscious level.

A Jungian technique called active imagination provides another way of using the imagination to constructively approach the unconscious.[6] Ignatius and others utilized aspects of this process long before researchers in neurology, psychology and philosophy "discovered" the giftedness of right-brained functions. Many writers have pointed to similarities between active imagination and imaginative contemplation. Both use dialogue with images or symbols that arise during the course of attentiveness. In prayer, this may mean dialoguing with persons within the scriptural scene. It may also mean conversing with aspects of the personality or dream figures.

Some women feel they have no imagination, at least no visual imagination. They fear it, hesitating to employ it in relation to prayer. Yet their imagination may be much more active than they realize. They might be invited to notice such commonplace life situations as planning what they will wear to their friend's wedding, organizing their day to make sure that the children get picked up or preparing what they will say at an important meeting. These simple exercises can expand their understanding of imagination and help them claim the kinds they do have. Nonthreatening guided exercises, symbolic fantasies, such as Anthony de Mello (1978) suggests, can prove both helpful and revealing, preparatory to scriptural prayer.

One guide relates a provocative example that occurred during a workshop on imaginative prayer. A woman was asked to imagine a sculptor had created a statue of her. In her imagination, she was to walk into a room where the covered statue waited and remove the sheet. She did so and was at first delighted by the likeness, but subsequently repulsed when she saw the statue portrayed her standing with her hands over her eyes, covering her face. Still following directions, she watched incredulously as workmen came in, lifted the statue and loaded it in to the back of a pickup truck. She followed the pickup to a familiar location—in actual life, her therapist's office. The workmen placed the statue in the waiting room and there, merging with the statue, she stood with her hands over her face. Children coming into the waiting room begged her to remove her hands, but she couldn't. Finally she was told that Jesus had entered the room and was standing in front of her. She couldn't see him. Suddenly she heard Jesus say words to her that she had often heard from her spiritual director: "Ann, look at me." He gently touched her immobile hands and took them away from her face. At that moment she began to feel differently about herself and God. This imaginative encounter triggered an awareness in her in a way that many other efforts had not succeeded in doing (Kelly 1991, 12).

There is nothing magic about this or several other helpful techniques such as "image guidance" or focusing.[7] When prayer seems blocked, it helps to explore whether images are the culprit. If one's images of the holy mystery of God are static, then chances are so is one's spiritual life.

## Examen: Prayer of Women's Consciousness

The particular examination, suitably adapted in form and focus, has the potential to become truly a prayer of women's experience. The seeker begins by acknowledging her own gifts and exploring the implications of her gifts. In this process, she also discovers the negative consequences of her choices. Rather than emphasizing areas of failure, however, women generally profit more from reflecting on areas of giftedness, graces, breakthroughs and successes, recognizing how God has brought fruit into all dimensions of life. Women often need time to acknowledge their gifts and to take responsibility for their own lives, since they may not habitually do so. They may need to get in touch with their own initiative and responsibility in response to an initiating, enlivening and loving God. The dailiness of the particular examination fosters this internalization.

Examen also fosters the realization that the present moment, ordinary as it may be, is the fruit of one's past choices and leads to future ones. It moves from a superficial survey of what happened in a day to a deeper sense of patterns in one's life. This first step, noticing, needs to be followed by analysis, judgment and choosing, for as one sees, one judges and acts. The practice of examen can evolve from exterior norms to interior movements, from individualistic assessment to communal and social responsibility, from a specific list of daily practices to a discerning way of life, from externally imposed norms to a sense of personal coresponsibility with God.

Self-knowledge plays a role in every great religious tradition, yet one can never become totally aware of everything about oneself. Sooner or later, the particular examen leads to the unconscious. The process of integration requires bringing to light aspects of the self kept out of consciousness, so as to use them in service of one's ultimate goal.

By definition, one has no awareness of what is unconscious. How does one notice what one does not notice? Clues do exist: in dreams, slips of the tongue, resistances and desires and projections, both positive and negative. Pertinent questions reveal pivotal insights. What are the "musts" in my life? Where do they come from? What if I disregard one of them? What do I really dislike in others? How is this quality present in me? What do I really desire, and how does it differ from what I have deemed an "acceptable" desire? What is going on when my response is out of proportion to the situation? When examen reaches this depth, it becomes par excellence a prayer of ongoing conversion.[8]

Examen can raise particular difficulties for women. They may come to this prayer with a stronger sense of being sinned against than of sinning. The important move then becomes the transition from being a victim to being a self-directed agent of one's own life, a shift that may take months or years. "Why is this taking so long? Why can't I just forgive and get on with my life?" they may say. Sensitive accompaniment will help them continue patiently through the process, rejoicing at each new degree of freedom.

Women can also notice too much, being blinded by detail. Learning to sift the wheat from the chaff and letting the less important go in service of the central can sometimes prove a difficult struggle. They may need an outside perspective, someone who helps them evaluate their experiences and choices in light of their deepest desires. The guide must exercise vigilance here by focusing on such questions as, Where does the deepest integrity of this person really lie? Am I reflecting the desire I want her to have, or is it really her desire, flowing from her integrity?

Practiced over time, examen can truly be a prayer of women's experience. As such, it becomes a source of revelation, not only for the individual woman, but ultimately, all persons.[9]

## Meditation: Using One's Mind as Prayer

Ignatius's presentation on discursive meditation [45–54] explicates more of a specific method than any kind of teaching on this form of prayer. Many women report disliking his outline of meditation. Some find it too heady or the structure cumbersome and artificial. Contemporary women may not need all the accompanying suggestions, preferring to prepare themselves for prayer by listening to appropriate music, utilizing body movement, yoga, fantasy or a simple breath prayer.

The second prelude remains significant for women: "asking for what I want and desire." The prelude focuses women in a healthy and helpful way and the reflective prayer itself may lead to deeper desires or wants. Recognizing and naming these desires encourages the process of self-appropriation.

Having the colloquy at the end seems to separate the affective element from intellectual activity, thus maintaining the dualism of head or heart prayer. On the contrary, one should view this necessary form of reflection from an affective perspective. Using one's mind is not an isolated endeavor any more than prayer of presence or of the heart is divorced from intellect. One brings the fullness of one's being to whatever form of prayer is employed.

Bringing her mind to bear on affective states can prove a revealing exercise, particularly when dealing with "negative" emotions. For example, spending a period of meditation "standing in one's anger" or journaling about it in the presence of Jesus can facilitate an enlightening and healing meditation, as can praying over Jesus' own anger in the temple (John 2:13–17). Body movement can also provide an expressive and prayerful medium (Fischer 1988, 190–92).

The rich tradition of discursive prayer prior to Ignatius began to deteriorate in the fourteenth century when reflection on religious or mystical experience was separated from the rest of theology. Prior to this time, theology implicitly contained the fruit of a profoundly prayerful life, as seen in the writings of Bernard of Clairvaux, Gregory of Nyssa, Bonaventure and others (W. Johnston 1995, 60–73). This separation greatly diminished the "base" of meditation, resulting in the contemporary need to broaden the human experience grounding this form. One effective way to do this is by reading widely: devotional classics or "spiritual reading," theology and literature, including novels and poetry. Drama, film, art and dance also add immeasurably to the depth and meaning of this or any form of prayer.

A second historical reality affecting prayer, still very much alive for many, is the perception of progressing in stages of prayer. In this model, meditation lies near the bottom of the ladder, implying a "second-class" status. Yet, real life does not bear out this approach to growth in prayer. Most of the great mystics or persons writing about prayer today report frequently using discursive prayer. Like any relationship, there are times of greater intellectual intensity as well as quiet and "being with."

Another antimeditation bias emerges from the more recent Eastern influence on contemporary prayer. Non-Christian and even Orthodox techniques generally focus on less activity by the pray-er and a gradual elimination of thought, image and symbol from consciousness. But both active and passive prayer have a place; the seasons and conditions of life change, calling forth a variety of prayer styles (Houdek 1995, 32).[10]

## Contemplation: Cultivating the Imagination

Drawing on a tradition of the late Middle Ages, Ignatius invites the seeker to envision a particular scene in Jesus' life as a kind of icon through which she moves and to become involved in Jesus' own life experience as a participant. The one making the Exercises consciously creates the scene and the persons involved and allows the story to unfold, prompted by the reading of scripture and the action of the Spirit.

One woman related the following. She had been praying with the story of the risen Christ appearing to Mary Magdalene (John 20:11–18). After listening to her describe her prayer, her Exercises guide remarked, "You know, I think you are looking *at* the story. You are not inside it. Why don't you let yourself *into* it?" With that encouragement, she returned to her prayer. The next day she reported, "I allowed myself to feel what I imagined Mary must have been feeling as she walked in the garden. Then Jesus turned around, and I recognized him, and he gave me the warmest, most loving hug!" She later observed, "I always thought I had no imagination. But it's not true—I have a great deal of imagination. I never knew Scripture could be so alive." The difference imagination can make in the feeling-tone of prayer may be life-changing.

Scripture, as noted, has a symbolic character. A Scripture text does not just provide a revelatory glimpse into the past, but a way of looking at oneself and others in the present. The events are mysteries that become alive and operative in the present. The story enters into one's own journey.

One author relates the experience of a woman asked to pray over the incident of Peter walking on the water (Matt 14:23–33). She had no difficulty getting into the boat, recognizing the presence of both Jesus and Peter, with whom she identified in her desire to be with the Master. Things went well for a time, but prayer seemed to "break down" when she attempted to get out of the boat. She told Jesus she could not do it and admitted to him she was scared because she could not swim. She then "felt" that Jesus was asking her if she thought he was making her do something beyond her capacity. She immediately replied, "Yes, you are…you often have." The deepest encounter took place as she realized she really did not trust Jesus because she did not know him well enough (Sheldrake 1987, 106). Her prayer did not really "break down," however, as the Spirit moved her in a direction she needed to go.

Imaginative contemplation does not mean slavishly sticking to the script, much less spending inordinate time on unnecessary details of the scene. Visualizing Jesus clearly is not important; a sense of presence is enough. Often communication is "felt" or intuited, rather than heard as ordinary conversation.[11]

Because many people equate the imagination with the ability to visualize, they feel they cannot do this type of prayer. But imagination does not rely only on sight. People can get in touch with their own imaginative process by focusing on the sound of car tires crunching on a gravel driveway or of rain pelting the roof, by smelling the odor of a bakery or a loved one's perfume, by feeling the soft, frowsy, wobbly head of an infant or the lushness of velvet, or by tasting a favorite dish or cold beer on a hot day. A simple fantasy may unloose the imagination: "You are on a beach…a hillside…sitting by a river.…Briefly describe the scene using different senses.…In the distance you see someone approaching.…Let the imagination take over." Success in such imaginative exercises gives courage to move beyond fear and anxiety and opens up for imaginative scriptural prayer.

Some women begin prayer by reflecting on their immediate life experience rather than on Scripture, but this procedure does not preclude imaginative contemplation. Jesus can be invited into the scene, to participate in the mystery of an individual's life, perhaps consoling, healing, challenging or drawing attention to a new perspective. The risen Jesus makes a past or present event the Word of God. More often, the seeker's lived experience, when probed with the guide, calls to mind a specific Scripture passage that can take on a whole new perspective in light of a daily happening. The seeker "backs into" Scripture, so to speak.

Some persons find themselves drawn to a more quiet, nondiscursive, imageless form of prayer, the classical notion of contemplation.[12] Persons drawn into this manner of prayer by way of solid discernment need not be excluded from the dynamic of the Exercises, which encourages the seeker to enter as she can and not according to rigid definitions or forms of prayer. Ignatius insists that the guide allow God to deal directly with the seeker [15].

The imaginative aspect of prayer may last for most of the time or be a relatively brief experience, possibly a threshold to something more quiet and reflective. Imagination is not an end in itself, but a powerful way of disposing one for an encounter with the living Christ who often speaks directly to a present situation or condition. Believing that God alone controls prayer gives one the freedom to follow wherever the Spirit leads.

## Application of the Senses: Embodiment in Prayer

Ignatius's terse description of Application of the Five Senses has opened a multidimensional approach to the senses, exterior and interior. The reflection on the five external senses within the First Method of Prayer [247–48] could well serve as a "priming" experience for most persons beginning the Spiritual Exercises.

The first and most immediate dimension of the Application of the Senses presumes an aliveness of the exterior bodily senses at the service of a faith perspective. The second dimension employs sense imagery by way of imagination and memory. The third dimension implies the activation of the interior senses by a Presence beyond human capacities to initiate.

The first dimension, awareness by the external physical senses, leads one beyond simple apprehension: "When we become present to and respectful of our bodily knowing and sensing, we become available for relationship with everything that is, including God" (Ruffing 1995, 105). This kind of openness may sound simple, but the fast pace of contemporary life carries with it a sensory numbing as one of its unhappy by-products. The deeper implications of a good part of experience get lost; life is not lived contemplatively.

One woman's recollection exemplifies how simple sensory awareness can lead to God and how all three dimensions coalesce:

> I recall when I was spending some time along the Icicle River.
> Whenever I have been in this picturesque area, surrounded by
> age-worn pines, the roar of the turbulent river in my ears, the
> scents of the season sharp in my nostrils—sun-toasted needles,
> naturally ripened blackberry vines—I have felt in my heart a
> great longing for God. As I contemplated the beauty of countless
> mountains surrounding the little valley through which the Icicle
> River flowed, I became aware that I had the privilege of seeing
> this beauty and of praising God for it. In a flash of insight I knew
> that God did not make all that wondrous scenery to get praised
> for it. I realized that God is so lavish as to make the beauty
> whether or not anyone ever even sees it! It was a momentary
> insight into the total meaning of things. I felt at-one with the
> earth and with my fellow inhabitants. The experience tapped into
> my interior creative sense, making me aware of my surroundings
> and, as my senses seemed to come alive, of my body's relationship
> with them. I saw for this moment the magnanimous nature of
> God, with plenty of room for inserting my gifts into life-with-
> God. I relinquished my need to be a "something," knowing that
> just to be, as the mountains just "are," was enough for this God.

Another woman making the Exercises was encouraged to
express grief in body movement. She was surprised to realize an
enormous unresolved anger emerging instead. The body registers
and remembers every experience, even if the mind is not conscious of
it. Thus, Application of the Senses becomes a way of honoring a
memory and either deepening and savoring it, or bringing it consciously to God for healing.

This first dimension also includes an awareness that goes beyond mere sensation. Imagination gives entry to the deepest realities because it approaches life in its wholeness: matter *and* spirit, not matter *or* spirit. Imagination establishes a relationship between the two, eliminating dualism and hierarchy. Rather, they fuse together in a kind of double vision or overlay of transparencies, allowing one to intuit the presence of mystery in the most ordinary things. The exterior senses become a portal to a deeper reality grasped only by faith. Imagination is integral to the living out of contemplation in action (Fischer, 1989, 23).

One woman's experience exemplifies this "double vision." She was literally confronted by her psychological "shadow" on a busy street in Chicago's South Side. A young woman approached and asked her "to take her home and give her something to eat." The immediacy of the request stung her at several levels: She felt compassion for the woman, overwhelmed by the intensity of the brief exchange and haunted by the "more" of the experience. Subsequent prayer helped her see God asking her to take care of herself instead of continually "pushing beyond" physical limitations. This first dimension of Application of the Senses, then, allows a person to enter fully into the present moment and be open to the deeper significance of immediate experience.

The second dimension moves inward, relying on the imaginative use of the senses along with memory, either reliving an experience such as the above or inserting oneself into a Gospel scene, an event in one's life or some artistic endeavor. Seasoned pray-ers will recognize moving into a mystery of Jesus' life as a participant—or even as Jesus—interacting with specific characters. Time demarcations blur and Jesus becomes present now, consoling, challenging, teaching, supporting or healing. A distinct affective quality usually marks this level of Application of the Senses.

Another woman contemplated the same scene in Matthew 14: 23–33, where Jesus invites Peter to walk on water:

> I was sitting in the open boat, feeling myself tossed from side to side, wet with the spray of crashing waves. I could not hear what my companions were yelling because of the noise of the storm. We were all terrified. I saw Jesus in the distance, coming across the water from the right, but I wasn't afraid of him at all. I wanted to get out of the boat to walk toward him but I was so exhausted I wasn't sure I could make it. I had waited so long for his coming! All of a sudden he seemed to be right beside me, calming both the water and the rapid palpitations of my heart. He didn't speak of any lack of faith, but told me not to worry...I had been walking on water for the last eight or nine years. But he assured me he had repeatedly kept me from "going under" both when I begged for help and when I simply needed it. I felt the blessed tears which for me are always a sign of God's presence. His words were so reassuring and vindicating in the midst of a storm of confusion, ambiguity and diminishment. I spent the remainder of prayer in deep gratitude and peace.

Previous dimensions, external sensation or internal imagery may move to a still deeper dimension beyond the active capability of the pray-er. The interior or "spiritual" sense metaphorically describes an ineffable immediate experience of the Divine. The Exercises themselves give only an extremely brief description of this dimension, but Ignatius's letter to Teresa Rejadell, a cloistered nun from Barcelona, sheds further light on it:

> For it frequently happens that our Lord moves and urges the soul to this or that activity. He begins by enlightening the soul;

that is to say, by speaking interiorly to it without the din of words, lifting it up wholly to His divine love and ourselves to His meaning without any possibility of resistance on our part, even should we wish to resist. (Young 1959, 22)

Ignatius's deepest dimension taps into a long tradition originating with Origen and later adopted by Augustine (K. Rahner 1979a, 1979b). Augustine's immortal passage illustrates well the interior senses (although it leaves some ambiguity about his understanding of the body). It seems clear, however, that God's use of the interior senses leads toward an appreciation of the concrete world, not away from it:

But what do I love when I love my God? Not material beauty or beauty of a temporal order; not the brilliance of earthy light, so welcome to our eyes; not the sweet melody of harmony and song; not the fragrance of flowers, perfumes, and spices; not manna or honey; not limbs such as the body delights to embrace. It is not these that I love when I love my God. And yet, when I love him, it is true that I love a light of a certain kind, a voice, a perfume, a food, an embrace; but they are of the kind that I love in my inner self, when my soul is bathed in light that is not bound by space; when it listens to sound that never dies away; when it breathes fragrance that is not borne on the wind; when it tastes food that is never consumed by the eating; when it clings to an embrace from which it is not severed by fulfillment of desire. This is what I love when I love my God (Augustine 1961, 211–12).

Ignatius says simply, "...smell the fragrance and taste the infinite sweetness and charm of the Divinity" [124]. What he speaks of cannot be taught, only received in gratefulness and awe. This gift of God obliterates any notion of dualism, consecrating once again the embodied spirit and the preciousness of the entire being. For Ignatius, "this form of the Application of the Senses was the very essence of *sentir*— the feeling for the things of God" (H. Rahner 1968, 2). Mystics characteristically use sensory imagery in describing their experience of God. For example, Teresa of Avila, a contemporary of Ignatius, is more explicit than he in describing one of her intense religious experiences:

> But when this most wealthy Spouse desires to enrich and comfort the bride still more, He draws her so closely to him that she is like one who swoons from excess of pleasure and joy and seems suspended in those Divine arms and drawn near to that sacred side and to those Divine breasts. Sustained by that Divine milk with which her Spouse continually nourishes her and growing in grace so that she may be enabled to receive His comfort, she can do nothing but rejoice....With what to compare this the soul knows not, save to the caresses of a mother who so dearly loves her child and feeds and caresses it. (Teresa of Jesus 1950, 384–85)

If Teresa were to make the Exercises today, how might the one guiding the Exercises respond? Experiences that defy gender and role stereotypes, that come clothed in a baroque mix of metaphors, could prove daunting to someone unacquainted with the classic mystics and the possibilities of divine initiative very much present in our era. Granted, no one today would use this type of language, yet the experience could be equally profound.[13]

A contemporary woman speaks simply of her experience, implicitly pointing to a common obstacle for many persons—intellectualizing:

> I have been hearing the music again. I mean, quite literally, I hear music, like I did as a child....[W]hen I play it, I am likely to

burst into tears, for its source is the Mystery, and I am playing something sacred that vibrates in places that are once again receiving light after many long years of darkness. I know that intellectualism has lost its grip on my being. What I do or what I become are not important so long as I listen to the music and dance.

Intellectualizing does not pose a trap just for men. Women too often interiorize cultural myths that honor only rational thinking and scientific proof. Persons who dismiss intuition and imagination approach life with an enormous handicap.

Application of the Senses, at whatever dimension, addresses a fully embodied way of knowing, not only through the intellect, but also the heart, feelings, intuition and imagination. The mind wants to know, to analyze and abstract, but the embodied spirit wants to be surprised and willingly risks encounter with the fullness of one's being. Knowing God in this way points not just to God in all of creation, but also to God within. The external senses are a threshold to awareness of how God touches, embraces and intimately creates each person, moment by moment, even if one does not feel it.

## The Three Methods of Prayer: Taking Adaptation Seriously

The literature on the Spiritual Exercises contains considerable discussion about whether these methods best suit "beginners" or those "advanced" in the spiritual life. The terms of the discussion come across as another form of hierarchy that makes value judgments about the rich diversity of prayer. Those who do not find their experience represented among the "valuable" prayer forms feel once again disenfranchised from their birthright. The guide has a responsibility to help the seeker find the most useful, indeed pleasurable, method of prayer, establish a faithful practice and adjust this practice in the face of the inevitable shifts that will occur as her relationship with God deepens.[14] A double-faceted corollary suggests itself: Whatever prayer form facilitates the dynamic movement of the Exercises may be used, whether or not Ignatius specifically suggests it, and the best kind of prayer is that which supports living one's everyday life with intentionality and integrity.[15] Guides face a subtle temptation here: to impose prayer forms they either like or know while subtly discouraging prayer forms they do not find helpful themselves.

Some modifications can make these methods of prayer more appropriate for contemporary women. Today ruminating on wisdom teachings such as the Beatitudes and prophetic calls issued by the church might replace an exclusive focus on the Ten Commandments. For example, the Barmen Declaration[16] or the Roman Catholic bishops' pastoral, *Economic Justice for All* (1986), can yield rich and fruitful prayer in relationship to issues of justice. Instead of reflecting on the Capital Sins, a focus on the virtues necessary for living in harmony with the entire planet may make more sense. Once again, Ignatius's focus on the individual can expand to include all the systems in which the seeker lives.

In contrast to a culture that fosters numbness, the prayers on the Three Powers of the Soul and on the Five Senses of the Body stir up and "befriend" all these aspects of the person. Sensory stimuli bombard the contemporary world. Traffic roars constantly in the background; even in rural areas, the night sky rarely becomes black because of the artificial light of cities; "musak" assaults the ears of persons in every elevator, waiting room and even over the telephone; commercials leap out from every radio, television and computer; and stimulants and other chemicals enter the body through overly processed food, to say nothing of the chemicals sought out to counter the deadness felt inside. No wonder our senses shut down: They never rest. A sabbath from overstimulation may prepare one to experience the senses anew; a simple fast from ordinary foods evokes a fresh, vivid taste of the first foods consumed.

In like manner, becoming aware of one's powers of memory, reasoning and choosing will prepare all these aspects of oneself to profit from the Exercises. These additional methods are not simply preparation for prayer, they *are* prayer in their own right.

A long section entitled "The Mysteries of the Life of Christ Our Lord" [261–312] immediately follows the Three Methods of Prayer. It does not contain a new method of prayer, but raises the issue of adaptation once again. It concerns presenting the biblical material in the Exercises and how it informs prayer.

Describing this section highlights how Ignatius uses Scripture. Numbers 261 through 312 consist of fifty-one additional Contemplations for use during the Second, Third and Fourth Weeks [162] or after the Exercises are completed. Each Contemplation centers on an event in the life of Christ and gives only the three central points, presuming the preparatory prayer, preludes and colloquy. The Spanish translations from the Latin *Vulgate* are Ignatius's own, and thus do not correspond exactly to contemporary versions (Ganss 1991, 421–22).

What Ignatius includes and omits has engendered much interest. He bases all but two Contemplations on Scripture: the appearances of the risen Christ to his mother [299], which he justifies with the statement that Jesus appeared to many others, and to Joseph of Arimathea [310], which he takes from the lives of the saints. The first eleven cover the infancy narratives. The final twenty-four cover passion and resurrection narratives, with two unexpected changes: he adds a "Thirteenth Apparition" based on 1 Corinthians 15:8 and excludes Pentecost (Egan 1987, 83).

Omissions from the sixteen remaining passages covering the public life of Christ are likewise glaring. There are no healings of the sick, blind or lame, no exorcisms, no forgiveness of sins, and no parables (Peters 1967, 114). The passages in which Jesus interacts with women are few (the Wedding Feast at Cana [276], the Conversion of Magdalene [282], the Raising of Lazarus [285], in which Mary and Martha are only supporting characters, and the Supper in Bethany [286]). Ignatius, like many others, equates Mary Magdalen with the unknown sinner.

Ignatius's biblical scholarship reflects his time. For example, he selects from several Gospels to construct the points for one contemplation, creating a kind of harmony. This procedure, usual in his day, has been eclipsed since the rise of modern form criticism. Clearly, a contemporary approach to the Spiritual Exercises must be undergirded by advances in biblical scholarship.

Ideally, the one making the Exercises will have internalized the fruits of modern biblical scholarship and make such shifts easily, but it is equally possible that a woman approaches the Scriptures without benefit of modern Scripture scholarship. She may find great consolation in a literal interpretation of Scripture, for example. She may have difficulty with Ignatian contemplation until she can resolve the theological issue of "correct" interpretation of Scripture. "That's not the Word of God, that's my imagination," she may insist. Yet, if not forced to identify Ignatian contemplation too facilely with her understanding of a biblical Word of God, she may still desire to experience what Jesus might want to say to her today. She may then willingly explore through active imagination how he might address her immediate needs. The biblical event simply frames this conversation. Once she experiences the immediate presence of the living Christ, her resistance to imaginative contemplation of Scripture may well lessen. Gentle and suitably framed suggestions about the ongoing and personal nature of God's revelation and the place of Scripture within this revelation will also help.

Even biblically literate women may be startled to uncover the patriarchy embedded in Scripture. If this discovery occurs during the course of the Exercises, the strong feelings evoked become important material for prayer. They may wish to abandon the biblical text as a source for prayer. They may need encouragement to stay with this unpleasant discovery rather than abandon the biblical text.

In accord with the principle that the Exercises should be adapted to each person, women may need a selection of mysteries adapted to their predilections and preferences in prayer. If they so desire, they should receive encouragement to pray with passages involving women or having particular relevance to women. Some likely pericopes include the woman taken in adultery (John 7:53–8:11), Jesus weeping over Jerusalem (Luke 13:34), the woman who causes Jesus to change his mind (Mark 7:24–30), the first resurrection appearance to Mary Magdalene (John 20:11–18), the cures of the bent-over woman (Luke 13:10–17), the woman with the hemorrhage and the raising of the little girl (Luke 8:40–56) and the women who follow Jesus (Luke 8:1–3). Other alternatives include inviting women to put themselves in the place of male characters, such as Zacchaeus, Lazarus or Peter or encouraging them to pray with a single Gospel and allowing the figure of Jesus to develop within its theology and spirituality.

Since the individuals making the Exercises will vary widely in their experiences, desires, biblical interpretation and theology, one cannot possibly propose a single list of texts women might find useful. The one giving the Exercises must have an ease with Scripture and knowledge of contemporary scholarship in order to move seamlessly between the biblical text and the particular needs of each person. There is no shortcut to this intimate acquaintance with the Scriptures.

## Wisdom for the One Giving the Exercises

Like many mystics, Ignatius does not elaborate a mystical theology or an extended teaching on prayer to undergird his work. He does not describe stages of prayer or nights of the senses and spirit as do his contemporaries Teresa of Avila or John of the Cross. He simply outlines forms of prayer, offering several possibilities that might appeal and lead one to God.

Within the Exercises he assembles a rich fare of prayer practices and techniques borrowed from the living tradition, adding his own particular emphasis on service as fruit of prayer. His stress on concreteness, the beauty of creation, embodied prayer, use of the imaginative faculty and openness to affectivity generally appeal to women, even if certain images are repugnant or outdated.

Ignatius's emphasis on disposing oneself for prayer should encompass music, yoga, body movement, fantasy and breath prayer, whatever techniques tend to move a woman toward centeredness and focus. A respectful use of Native American and Eastern practices has helped many persons. Those women out of touch with the gift of the senses or who tend to intellectualize might find Ignatius's Prayer on the Five Senses of the Body [247] or adaptations thereof helpful. Often women use art work, poetry or even body movement to report back to their guide. These media are significant because, by their very nature, they operate at a heart level.

In moving into the dynamic of the Exercises, some women are so intent on praying correctly that they violate their own spirituality. Anyone making the Exercises must be in tune with where God leads and seems to be present rather than rigidly adhere to the specific form of prayer suggested. For example, in Jesus' healing of blind Bartimaeus (Mark 10:46–52) one can move into prayer with a word or phrase that becomes a mantra. Alternately, one can simply be present to the God-in-Jesus who heals or recall an event in life where one was healed of blindness or perhaps assisted another in this way. Whatever prayer form facilitates the dynamic movement of the Exercises should be used [2, 15, 76]. This flexibility seems to reflect the mind of Ignatius: prayer forms are not sacred—the relationship with God is. Ignatius's chief concern lies in assisting others to experience God and subsequently to go out in service to others.[17]

Finding ways that are "pleasurable" [238] does not simply mean experiencing comfort and warmth. It may mean confronting the need to take care of the earth, to probe questionable policies in church or government, or to go to that person with whom one violently disagrees. The one making the Exercises should remain open to these new possibilities. Unfortunately, prayer itself can be an idol, substituting for the living God. The way God desires to be found *now* may be different than in the past.

A related issue concerns a hierarchy that judges some prayer as better than others. Theologian Karl Rahner maintained that mystical experience does not mark a higher stage of the Christian life, but rather expresses the *psychology* of individual persons. Extraordinary mystical phenomena may reveal God's intimate presence, but may use the language of the pray-er's psychosomatic structure. Theologically, the experience of God in meditation or in classical infused contemplation is the same gift of God (K. Rahner, 1986, 75–77). God comes through any form of prayer.

Thus, persons who apprehend life in Ruth Burrows's "lights on" modality consciously experience God's presence and action at least some of the time. Others grow through the darkness and nakedness of pure faith in what Burrows (1980) calls "lights off" or Karl Rahner terms "winter grace." Neither journey is better: it simply is what it is by the grace and gift of God. Many experience a combination of both.

The body of Ignatius's writing does not seem to advocate any one form of prayer. He was not concerned whether a prayer form was more "advanced" but whether it was authentic for an individual and a wellspring of integrity and service. The ultimate criteria of any prayer or religious experience or lack thereof lies in the quality of one's life and the ability to go out in love and compassion to others, oneself and to our earth. Fidelity to prayer and a desire for God marks any authentic relationship with God. It matters not whether the prayer is characterized by parapsychological phenomena, rich affect or complete blankness. Outward indications of authentic prayer, however described, are recognizable over time: interior freedom and trust of God, self and others; greater flexibility and less judgmentalism; lessening of various kinds of fear; a mellowing-out or gentleness; absence of defensiveness; and of course, peace and joy.

The guide, too, needs to be a person of deep prayer who grants others the freedom to pray as they can. He or she need to be able to intuit when God invites the one making the Exercises to a different prayer form, which may elicit some initial fear and hesitancy. This sensitivity by the guide to God's action presumes an awareness of the subtleties of the Rules for the Discernment of Spirits, as well as a knowledge of the broader tradition of prayer. It is a knowledge born of personal experience and study, coupled with total reliance on the Spirit.

# Notes

1. Our assumption remains despite a burst of writing on prayer in the Spiritual Exercises that spurred their contemporary renewal. See, for example, Thomas Burke, *Methods of Prayer in the Spiritual Exercises* (Jersey City, N.J.: Program to Adapt the Spiritual Exercises, n.d.); Joseph Conwell, *Contemplation in Action: A Study in Ignatian Prayer* (Spokane, Wash.: Gonzaga University, 1957); Joseph de Guibert, *The Jesuits, Their Spiritual Doctrine and Practice: A Historical Study* (St. Louis: Institute of Jesuit Studies, 1964); and Peters (1967). More recent collections of articles such as those in the *Way Supplements* 16 (1972) and 82 (1995) reach few persons other than specialists in spirituality.

For contemporary adaptations and presentations of prayer forms within the Spiritual Exercises intended for wider readership, see the Take and Receive series by Jacqueline Bergan and Marie Schwan, *Love,* (1985), *Forgiveness* (1985), *Birth* (1985), *Surrender* (1986), and *Freedom* (1988) (Winona, Minn.: St. Mary's Press); Jacqueline Syrup Bergan and Marie Schwan, *Praying with Ignatius of Loyola* (Winona, Minn.: St. Mary's Press, 1991); Thomas Green, *A Vacation with the Lord* (Notre Dame, Ind.: Ave Maria Press, 1986); R. Huelsman, *Pray: Participant's and Moderator's Manuals* (New York: Paulist, 1976); Mark Link, *Challenge: A Meditation Program Based on The Spiritual Exercises of St. Ignatius* (Valencia, Calif.: Tabor Publishing, 1988); de Mello (1978); George Schemel, ed. *Focusing Group Energies: Common Ground for Leadership, Organization, Spirituality* (Scranton, Pa.: University of Scranton, 1992, formerly titled *Ignatian Spiritual Exercises for the Corporate Person: Structured Resources for Group Development,* 1987); and Joseph Tetlow, *Choosing Christ in the World* (St. Louis: Institute of Jesuit Sources, 1989).

2. See also Dennis Hamm, "Rummaging for God: Praying Backward Through Your Day," *America* 170 (May 14, 1994): 22–23 and Tad Dunne, *Spiritual Exercises for Today* (San Francisco: Harper, 1991), 122–27.

3. Joseph A Tetlow, S.J. "The Most Postmodern Prayer: American Jesuit Identity and the Examen of Conscience, 1920–1990," *Studies in the*

*Spirituality of Jesuits* 26 (January 1994) offers an analysis of the shifts in philosophy, theology and American culture in this century and chronicles their effects on the examination of conscience.

4. The lack of clarity about Application of the Senses dates from the *Official Directory* of 1599, which summarily dismissed Application of the Senses as a method suitable for beginners or those fatigued by earlier prayer periods (Palmer 1996, 321–23). This interpretation gained ascendancy despite Juan de Polanco's own *Directory* dated 1574. Polanco, who had served as Ignatius's personal secretary from 1547 on and presumably knew his mind on the Exercises, differentiates two understandings of Application of the Senses: a simple use of imagination and a form of infused contemplation (Alexandre Brou, *Ignatian Methods of Prayer* [Milwaukee: Bruce, 1949], 162). For an excellent and detailed analysis of the discussion within the Society of Jesus on Application of the Senses, see also Hugo Rahner (1968), chapter 5; and Philip Endean, "The Ignatian Prayer of the Senses" *Heythrop Journal* 31 (1990): 391–418.

5. For further discussion on imagination and spirituality, see Kathleen Fischer, "The Imagination in Spirituality," *The Way Supplement* 66 (Autumn 1989): 96. For an excellent explication of imagination in general, see Ann and Barry Ulanov, *The Healing Imagination* (New York: Paulist, 1991).

6. Two excellent resources on active imagination are Robert Johnson, *Inner Work* (San Francisco: Harper and Row, 1986) and Barbara Hannah, *Encounters with the Soul: Active Imagination* (Santa Maria: Sigo Press, 1981).

7. See Eugene Gendlin (1979); Peter Campbell and Edwin McMahon, *Biospirituality* (Chicago: Loyola University Press, 1985) and Elizabeth Anne Vanek, *Image Guidance* (New York: Paulist, 1992).

8. On this point, see Judith A Roemer's "Examination of Unconsciousness," *Human Development* 6 (Fall, 1985): 50–52.

9. We suggest the following abbreviated form of examen used by the Spiritual Exercises in the Everyday Life Program, Seattle, Washington:

A Daily Check-in

Jesus
you have been present with me
in my life today
Be near, now.

Let us look together at my day.
Let me see through your loving
eyes…
When did I listen to your voice
today?
When did I resist listening to you
today?

Jesus,
everything is gift from you.
I give you thanks and praise
for the gifts of this day…

I ask your healing in…
I ask your forgiveness and
mercy for…

Jesus,
continue to be present with me
in my life each day.

We also recommend Dennis Linn, Sheila Fabricant Linn and Matthew Linn, *Sleeping with Bread: Holding What Gives Us Life* (New York: Paulist, 1995) for an excellent treatment of examen, and adaptations for various individual and group times of prayer.

10. A very interesting comparison between contemporary prayer forms and classical contemplation is Ernest E Larkin, "Today's Contemplative Prayer Forms: Are they Contemplation?" *Review for Religious* 57 (Jan/Feb 1998): 77–87.

11. For further discussion of imaginative contemplation, see John Wickham, "Ignatian Contemplation Today," in *The Way of Ignatius Loyola,* ed. Philip Sheldrake (St. Louis: Institute of Jesuit Sources, 1991), 145–53 and Kathleen Fischer, *Inner Rainbow* (New York: Paulist, 1983), 70–88.

12. For a concise article on working with a person utilizing the prayer of faith see Dermot Mansfield, "The Exercises and Contemplative Prayer," in *The Way of Ignatius of Loyola,* ed. Philip Sheldrake (St. Louis: Institute of Jesuit Sources, 1991), 191–202.

13. On the phenomenology of mysticism, see Nelson Pike, *Mystic Union* (Ithaca, N.Y.: Cornell University Press, 1992); and Janet Ruffing, "Encountering Love Mysticism," *Presence* 1 (January 1995): 20–33, and *Spiritual Direction: Beyond the Beginnings* (New York: Paulist, 2000).

14. A particularly sensitive treatment of these shifts can be found in Mary Sharon Riley, "Women and Contemplation," *The Way Supplement* 82 (Spring 1995): 35–43.

15. The question of what constitutes "Ignatian Prayer" and its relationship to the so-called degrees of prayer appears regularly in the literature on the Exercises. A particularly well-framed articulation of the position held here can be found in Veale (1995).

16. This document was issued in May 1934 by representatives of the Lutheran, Reformed and United Churches, to define the Christian opposition to National Socialism in Germany. It was a precursor to the formation of the Confessing Church. See Hubert G. Locke, *The Church Confronts the Nazis: Barmen Then and Now* (Lewiston: Edwin Mellen Press, 1984). The text may be found in *The Constitution of the Presbyterian Church* (U.S.A.): Part I: Book of Confessions (Louisville: Office of the General Assembly, 1996).

17. Excellent articles on this question include Veale (1995), and Frank Houdek, "The Limitations of Ignatian Prayer" *The Way Supplement* 82 (Spring, 1995): 26–43.

# PART III:

# Exercises

PART III:

Exercises

# Chapter 6

# Surrounded by Love:
# Exercises of the First Week

*...that I may feel an interior knowledge of my sins and also an abhorrence of them;*

*...that I may perceive the disorder of my actions in order to detest them, amend myself, and put myself in order;*

*...that I may have knowledge of the world, in order to detest it and rid myself of all that is worldly and vain.*

—Spiritual Exercises [63]

*Mortal and venial sin, compounded by stories of the fires of hell, are the antithesis of my belief about a loving and compassionate God. The content of the first week of the Exercises as well as its reasoned and rigid structures is repugnant to me.*

—A Contemporary Woman

The loved sinner stands at the center of the First Week of the Spiritual Exercises. Although sin provides the focus, the First Week really dwells on love, God's love, which is greater than human sin. This Week moves from awareness of and responsibility for sin to awareness of God's gracious love, a love that forgives sin and welcomes the sinner, like the forgiving and prodigal parent who embraces and welcomes home an erring offspring. Stories provide an avenue for this discovery.

In the First Week, cosmic and personal stories of conflict, alienation and destruction tend to disturb and disorient. Thus, the one making the Exercises immediately has to decide whether to trust the storytelling mode that grounds the Exercises and thus enter the narrative herself or to remain an observer. To continue implies confidence that the insight and self-understanding flowing from this reflection can move one toward the goal of personal freedom and not toward irrelevance, self-negation or unhealthy guilt. A decision to probe these stories in faith-filled attentiveness can reveal a new understanding of God's mystery present in the power of narrative. Difficult stories also have potential for revelation and transformation. An attentive ear, listening to the truth in both the cosmic and personal stories, combined with a confident voice willing to engage in spiritual conversation, can uncover deeper levels of meaning and direction.

## Material and Dynamics of the First Week

Two questions may quickly arise: What are the First Week exercises about? What is going to happen to me? These questions touch on context and process.

Answering these serious questions requires that one remember that God's gifts and hopes for humanity depend on one's free response to a personal call. Biblically based and imaginative stories reveal the cosmic struggle between good and evil, leading the one making the Exercises to the liberating discovery of God as compassionate Creator. In other words, the seeker experiences the story of sin and grace.

This awareness marks the major consciousness evoked in the First Week. As the one praying the Exercises becomes aware of multiple inner movements, she gains a clearer sense of what is of God and what is not of God. The God who creates and cares, Divine Majesty and Infinite Goodness, grounds one's deepest desires and deserves one's trust. Christ on the cross labors and saves. Each person, created in God's image and gifted in the mutuality of creation, is bound both by personal sin and, in some mysterious way, by the power of sin in the world. Such a realization can evoke tears, sorrow, confusion, helplessness and repentance. The God of love and mercy calls to conversion.

Frequently, those making the Exercises struggle between opposites; they feel tempted to trivialize and deny sin or to become overwhelmed at its enormity. Yet the movement of the Exercises continues: from avoiding to encountering and finally to accepting and understanding sin as a reality of faith. Paradoxically, in confronting sin, the presence of goodness becomes more visible, causing an aversion to everything not of God. In the First Week, a person's prayer moves from awareness, confusion and sorrow to a response of deep gratitude and love. The grace of the First Week emerges when personal desires come gradually into greater harmony with God's will and desire.

A closer look shows that the first exercise concentrates on the cosmic scope of sin in three stories of choice involving the angels, Adam and Eve and an anonymous sinner. The second exercise invites the one making the Exercises to move from observer to participant. She takes center stage in her own dramatic struggle to choose the direction of her life through memories of her personal "sin stories." She ponders her personal environment, her relationships and her work. Where has she lived? Who has she lived with? What has she been doing with her life? In the third and fourth exercises, utilizing repetition, she returns to the subject matter of her prior meditations, specifically her experiences of inner movement, both positive and negative, that potentially lead to greater insight and affection. The First Week concludes with the fifth exercise, a meditation on hell that draws upon the symbolic memory of all the senses (seeing, hearing, tasting, touching and smelling), graphically dramatizing the ultimate human evil imaginable—hell and whatever that suggests to the individual. There, in stark contrast, she realizes the unfathomable love of God. The graces of the First Week evolve from a more objective awareness and understanding of sin and its effect, to a deep personal realization that she is a loved and forgiven sinner. The pain of truth leads to the process of healing and the response of gratitude.

Human finitude and its redemption comprise the content of the First Week meditations. Meditation calls upon memory, imagination, reason and will in considering the reality of cosmic and personal sin. Repetition provides an opportunity to circle the material, allowing feelings of attraction or resistance to lead toward deeper insight and affectivity. The meditation on hell activates sensory awareness as a prayer of the whole person.

## Problems and Possibilities for Women

The First Week seems clear and the dynamic consistent. Yet women's realities raise probing questions and troubling issues. Some of the factors women identify as blocking entry into the First Week include the negative tone of the material, their dissatisfaction in praying with the Bible and their lack of imagination. One might say "I want to get out of my head," another, "I don't know what I want or desire." Such concerns can pose problems.

Some difficulties flow from rigid sense of structure, that is, How do I do it right? Some have gotten the impression, even prior to the Exercises, that a person must fit into a pattern and perform according to a script and that she will be evaluated on successful accomplishment of the tasks. This distorts the Spiritual Exercises, making them into a grueling regimen with predetermined tasks to accomplish, obstacles to overcome and goals to reach. The one making the Exercises may also find the subject matter of sin and hell distasteful, the desired emotions of shame and confusion fearful and some prayer forms artificial.

Reexamining the process and content of the First Week, however, will provide women with an alternative perspective. A contemporary worldview can open up a deeper realization about the interdependence of all creation and foster the basic recognition that she is not God. This assent leads to a growing sense of truth about self and God in light of the "creation and fall." The actual meditations provide starting points for an affective response arising from prayer, not necessarily ends in themselves. Additional biblical stories, personal experiences, images and insights beyond those suggested by the text can emerge as fruitful material for prayer of the First Week.

## Images of Self and God

Those giving the Exercises know that the texts of the Spiritual Exercises, particularly those passages describing the self envisioned by the Exercises, require critiquing. This critique is critical when the "self" is a woman, because meditating on this material can create hazards for both self-concept and God-image. Women especially react to the self-deprecation underlying the suggestion "to consider my soul as imprisoned in this corruptible body, and my whole compound self as an exile in this valley [of tears] among brute animals" [47]. Another text raises similar problems:

> I will reflect upon myself, by using examples which humble me:
> First what am I when compared with all other human
> beings?...I will look at all the corruption and foulness of my

body....I will look upon myself as a sore or abscess from which
have issued great sins and iniquities and such foul poison. [58]

While this dramatic statement of mortality may have startled
Ignatius's audience or echoed experiences of the early Companions,[1] it
seems to offer little of positive value for contemporary women.

Entering the Spiritual Exercises with a positive self-image and a
holistic understanding of the human person engenders a positive val-
uation of oneself as a whole being with a body, mind, spirit, emotions
and relationships. In this way, relationship and connection replace
dualism and polarization. When the one making the Exercises discovers and appreciates her own story and uses her own voice to tell it,
she contributes powerfully to the larger story of faith.

Listening becomes an essential skill for the one making the
Exercises. She must first learn to discern and honor her own authentic inner voice. This awareness and acceptance can prove difficult, as
the most familiar voices she may hear are the loud dominating voices
of external authority or the strident voice of her own inner critic.
Claiming the authority of her own voice becomes a prerequisite for
personal authenticity and for contributing to the wisdom of the faith
community. Thus, each woman's self-identity questions relate to concepts of self-image and God-image and make up an essential dynamic
of this First Week. She is encouraged to reflect on her self-image: self
as personal and as public but always as relational. The Exercises assume
the importance of self-definition leading to self-understanding. Each of
the Weeks move toward a greater self-reflexivity and therefore relate
to the dynamic direction of human development.

The actual dynamics of the First Week demonstrate how Ignatius
starts with the "big picture," a cosmic perspective, and gradually
moves toward the personal and specific. Personal responsibility, or
lack of it, is also viewed according to its impact on the greater reality.

The more self-reflexive one is, the more one sees one's personal role in the dynamics of creation. Reflecting on self-image remains impossible without relating to God.

The harmful effects of negative imagery extend beyond self-concept to God-concept, particularly in relationship to sin. When the woman making the Exercises perceives God primarily as Patriarchal King, Lord and Judge, she may base her sense of sin largely on submission and judgment. Classifying sin as mortal and venial assesses responsibility according to an exterior moral hierarchy. "Contemplating my many sins" may be exactly what a given woman should *not* do until she broadens her sense of sin and interprets it in light of a loving God. Perhaps an authentic conversion in the First Week reveals an inner experience of knowing oneself as loved by God and rejecting any internalized self-hatred. Conversion may uniquely relate to ordinary events of daily life and its missed possibilities for growth.

Ignatius uses a limited range of names for God in the Exercises, but these need not limit the possibilities for contemporary women. Images of God depend on one's experience of God, and how God acts in human history. Who am I? Who is God? remain constant underlying questions. The Principle and Foundation invited the seeker to consider the God of love and mercy as integral to her personal worldview. The subsequent movement of the Exercises, namely, awareness of the self as loved by God and the corresponding opportunity to respond in grateful loving service of others, invites one to love with greater and greater freedom. Even when employing Ignatius's names for God, contemporary women can reappropriate them. For example, naming the relationship of creature and Creator does not necessarily imply that the one making the Exercises find herself near the bottom of the pyramid model of creation, which reflects an older cosmology. In fact, she participates in a network of interconnected life and creation where God constantly creates and initiates. Many metaphors try to describe this

Holy Mystery of God: friend, lover, healer, father, mother, teacher, source of life and energy. As one's awareness grows, one responds in praise and thanksgiving, recognizing the God of mercy and forgiveness.

Christ is mentioned several times in the First Week. One powerful image encourages talking to him as friend to friend. Another suggests God's relationship to humankind in Jesus, a God of love and forgiveness. If one's sense of God flows from the experience of Jesus, who called God "Abba" and who compared God to a shepherd searching for a lost sheep or to a woman searching for a lost coin, then a more recent understanding of sin in terms of a fundamental option makes sense.[2] In this instance, the pattern of choices reveals a person's life direction more than isolated and individual acts. Those in touch with the cosmic Christ sense that Christ implicitly continues to act in creation. The First Week also refers explicitly to Christ on the cross, the traditional symbol of sin and salvation, but, even more, of gratuitous love.

However diverse the words or images used by the one making the Exercises, the grace of the First Week remains clear: to know God, source of merciful forgiveness and compassionate love, and to know oneself in relation to God. Praise, service, wonder and gratitude well up when encountering the God who knows each person more intimately than she knows herself.

## Sin, Personal and Social

Ignatius's understanding of sin grew from his own conversion story. For him sin was "iniquity, disorder, ingratitude and slavery to Satan," and he wished to integrate all the "biblical ways of expressing what is evil into one dynamic consideration of the history of sin" (Cusson 1988, 141).

One's understanding of sin depends on one's worldview, sense of God and human relationships, and degree of freedom and responsibility. Because an understanding of sin implies a wide range of culpability, conscience formation and education likewise exert significant influence. Some equate sin with disobedience to laws and transgressions of rules. This lack of nuance in the categories of sin has taken its toll. One woman said tellingly, "I grew up thinking and feeling that almost everything was a sin, venial or mortal, especially mortal if it looked, sounded, smelled or felt good. Now I realize that this belief was the sin I committed against myself." Others understand sin as infidelity to or breaking a covenant relationship of love. As Fischer and Hart (1995, 118) express it: "Sin or moral evil is the use of this capacity for free decision in ways that destroy our relationship with self, others and God—in fact with all of creation."

By pondering her culpability rather than exclusively contemplating her "many sins," the seeker can more productively reflect upon the First Week. Such consciousness asks each person to develop a true sense of sin and self before the reality of a living, loving, relational God. Each woman needs to let God reveal where she refuses love. Since the First Week deals with sin and salvation, it also touches on God's love and forgiveness. Only persons of faith can comprehend the depth of the reality of sin. Indeed, saints seem to be the experts on sin, as Julian of Norwich illustrates:

> ...it is God's will that we recognize sin, and pray busily and labour willingly and seek meekly for teaching, so that we do not fall blindly into it, and if we fall, so that we quickly rise. For the greatest pain that the soul can have is at any time to turn from God through sin. (Colledge and Walsh 1978, 328)

In the process of the First Week, the person living the Exercises moves from the more objective meditations on sin as a cosmic and historical reality to its personal reality. At the same time, the perspective shifts from observer to participant, eliciting a greater sense of responsibility for exercising personal freedom. Women can be encouraged to take responsibility for personal sin in ways that have meaning for their lives. For example, a woman may understand sin as whatever lessens humanity, decreases the capacity to love, or gets in the way of developing her potential as an image of God. Sin ultimately goes against her own being, for its roots are relational. Thus, sin includes both individual and social responsibility.

Traditionally, specific acts such as lying, cheating, stealing, inflicting bodily harm on another were termed sinful. Yet sinful situations, such as sexism and racism or the voracious consumption of the planet's limited natural resources also constitute sin. Middle- and upper-class women face several particular challenges from the First Week as they reflect on sin. They can unconsciously maintain a situation of privilege while avoiding awareness of the interrelationship of oppression, racism, classism, sexism and of their complicity in such social sin. Clues to this complicity can be as subtle as assuming that "flesh"-colored bandages match one's own skin and that local newspapers and television will reflect mainly people of one's own race.[3] A growing grasp of the personal and collective nature of sin initiates conversion and the desire, with God's grace, to right the wrongs in one's personal life and in the larger society.

Again, the Spiritual Exercises invite the seeker to engage prayerfully in the graced and sinful moments of the larger human story. The dialogue between the past cosmic story and personal stories of sin and grace has implications for the larger human and earth community; personal sin has social and planetary repercussions.

This expanding awareness of human sin fosters a greater sensitivity to global realities. Whereas before one might have reflected only on individual acts of commission and omission, a contemporary examination of consciousness moves one toward an awareness of the transcendent and of the intimate connection to all created reality. Theologian Marjorie Suchocki describes sin as violence acted out in the variety of ways of inflicting "ill-being" on oneself, one another and the earth.

> [F]eminist scholars see the sin of pride as describing the sins of the powerful who refuse to recognize the rightful boundaries of others, and the sin of hiding as the refusal of the responsibility to become a self that is so often the plight of women and men who are not in positions of power. (1995, 32)

Interestingly, the way to transcendence, which Suchocki (1995, 36) equates with well-being as opposed to ill-being, consists of the three-fold use of memory, empathy and imagination, a complement to an Ignatian perspective.

Sin, therefore, extends beyond the personal to the "structural." Although one may not be a conscious agent, one still participates at a level that perpetuates social and global sin. The challenge of the First Week includes becoming aware of the inadvertent, unconscious and inevitable collusion in structural sin. The question becomes crucial: How am I benefiting from other's oppression or my desire to maintain a privileged status quo? Sins against creation and the destruction of the earth exemplify the universal participation in sin. "The tendency to violence that persists in human nature is the ground of sin....Through organic solidarity of the race, we are affected by the sins of others, and our own sins likewise have an effect upon all others" (Suchocki 1995, 101).

Since the Second Vatican Council, sin cannot be considered without simultaneously understanding the universal call to holiness.[4] Holiness today means living love—love of God expressed by love of neighbor, contributing to the world here and now. Sin disrupts love, bringing disorder and disharmony to relationships.

Relating the call to holiness and the disorder of sin in the First Week of the Exercises makes the prayer experience more immediate and contemporary. Conversion, healing and transformation all comprise part of the process of the First Week's movement toward freedom. As a woman moves from a privatized sense of sin to a more relational perspective, she increasingly understands sin not just as individual isolated actions but as choices that affect many. Like throwing a rock into a pool of water, her decisions ripple outward to touch others.

## An Understanding of Sin from a Feminist Perspective

Studies in feminist theology and psychology suggest an evolution in understanding women's experience of sin and its effects on their lives. The pioneering work of Valerie Saiving in 1960 recognized that the experience of men and women differs in significant ways. She noted that establishing male experience as normative is inadequate for women's self-understanding and that the traditional categories of sin do not address the situation of women. She challenged the notion of "pride and the will-to-power" as the primary offense (Saiving 1992).[5]

Following the work of Saiving, feminist thinker Judith Plaskow challenges the assumption that equates sin with pride and egoistic self-assertion, suggesting that this norm better describes the experience of men. She notes the impact of cultural expectations in defining "the feminine": "The 'sin' which the feminine role in modern society creates and encourages in women, is not illegitimate self-centeredness but failure to center the self, the failure to take responsibility for one's own life" (Plaskow 1980, 92).

Theologian Anne Carr (1996) points out the need to reinterpret Christian categories of sin in light of the experience of women. She concludes that women's sin manifests itself in a lack of self-assertion in the face of society and culture's expectations. A woman's sin often consists not of what she does, but of what she fails to do, such as failing to assume responsibility for choices and naming her own values and gifts (8).[6] Carr reiterates that a male theological perspective has dominated the definition of sin as pride and rebellion and has failed to pay attention to the sin "of those who are powerless, who lack agency, selfhood, and responsibility, and who have suffered violence and abuse" (186). She recognizes that as contemporary women assume more "masculine" roles in society, they will also take on the "sin" of the masculine culture. Yet, she still believes that women's formation neglects to emphasize women's sin of "passive failure to develop a sense of self, a sense of agency and responsibility" (186). Carr defines sin from a feminist perspective as "the breaking of relationship with both God and with human beings that can take the form of weakness as well as pride in its denial of the importance of human responsibility in both the personal and the political realms" (186).

Author Mary Potter Engel (1990, 152–54) extends the notion of sin by drawing attention to women whose primary experience of sin has been as victims of violence, particularly as survivors of domestic and sexual abuse. In naming the evil present in systems of domination and oppression, she also identifies the pervasive reality of sin as those choices causing violence to both victim and perpetrator: "those free, discrete acts of responsible individuals that create or reinforce these structures of oppression" (155). While not blaming the victim, Potter Engel raises awareness that some victims unwittingly contribute to oppression in their own situations and invites serious consideration about ways of responsible action.[7] These four authors suggest an evolution of thought regarding the interplay between sin and women's issues and the implications for foundational theology and pastoral practice.

Growth in feminist consciousness brings on awareness of situations always present in society but only now coming to public attention. In this climate, women often identify themselves not first as sinners but as victims of sin and oppression. This self-identification leads to a personal form of prayer, lament. In lament one names her suffering, caused by injustice, evil and pain, and cries out for God's help. Naming the trouble begins the healing; turning to God in faith and hope opens one to grace. Through the prayer of lament, the seeker shifts her understanding of sin from her own experience of being sinned against to important new questions: What is sin for me? How do I understand myself as good? How do I avoid taking responsibility for my life? How is God an integral partner in all this? Therefore, a prayer of lament may prove a more appropriate starting point for the First Week of the Exercises than a prayer of contrition.

Contemporary women's frequent experience of violence and victimization calls forth the memory of biblical women, also victims. Some of them, such as Susanna, were vindicated. Others remained forgotten until a later generation cried "Enough!" The Levite's concubine (Judg 19:1–30) and the violent revenge done to the women of the tribe of Benjamin tell tales of horror either too often forgotten or repeated unreflectively throughout history.[8] Today's suffering women more typically cry out against the evil that has touched their lives, acknowledging and naming their grief, sorrow, pain and oppression. From here they can move to a freer, deeper and more authentic awareness of personal sin.

## Biblical Passages and Interpretation

Persons of faith reverence "God's Word" as a source of revelation, yet rarely do they probe how the process of personal formation ties into biblically based religious imagery. If a person making the

Exercises asked herself, "What are the sources of my knowledge and feelings about the Bible?" she would realize both the strengths and the limits of her biblical understanding. This realization will surely assist her engagement with the material of the First Week.

For some, emphasis on selective biblical references and personal stories of sin have precipitated a negative self-preoccupation and a legalistic or privatistic spirituality. For others, the particular biblical images and stories of the First Week fall into the category of fantasy rather than revelation. Another potential pitfall lies in traditional interpretation, such as the example of Adam and Eve's story, which isolates women as a source of sin and temptation and reveals an image deeply imbedded in the recesses of the religious imagination of both women and men. Persons come to these First Week meditations with unconscious assumptions and attitudes about the biblical material. However, they often fail to examine their degree of familiarity with the stories and the way they have interpreted them. For example, they may reflect on a familiar and long-remembered story and, in praying over the actual biblical text, discover something new and surprising.

The earlier discussion of biblical hermeneutics highlighted the fact that biblical stories in the Exercises must first be critiqued before being retrieved; critical consciousness and constructive recovery can coexist in the experiences of the Exercises. Mining scripture uncovers valuable sources of Christian imagery and a rich vein of possibility for women.

Artists' interpretations of the biblical characters and events with their recurring depictions of the great questions of life, death and destiny have deeply formed contemporary religious imagination. For example, cathedrals serve as repositories of art and culture and form spirituality. Stained-glass windows, carved and colorful statues and painted walls and ceilings chronicle the biblical stories of God and humankind. Artists and preachers function as influential interpreters of the Bible for the vast majority of the "faithful," just as they did in Ignatius's time.

Today few persons making the Spiritual Exercises come to the meditation topics of angels, Adam and Eve and sin without preconceived ideas derived from either the tradition or today's popular culture. Popular culture presents images that probe life's meaning and open up new possibilities for understanding old ideas. The current appeal of angels, for example, reveals a deep human desire to touch the divine and to stretch the limits of humanity.[9] Relationships between the sexes and the struggle of good against evil still hold a fascination in modern communications. Anyone can access religious information at a popular level in religion columns in news magazines, the internet, books and television, educational programs or even office jokes. Any conversation between the guide and the one making the Exercises needs to raise consciousness about these less obvious aspects of biblical formation.

In light of this realization, consider the creation story. Humans are created in God's image, male and female (Gen 1:26–28), but the religious imagery for Eve is much more ambiguous than for Adam. Artistic representations reinforce two diverse interpretations of Eve, which have implications for the image of women: Eve as temptress and source of man's sin, often pictured as naked and talking to a snake or, more positively, as "a power equal to man" (Freedman 1983, 56).

An important strand of the ancient tradition offers a favorable image of Eve, placing her in continuity with Mary. The crypt of the Church of the Dormition in Jerusalem stresses the continuity, where a brilliant ceiling mosaic depicts heroic biblical women surrounding the central image of Mary. Mary's significance cannot be separated from her foremothers, including the first mother. Despite this positive tradition, however, Mary and Eve are often opposed to one another. Mary became elevated to the most holy woman while Eve represented the most sinful. Eve personified everything evil in women, especially sexual sin, lust and temptation; she reflected cultural stereotypes that identified women as less rational than men and therefore as "the weaker sex."[10]

References to this negative understanding of Eve abound in the apocryphal literature and in patristic sermons and writings, as well as in the New Testament itself. In giving directives about women's dress and demeanor, the first letter of Timothy states: "I permit no woman to teach or to have authority over a man; she is to keep silent. For Adam was formed first, then Eve: and Adam was not deceived, but the woman was deceived and became a transgressor" (1 Tim 2:12–14). Tertullian furthers this line of interpretation as he addresses a third-century female audience in *On the Dress of Women*. "She would carry herself around like Eve, mourning and penitent, that she might more fully expiate by each garment of penitence that which she acquired from Eve—I mean the degradation of the first sin and the hatefulness of human perdition" (Clark 1983, 39).

Because Eve's many faces in art, literature and theology[11] frequently reinforce a negative image, a stereotype of Eve as the cause of "man's downfall" has been projected onto women. Yet the more positive image of Eve, also based in the tradition, suggests that the "original sin" consisted in the rupture of right relationships between women and men. The loss of this insight about original sin reinforced patriarchy as a model for systems of domination and oppression. A way forward lies in recognizing universal human dignity lived out in right relationships.

## Hell

The theological issue of hell in the First Week provokes continuing dialogue, and the fifth and final meditation on hell often causes much resistance and consternation. For some, the idea of hell belongs to an unreal world instead of life today. Unfortunately, this meditation has too often become an exercise in literalism, where the residue of traditional preaching of fire and brimstone distorts and limits conscious reflection on its reality. In spite of these negative aspects, hell reappears often in the imaginations of artists and the debates of theologians.

Author Alice K. Turner (1993), who recently explored the history of hell, maintains that no world religions equal Christianity in giving such importance to hell: a "fantastic underground kingdom of cruelty, surrounded by dense strata of legend, myth, religious creed, and what, from a distance, we might call dubious psychology." She notes that poets and artists have taken an "immoderate interest in Hell" (1993, 3) while theologically, hell fades in and out of favor. Two factors remain constant: the desire for cosmic justice where evil is punished and fear as a fall-back motivator for virtuous living when love is not enough. One question remains: How can praying about hell be a grace-filled experience for contemporary women?

Hell means different things to different people. Ignatius suggests one approach to hell, but other ways may prove more profitable. Rather than simply assume or jettison the traditional mythology, one person might try to imagine the opposite of God or might imagine her own personal hell. Another might prefer to reflect on the iconic representation of Jesus' descent into hell, echoed in the creed, which suggests the divine confrontation of evil, sin and death and the ultimate triumph of love. Or another might profit from returning to the writings of traditional wisdom figures who themselves reflected on this mystery.

For example, Teresa of Avila recounts what she calls a "copy of hell," noting prayer brought anguish and torment without knowing why. Later in the same work, she narrates in more detail her vision and understanding of hell. She uses descriptions full of sensory images: a long and narrow alleyway like an oven "low and dark," the floor consisting of "dirty muddy water emitting a foul stench and swarming with putrid vermin," followed by her sense of being placed in a small cupboard in a cramped position. This was combined with an interior fire and "despairing and tormenting unhappiness." She calls this experience of prayer one of the greatest favors God gave her "because it helped me very much to lose fear of the tribulations and contradictions of this life as well as to grow strong enough to suffer these and give thanks to the Lord who freed me." As a result, she had a great desire to "help souls, to free them from such torment" (Teresa of Avila 1976, 199, 213–15).

A middle-aged religious who ministers to street children describes her modern version of hell: "Sometimes when I am on the street with the kids of Brazil, I feel like I'm in hell." Today, the meditation on hell invites each person making the Exercises to enter into the worst possible scenario not for its own sake or to induce guilt, but to assure oneself that one does not experience hell alone. Paradoxically, Ignatius wanted to facilitate an experience of God's profound depth of love through internalizing the truth of personal experience with the meditation.

Women's stories may reveal hell as an experience or situation or even an interior awareness. Some contemporary women name the violence done to themselves and/or others as hell on earth: sexual abuse, domestic violence, a degrading life below the poverty level, homelessness while raising children, genocide, starvation, poisoned air and water, disabling physical or mental conditions. Images and stories about sin and hell cluster around broken relationships, past and present. Such an approach may open up further profitable reflection, always in the context of the grace of the Week.

## Wisdom for Those Giving the Exercises

Various themes appear in the First Week in story, symbol and religious imagination. Three areas that touch specifically on the one giving the Exercises include refining the relationship between the persons giving and making the Exercises, affective and intellectual transformation, and discerning areas of confirmation and challenge.

### Refining Relationships

The relationship between the one giving and the one receiving the Exercises develops in depth during the First Week, when each grows in ease, trust, openness to God and desire for the graces of the Week. As each recognizes the mutuality of gifts and limitations, a trusting relationship provides for effective communication and feedback. As they need to pay less attention to clarifying their relationship, they can pay more attention to the seeker's growing relationship with God.

Hospitality in spiritual conversation assumes that words bring greater understanding. A wise companion will ask herself, "How do my words and language welcome the presence and the experience of the other?" Women making the Exercises need to trust their own stories and to probe their deeper meaning, but this trust can only grow when women claim their voices and tell their stories. The guide's role in dismantling the stone wall that excludes women's stories and in creating stepping-stones toward women's empowerment cannot be underestimated. Only then can women's stories liberate personal power, inner strength and sense of self expressed in relationships of freedom and purposeful action.

The First Week, which deals with difficult stories from Scripture and life, requires receptive and nonjudgmental listening from the guide in order to create a trusting relationship. A woman who discloses sinful experiences may fear rejection. Therefore sensitive listening by the person giving the Exercises may manifest the love and forgiveness of God.

## Affective and Intellectual Transformation

Also crucial to the transformative dynamic of the First Week is attentiveness to any deceleration of forward movement. The deepening of the First Week may be marked by hesitation, fear of a rigid and imposed structure, uncertainty and even doubt about the value of personal experience. The one making the Exercises needs to understand that "doing" certain actions suggested in the Exercises does not matter; experiencing the underlying dynamic does.

The guide needs to attend to any content of the First Weeks that proves difficult for a woman. In such cases, the guide needs to notice how she experiences problems. Does she have trouble/difficulty with the biblically based stories or their interpretation, her personal sin story or the anticipation of the meditations on sin and hell? Alert to the temptation to either dismiss or overemphasize, a wise guide will respond sensitively, preferring to say: "How can we use this material profitably?" rather than an unequivocal, "We can't use this." The conversation thus can lead to further exploration: "What can you learn from these stories? Can you allow yourself to be open to discover a threshold of insight?"

The person giving the Exercises might find particular manifestations of sin surprising. Ironically, these sins may be the very things for which women have been lauded: passivity or indirect influence; staying in the background (the "behind every great man is a woman" syndrome); quietness, dependence, self-effacement, feeling rather than thinking; self-sacrificing to the detriment of self; or denial of one's gifts. At times, gifts waiting to be developed will be understood as sinful; for example, justified and liberating anger, assertiveness, leadership or independence. Other times, women may avoid naming some things as sin, especially inaction or fear of failure. "That which I have failed to do" is as important as "that which I have done."

Although the guide should focus on gender's influence on interpreting sin, it is not the only important factor to consider. Often the sin and conversion experiences of those who belong to the dominant culture and those outside it differ. When the Exercises call attention to "pride, riches and honor" [142] as leading to sinful ways, a contemporary reading might highlight classism, racism and sexism. Conversations between women professionals in business, law and medicine and women who constitute their support staff—secretaries, receptionists, nurses—reveal oppressive relationships among women in the workplace, sometimes subtle and other times blatant. Women's workplace also includes the home and those who serve there. The topic of women and sin has significant implications for the lives and self-perception of women and deserves continued reflection and discussion.[12]

The dynamics of the First Week may evoke deep feelings, including sorrow, confusion, helplessness and repentance as well as a deepfelt knowledge of God's loving presence. Their expression is necessary. The guide also needs to pay attention to feelings of liberation that women themselves may hesitate to acknowledge and receive. An experience of being a loved sinner, for example, can liberate one for a qualitatively new level of responsibility for one's own life.

## Discerning Areas of Confirmation and Challenge

Another responsibility of the person guiding the Exercises lies in the ongoing discernment of when to encourage, affirm and challenge in response to the movement of the First Week. Those making the First Week exercises will often need to struggle before things become clear; struggle by itself does not indicate the absence of the Holy

Spirit. It simply may surround coming to terms with what truly constitutes good and evil, heaven and hell, freedom and bondage, acceptance and rejection, gratitude and fear.

Sometimes, however, the struggle manifests itself in deadening silence, getting "stuck," or staying in superficial or heady responses. Usually the guide can pick up enough material through intuition and careful listening to ascertain whether this is the case. When the situation is ambiguous and the guide needs clarification, one or two open-ended questions can aid discernment: What is your favorite image of God? Why? Tell me what you know and feel about angels? What would you have to say about Adam and Eve? Where did you learn about hell and how have your ideas changed? How much do you reflect about sin? What difference do any of these topics—angels, Adam and Eve, sin, hell—make in your spiritual life? Conversing about these or similar questions makes conscious the formative power of these stories and themes in spirituality and gives an opportunity to assess their present value. The way persons read sacred stories in Ignatius's time and today may differ. Yet the search for a living, empowering word remains the same.

The companion giving the Exercises can make a significant contribution by providing alternative stories from the tradition or from film, television, novels, drama, daily newspapers and magazines to expand possibilities for prayer in the First Week. Some find meditating on the stories of Sarah and Hagar valuable. Others have fruitfully pondered the stories of the women in Matthew's genealogy—Tamar, Rahab, Ruth, Bathsheba—women who transcend their sin and witness to the power and plan of God. At other times, women have found solace and courage in various psalms that voice their experience of sin and salvation as well as God's loving mercy and forgiveness.[13] Others find that art and literature stimulates their imagination and opens their hearts to new possibilities for prayer and insight. Whatever means are used, they should never present sin in order to break the spirit or evoke guilt, but only to help in truthfully portraying oneself in the world.

If listening to the stories of others is so significant, paying attention to one's own story proves even more so. Thus, the importance of language magnifies as the person becomes engaged as the subject of her own sacred story. The power to name oneself and God forms the basis of self-identity. The person giving the Exercises may need to invite the woman living the Exercises to expand her concept of God beyond a traditional understanding of "God-He" by suggesting other metaphors for God beyond male imagery. The vocabulary of prayer can also provide alternatives. For example, the person making the Exercises might pay attention to the words of the Jesus prayer or the liturgical penitential rite or biblical phrases of the fraction rite, "Lamb of God," or Psalm 51, or she might reflect on the familiar words of the prayer that Jesus taught, "forgive us our trespasses as we forgive those who trespass against us." Each phrase or prayer gives a different nuance about who God is and who she is. In naming oneself and God, the choice of words matters. While such a personal perspective provides the starting point for reflection, it may not be the ending point. Wise guides can suggest various ideas for persons for reflection in light of their experience, and then encourage them to let go enough to share another's experience without crossing personal boundaries.

The last issue for the one giving the Exercises moves from depth of the personal reflection to the breadth of the theological foundations inherent in the First Week, which can paralyze even the most experienced companion. Accompanying someone through sin and sinfulness in a constructive way can be daunting. Women can put false guilt on themselves instead of cultivating a mature and authentic conscience. Distinguishing authentic anger that energizes and directs action for good from self-destructive anger that leads to depletion and despair demands serious discernment. In-depth spiritual conversation around topics of God's reality, God's will, human realities of freedom, sin, salvation, and the person and the role of Christ can prove invaluable. For all these issues, those giving the Exercises can profit from a commitment to their own continuing education and supervision.

## Conclusion

The First Week centers on God's graciousness and the seeker's lack of gratitude. The dynamic of the First Week leads to gratitude, the result of a deep and personal understanding of one's place in the cosmic order, as well as to a realization of one's use or misuse of God's gifts. This entire process leads to a deep experience of God's unconditional and passionate love.

As the First Week concludes, the guide may again recall the various motivations that women bring to the Spiritual Exercises. Whether a sixteenth-century woman of Alcalá or a twenty-first-century woman of Seattle, questions of meaning emerge from life changes, transition experiences or a sense of one's own mortality. Situations arise in family life, work, economic circumstances or church participation that disrupt the familiar sense of identity and relationships and call for a response. A desire for a deeper spirituality results from an initial or renewed discovery of God. Whatever the reason propelling them toward the Spiritual Exercises across the centuries, women acknowledge both rich resources and ambiguity in them. Contemporary women's significant interest and participation in the Spiritual Exercises may reveal important insights about the Spirit's call to the church in modern times.

# Notes

1. The life of Francis Borgia attests to this kind of conversion experience. Borgia identified the disfigured and decomposing corpse of the empress Isabel, whose beauty and vivacity had been so precious to him, and he exclaimed: "Never more, never more will I serve a master who can die" (de Dalmases 1991, 16).

2. See Brian V. Johnstone, "Fundamental Option," in *The New Dictionary of Theology,* ed. Mary Collins, Joseph Komonchak and Dermot Lane (Wilmington, Del.: Michael Glazier, 1987): 407–8. Fundamental option is presented as a corrective to a more legalistic approach to moral life. According to Johnstone, fundamental option can best be understood as an orientation to life as a unified dynamic process where one's choices set a direction, which, according to human freedom, can be changed, deepened or reversed. For example, a person's basic orientation is toward or away from God. Further discussion on fundamental option occurs in chapter 10; see also n. 4 for further reading.

3. Dr. Peggy McIntosh, Wellesley College Center for Research on Women, has explored this dynamic in detail in her paper "White Privilege Male Privilege." Excerpts are taken from *Spotlight,* American Friends Service Committee (winter 1989): 2–3.

4. Vatican Council II describes this "Universal Call to Holiness" in *Lumen Gentium* (Dogmatic Constitution on the Church), chapter 5. The document stresses that holiness is a vocation, a lifetime "calling" for the believer. All persons, regardless of age or particular life choices and work, are called to live a life based on love of God and neighbor, contributing through their gifts to the betterment of society.

5. According to Saiving (1992, 37), women's sins are better suggested by triviality, distractibility and diffuseness. She notes that women often depend on others for their own self-definition or use tolerance as an excuse for avoiding the demands of excellence. Women's mistrust of reason is another demonstration of the underdevelopment or negation of the self.

6. Also in relation to the first exercise of the First Week and its biblical content, Carr calls for a critique of the literal reading of the story of Adam and Eve and its centuries of preaching and theological interpretation, and suggests a feminist reinterpretation of the Genesis story of sin and its meaning in relation to women.

7. Potter Engel (1990, 156–62) offers four ways to think about sin in situations of abuse: sin as distortion of feeling or hardness of heart that denies authentic anger, sin as betrayal of trust or inability to learn and practice trust, sin as lack of care of oneself, and sin as lack of consent to vulnerability or equating honest dependence with subjection.

8. See Miriam Therese Winter, *WomenWisdom: A Feminist Lectionary and Psalter—Women of the Hebrew Scripture* (New York: Crossroad, 1991), 142–55, as a contemporary example of response to violence against women.

9. Tony Kushner's Pulitzer Prize–winning drama, *Angels in America* (New York: Theatre Communications Group, 1992), demonstrates this interest. Human interaction with angels provides the dramatic elements of this popular contemporary play.

10. See Antonia Fraser, *The Weaker Vessel* (New York: Vintage Books, 1984) for an exploration of the specific situation of women in the seventeenth century. Fraser documents the understanding of the phrase "the weaker vessel." She interprets the phrase not only as applied to the realm of physical prowess but, by association, to morality as well.

11. See John A. Phillips, *Eve: The History of an Idea* (San Francisco: Harper and Row, 1984). Phillips examines Eve's treatment in Scripture, theological treatises and literary works to illuminate the tradition that blames Eve for the "Fall" in both Catholic and Protestant theology. His sources include artistic illustrations covering 2500 years.

12. See Sally Ann McReynolds and Ann O'Hara Graff, "Sin—When Women Are the Context," in *In the Embrace of God: Feminist Approaches to Theological Anthropology* (Maryknoll, N.Y.: Orbis Books, 1995), 161–72 and the discussion of women's experience of sin and grace in Georgia Masters Keightley, "The Challenge of Feminist Theology," in *Horizons on Catholic Feminist Theology,* ed. Joann Wolski Conn and Walter E. Conn (Washington,

D.C.: Georgetown University Press, 1992), 37–60. The specific section is titled "Woman's Experience: The Discussion of Sin and Grace."

13. At least two adaptations exist in which psalms are suggested as the basis for praying the Spiritual Exercises. See Juan Benitz, *Los Ejercicios Espirituales: Meditados con los Salmos* (Bilbao: Mensajero del Corazon de Jesus, 1965) and Luis Alonso Schökel, *Contempladlo y Quedaréis Radiantes: Salmos y Ejercicios* (Santander: Editorial Sal Terrae, 1996). For an English translation of the suggested psalms and Exercises, see John Endres and Elizabeth Liebert's *A Retreat with the Psalms: Resources for Personal and Communal Prayer* (Mahwah, N.J.: Paulist Press, 2001), appendix 2.

# Chapter 7

# Who Do You Say That I Am?: Exercises of the Second Week

*...to ask for an interior knowledge of our Lord, who became human for me, that I may love him more intensely and follow him more closely.*

—Spiritual Exercises [104]

*I read about the call of the disciples and they are all men. The women who follow Jesus seem to come to him because they have something wrong with them that he has to fix.*

—A Contemporary Woman

"Now we will begin the Second Week." These words often elicit a sigh of relief both from the one receiving and the one giving the Spiritual Exercises. For some, the First Week seems like a qualifying exam or probation, "Whew, the hard part is over, I've made it through." Others struggle and learn about faithful presence: "I know God's faithful love in a way I've never realized before." Whatever the First Week experience, the transition from the First to the Second Week and the anticipation of praying over the life of Christ opens a new set of feelings and expectations. Most persons who make the Exercises are searching for opportunities to reflect more closely on the person of Jesus and to deepen their personal relationship with him. Indeed, the grace of the Second Week consists of finding "an interior knowledge of our Lord" so as to "love him more intensely and follow him more closely" [104].

## Material and Dynamics of the Second Week

How does one enter into the Second Week? The meditations and contemplations strategically placed throughout the week help in refining one's ability to make freer choices in following Christ. The Second Week exercises directed toward this process include the Call of the King [91–100], the Two Standards [136–48], Three Classes of Persons [149–57] and Three Ways of Being Humble [165–68]. First, the Call of the King considers discipleship and invites the seeker to cast her lot with Jesus. Yet life includes struggle and, sooner or later, all must answer the questions raised by the meditation on the Two Standards: Whose side are you on? and How do you know this? The two additional exercises offer nuances to this invitation to discipleship. Even when not making life-changing decisions, an "Election," one finds that daily choices ultimately form the pattern of ongoing fidelity to Jesus.

The Ignatian contemplations in the Second Week focus attention on the mysteries of Christ [101–34, 158–64], moving the seeker from self-preoccupation to the mystery of God who shares in our humanity. The Gospel contemplations proceed from Jesus' birth to his death, linking the mysteries of the Life of Christ with the mystery of God's presence in one's own life. Entering the Gospel scenes imaginatively brings one into contact with Jesus in Nazareth, by the Sea of Galilee or in Jerusalem. One imagines his actions, his words and how he touches people's lives. Contemplative awareness allows one to really see people, listen to their voices, share in their experiences and respond in faith to the myriad ways of God-with-us. Consciousness of one's life before God gives a momentary glimpse into the mystery of God at unexpected times: walking, working, eating, resting. Paradoxically, distractions and busy thoughts may also provide insight.

At the beginning of the Second Week, prayer focuses around hearing God's call and listening attentively and lovingly to God's revelation of Love incarnate, Jesus. Imagining the Trinity's perspective of a sinful yet loved world leading God to "dwell with us" situates the Second Week within the mystery of the incarnation. Traveling the road from Nazareth to Bethlehem engages one with the reality of Jesus' birth and the vulnerability of God who chooses to enter human history. The seeker accompanies Jesus as he journeys through "cities and villages, proclaiming and bringing the good news of the kingdom of God" (Luke 8:1).

The grace of the Second Week, a deepening relationship with Jesus, offers new ways of knowing, loving and following. What may have begun as an individual "Jesus and me" piety can develop into an intimate relationship of love overflowing into service; the Second Week is about words and actions. The first question, Who do you say that I am? leads to the next, Where do you stand and with whom will you walk? Both questions require a response.

## To Know, Love and Serve Christ Our Lord

Christ is central to both Ignatius and the Spiritual Exercises, yet persons receiving the Exercises today don't always know how to answer the question "Who do you say that I am?" They say, "Which Christ?" Some stress the divinity of Christ and tend to emphasize a Christology from "above"; others stress the humanity of Jesus, a Christology from "below." Many names and images present themselves to the contemporary believer, both as inheritance from the

Christian past and fruit of the current christological debates. How can Ignatius's understanding and experience of Christ in his historical and cultural context illumine contemporary experience without confining the Spirit of God?[1] What will help contemporary seekers discover the identity of "Christ Our Lord" for today?

Ignatius blends together the Gospel accounts and the writings of Paul displaying a quite different sensibility than that of the modern Scripture scholar who differentiates the distinct understandings of Jesus presented in the New Testament. For today's seeker, any one of the following could provide an entry point: Scripture, worship, liturgy or the arts. Each forms one's image of Jesus, creating a variety of Christologies. Doctrine, debated or professed, along with conscious or unconscious belief patterns influence personal and public understanding. Questions continue to challenge and enrich the believer today.

The specific images of Jesus the Christ in the contemplations of the Second Week differ according to their placement in the hidden life or public life. One considers first the pregnant Mary, the infant Jesus, the Lord born in poverty, the eternal Word, Christ our Lord and the child Jesus. The Meditation on the Two Standards presents "Christ our Supreme Commander and Lord," and the remaining contemplations name him as "Christ our Lord." Ignatius uses this title most frequently even when referring to the historical Jesus. Regardless of the name, the grace remains the same: attaining an "interior knowledge of Our Lord, who became human for me" [104].

Today's believers, conscious of the distinctions between the Jesus of history and the Christ of faith, may more often assume the perspective of a postresurrection Christian in the presence of the Spirit of Christ the Lord. They wish to move beyond the limitations of an exclusive emphasis on the physical maleness of Jesus and its patriarchal association with male domination. Consequently, some women continue to raise fundamental issues concerning the relationship of women to "Christ Our Lord."

## Problems and Possibilities Raised by Christology

Individual women's critique of Christology usually begins tentatively as church and culture tend to resist such critique. Some find themselves unable to relate to Jesus of the distant past; biblical stories seem irrelevant to their lives. Others struggle with the temptation to settle for a private, idiosyncratic relationship with Jesus and hesitate to make a deeper public commitment, given its attendant conflict. Others find the language associated with Christ so irritating that it blocks them: For example, the Nicene Creed's English translation reads "I believe in Jesus Christ, who for us *men* and for our salvation...was made *man*." The first reference to "men" emphasizes exclusive male language and the subsequent "man" emphasizes the maleness of Jesus rather than his humanity.

Many reject the image of Jesus as a blue-eyed, light-haired, white European male. Others react similarly to the stern Pantocrator overseeing the worshiping community from an ancient apse. They perceive images that idealize men, distance the divine and, more often than not, portray Jesus Christ in the image of men in the dominant culture. Other images go to the opposite extreme and place Jesus in domestic scenes emphasizing the gentleness and meekness associated with women; "feminizing" Christ also elicits a negative reaction. Few images of Jesus interacting in the historical, cultural, religious events of his times include women. Whatever the sources of their intellectual and spiritual formation in Christology, many contemporary women admit that their experience of Jesus the Christ simultaneously oppresses and liberates.

Theologian Elizabeth Johnson explores another problem in her article "The Maleness of Christ" (1991). If Jesus is the revelation of

God, then when "the Christ symbol points to maleness as an essential characteristic of divine being itself," the exclusive use of Father-Son imagery to describe the relationship reinforces these exclusive symbols (108). Because the "Word made flesh" dwelt among us as male, men more closely identify with Christ than women because of their natural physical resemblance. If male human beings represent Christ more fully than female, then reconciling the theological dictum, "What is not assumed is not healed," with women's experience becomes impossible (109).[2]

Although the emphasis on the maleness of Jesus has proved problematic for some, Johnson rejects a "naive physicalism which collapses the totality of the Christ into the human man Jesus" (113). She underscores the importance of sexuality in all human experience. "The fact that Jesus of Nazareth was a male human being is not in question. His sex was a constitutive element of his historical person along with other particularities such as his Jewish racial identity, his location in the world of first-century Galilee" (Johnson 1991, 108).

Johnson further states that appreciating Jesus' maleness as a historical reality does not determine his identity theologically as the Christ nor does it establish his maleness as normative in any way for members of the Christian community (Johnson 1991, 115). Both Scripture and baptism remind the believing Christian community that baptism into Christ obliterates all distinction based on sex, race or class, for all are one in Christ Jesus (Gal 3:28). Both seeker and guide need to develop this consciousness so that the "maleness" of Jesus does not become an obstacle to a woman's ability to grow in the knowledge of Christ, loving more deeply and following more closely in discipleship.

Other feminist theologians of various countries and cultures, of different races and economic classes and from various Christian churches bring additional responses to the question "Who do you say that I am?" Jacquelyn Grant speaks of the experience of African

American women noting the marginalization of women by sex and race and class. Oppressed women identify with Jesus as cosufferer.

> The pervasiveness and interconnectedness of racism, sexism, classism and other forms of oppression which define a good portion of the lives of black women make "trouble" inescapable. Jesus, for many black women, has been the consistent force which has enabled them not only to survive the troubles of the world, but to move beyond them. (Grant 1993, 56)

For them, Jesus becomes cosufferer, equalizer and liberator.

Virginia Fabella (1989), reflecting an Asian woman's perspective, notes that the question is not Who is Jesus? but Where is Jesus found? And she has an answer: Jesus dwells in solidarity with suffering people. Jesus must be "not only healer, exorciser, consoler, friend; he will also be transformer" (113). Jesus stands as a liberating figure for those women and men who do not take issue with "the maleness of Jesus," who understand the gender of Jesus as accidental to the liberation process.

Marina Herrera compares her experience growing up in Latin America with her adult life in the United States and reflects on images of Jesus meaningful for her. "I prefer to think of 'Son of Man' not as a title that merely stresses or highlights Jesus' maleness, but as one which underscores his relationship, duties, responsibilities and privileges as first born of the New Dispensation" (Herrera 1993, 88). She prefers to speak of Emmanuel, God-With-Us, because this name emphasizes the relational qualities she considers most important. Noting that she encountered the image of Jesus as King and other triumphant male images only after she came to the United States, she never made them part of her spirituality. Images that remain consistent for her are those in which Jesus serves as a nonviolent model. She challenges feminist theologians to extend the critique beyond the feminist viewpoint as it does not include enough of what needs reworking. She remarks that giving birth to a new Christology must include an "Americanist critique" of the Westernization of Jesus and his message (82). Consequently, rather than engaging in abstract controversies about the historical Jesus versus the Christ of faith or the traditional titles of "Son of God," " Son of Man" and "Lord," women need to understand their struggle in the context of the larger struggle of all marginalized and oppressed people who claim Jesus primarily as liberator.

Other feminist theologians have taken seriously women's response to classical formulations of Christology. They have directed their scholarly work toward naming the sexist and androcentric bias of doctrine and symbols of Christology; at the same time they search for other expressions more liberating for women,[3] frequently discovering Jesus' relational qualities as their common theme rather than emphasizing gender and cultural images of him.

Still, for Ignatius, "Christ the Lord," the central focus of Christian faith, is the Christ of the Second Week revealed through the mystery of God, Divine Majesty and Trinity. Jesus of Nazareth is revealed in his life, message, ministry, suffering, death and resurrection and the proclamation by the community of faithful believers. As contemporary women bring the skills of critical reflection to the Christ images of the Exercises, they name themselves as resurrection Christians, believers recognizing the risen Christ in their midst today. They need to bring to conscious awareness the assumptions they hold about Jesus Christ and the ways they experience convergence or conflict with the Christ images of the Exercises. Like members of the early church, contemporary persons of faith identify signs of the Spirit in Scripture, sacraments, worship, symbols, religious experience and personal transformation.

Specific aspects of the Second Week attractive to women include prayerful exploration of the "hidden life" of Jesus. The daily world of family reminds them of the importance of mothers and parental care of vulnerable children. Many of the early contemplations involve domestic scenes, giving glimpses into Jesus' human formation: experiences of dependency, nurturing and learning. Community and familial relationships across generations, occasional travel and everyday religious and cultural norms provide a familiar and reassuring context for prayer.

Other women feel drawn to Jesus' public life and his inclusive call to discipleship, issued to both women and men and lived out through deepening knowledge and loving commitment. They identify with his strong and focused relationships and the sense of mission he developed as he discovered his own "Principle and Foundation." His relationship with the land, the people and the events of his life in the desert, towns, mountaintops or at table all formed his own sense of identity and shaped the way he related with others.

In addition to Scripture, the writing of the mystics and religious and liturgical practice reveal additional images. Images of Jesus as prophet, teacher and healer appeal to those who desire more holistic interpretations as well as the ancient but relatively unknown image of Jesus as Mother,[4] which opens up a new perspective on Jesus the Christ. Matthew compares Jesus to a mother hen, crying out his anguished desire to gather the children to his protective care (Matt 23:37). Julian of Norwich calls Jesus Mother: "So Jesus Christ, who opposes good to evil, is our true Mother. We have our being from him, where the foundation of motherhood begins, with all the sweet protection of love which endlessly follows" (Colledge and Walsh 1978, 295). Some women discover great profit in following the liturgical seasons in companionship with Christ while a few have the opportunity to visit the actual sites of Jerusalem and Galilee on pilgrimage.

The grace of the Second Week invites one to know, love and follow Jesus. Many who receive this grace find the experience diffused with various images and experiences as revelatory. Regardless of the image, the grace of the Second Week remains constant. As a transition from the First Week into the Second Week the seeker is invited to pause and ponder what captures her passion, her heart, and invites her to go beyond what she can imagine to discover her deepest desires.

## Call of the King

Steeped in medieval metaphor, Ignatius remembered his former life and the romance novels that motivated his fantasy and directed his desires. The Call of the King draws on this experience and begins with a parable of a temporal king, then shifts attention to the eternal King. Ignatius knew the magnetism of a powerful and appealing leader. Just as a temporal king could capture one's heart, energy and commitment, so the call of Christ the eternal King would elicit great desires to follow the way of discipleship and be transformed by entering a deeper and more intimate relationship. Thus the grace of the week, to know, love and serve the eternal King, depends on the seeker's desire to hear the personal call of Christ and to respond generously. The metaphor of King and Kingdom suggests a reality deeper than literal meaning. Beneath the image of King and Kingdom lies the truth of commitment, single-heartedness, sacrifice and freedom. While the call of "Christ our Lord" suggests a global image of the "world assembled," it is also intimately personal. As one moves more deeply into prayer, Christ shares his desire to bring about the Reign of God while the seeker considers her free response to this invitation to participate in God's project.

Ignatius's own life clarifies the intent of this consideration. The metaphors of monarchy and politics were intrinsic to his life, just as they were for noblewomen such as Juana of Spain, sister of King Philip. The parable associating a temporal king with Christ the King expressed a natural link for Ignatius, whose daily life included kings and battles, victories and defeats as well as courage, loyalty and commitment. For Ignatius, comparing an earthly king with Christ as King was not a question of opposition but of transference, for Ignatius assumed if a subject has an experience or memory of a good and powerful king to whom she owes loyalty and service, she can transfer that energy and desire to her commitment to the eternal King. The centrality of the king to the life of the people pervades the spirituality of the times, touching rich and poor.[5]

This consideration transitions between the First and Second Weeks, and its placement is important, for it sets the stage for the Second Week of the Exercises. While similar to the Principle and Foundation, it specifically situates the person in relationship to Christ while encouraging dispositions of openness and attentiveness. Yet, language and images central to the Call of the King can be problematic for seekers in the twenty-first century.

## Problems and Possibilities in the Call of the King

Structures of contemporary life champion democracy, not monarchy. The language and images referring to Christ in this consideration are striking. At best, they elicit ambivalence and to some they seem repugnant. Although the language of God's kingship has a strong biblical base, its usage in this context tends to emphasize God as male conqueror. A God associated with violence and domination claims victory and defeats enemies, implying the holiness of war. Many women reject the militaristic language and the underlying concepts: obeying a temporal king, conquering infidels, participating in the victory, being a good subject or an unworthy knight for an eternal King who wishes "to conquer the whole world and all my enemies" [95]. This triumphalistic language and images of kings and knights seem far removed from the experience of the modern world. The metaphors suggest that women should be in relationship with a powerful male and with a hierarchical and impersonal system that expects unquestioning allegiance and self-surrender.

Not only is the metaphor of the king problematic, the expression, "Kingdom of God" further alienates those resistant to militaristic language. When a person finds the metaphor so distasteful, she may also find that its use blocks a positive affective or relational response. When this happens, it eliminates the possibility of encountering the deeper meaning of the image.

Reclaiming this notion of king and kingdom means expanding one's biblical perspective. Some who search more deeply note that Jesus himself resisted the title of "King." Others gave him that name; he did not use it to define himself. Some emphasize Jesus' continuity with the Old Testament kingly tradition, alluded to in the Angel's message to Mary, "...the Lord God will give to him the throne of his ancestor David. He will reign over the house of Jacob forever, and of his kingdom there will be no end" (Luke 1:32–33). The Fourth Gospel's account of Jesus' death on the cross includes the inscription, "Jesus of Nazareth, the King of the Jews" (John 19:19), an image kept alive through the apocalyptic vision of Revelation: "The kingdom of the world has become the kingdom of our Lord and of his Messiah, and he will reign forever and ever" (Rev 11:15). Thus two images of "king" emerge, one problematic in its militarism and one with possibilities suggesting the power of God achieving a reign of peace and justice. Each image illustrates an understanding of Jesus as King in "historical variations and permutations" (Pelikan 1985, 47).[6]

The Call of the King, then, can elicit two responses. Some might perceive this meditation as irrelevant, meaningless, perhaps even a contradictory example and detrimental for women's spiritual growth. Or, by confronting the historical limitations, one can discover a parable that today, as yesterday, has possibilities for transformation by posing these questions: Does this image free us to find God? Could it help us to find God in the future? Story and myth provide an avenue for interpreting the Call of the King not as literal history but as entry into truths that lie deep within the human spirit. Kings and queens, gods and goddesses, magicians, shamans, healers, heroes and villains dwell in the depths of the human psyche. The magnetism of special leaders continues to capture the human imagination as they touch the deep human desire for good to triumph over evil.

Finding and following a charismatic leader reveals qualities associated with discipleship. What if, like Ignatius, one recalled a person who unleashed one's admiration and loyalty in a relationship that elicited personal "greatness." Such a relationship could become a catalyst of great desires—sharing vision, hopes, struggles, resources, sacrifices, risks, work, commitment and success. Could not this personal motivation and relationship be understood as the necessary disposition for entering into the Call of the King today? Zeal, loyalty, active engagement in a life project, living for a goal bigger than one's personal gain, making sacrifices for the common good—all these values still merit admiration in contemporary life, even in their finitude. Opening up and out to Someone beyond oneself, yielding in love, can be a contemporary and equally compelling Call of the King.

Many models in our religious traditions pertinent to the relationship between God and the world emphasize God's transcendence and minimize God's palpable presence in concrete reality. In light of this, reconstructing the Call of the King might involve reflecting on the actions of this King as the one who sustains life, defends the poor, is present to and engaged in the life of the people. Why not deemphasize the image of "king" as powerful but self-serving and emphasize a powerful king ruling for the benefit of the people?

The parables provide an avenue to make this shift. Parables raise awareness of God's desires for inclusion, peace and justice for the people and the land. They highlight the reality that God's reign exists as a way of living and being, not as a physical place, geographical location or even a political system. Jesus spoke of the Kingdom of God as like a mustard seed, or yeast, and even a banquet.

An ecological awareness presents an additional possibility for reclaiming this concept of God's reign. Naming the earth as God's Body expands the reign of God to include the care of the earth, as well as its people. This image may capture the imagination of those who find it hard to relate to God because they do not have any lively imaginative picture of how God and the world *as they know it* are connected. Using this ancient image of the earth as God's Body stresses the incarnational, sacramental understanding of our world. It also underscores our human responsibility for the care and reverence of that body, not as dominators but as members of a common community.[7]

After reconstructing images of king and kingdom to assume God's reign of peace and justice, battle images become more fitting. War must be waged against injustice and oppression of people and the earth. Oppressed people must struggle, even mightily, for dignity and human rights, often giving their lives in the process. Today's interest in political and ecological theology illuminates this meditation in new ways, for it requires that Christian faith permeate the projects of those who desire to establish a more just society.

## Two Standards

The meditation on the Two Standards marks the transition from the contemplations on the hidden life to those on the public life of

Jesus. This meditation reminds the one making the Exercises that the call usually entails struggle.

The meditation on the Two Standards extends the invitation to follow the pathway of discipleship, focusing not so much on choice as on the discernment essential to making choices. Ignatius points to this discernment in the third prelude [139] where the one making the Exercises is directed to ask for what she needs. In this instance, the desire consists of "insight into the deceits of the evil leader, and for help to guard myself against them; and further, for insight into the genuine life which the supreme and truthful commander sets forth and grace to imitate him."

The one making the Exercises must carefully discern what reinforces and sustains her call to discipleship and what hinders deeper commitment. The standard or banner is not always easy to see in the heat of the day. Ascertaining what is life-giving or death-dealing to self and others remains a continual challenge. The underlying touchstone, of course, is always the life and death of Jesus and openness to his Spirit. Discernment in the Two Standards acts like a tuning fork for discerning the realities of life, indicating resonance or dissonance with the God who dwells within.

This meditation draws on the deep power of myth, vividly contrasting the characters of Christ and Lucifer in cosmic confrontation. The text describes a concrete place, complete with graphic imagery and imaginative design. Yet this cosmic struggle echoes within each person and a world marked by the continuing struggle between truth and deception.

Whether clothed in the imagery of the Two Standards or not, struggle pervades all conflict between nations, in families, churches, societies or one's own self. Paul recognized this reality when he acknowledged: "I do not understand my own actions. For I do not do what I want, but I do the very thing I hate" (Rom 7:15). The Two

Standards unmasks every person's need for God and the cost of choosing to follow Jesus. This discernment leads to greater commitment, which Ignatius recognizes by the presence of three virtues: poverty rather than riches, reproaches or contempt rather than honor, and humility rather than pride [146]. According to Ignatius, all other virtues flow from these three.

## Problems and Possibilities in the Two Standards

"I want to scream every time I hear the phrase 'Two Standards,'" reports one woman who rejects the graphic imagery of this Exercise. Indeed many women struggle with language that appears to affirm war and valorize virtues they equate with their oppression. Those affiliated with Christ are also invited to choose spiritual and material poverty as well as reproaches and contempt leading to humility. Such emphasis on the traditional categories of pride and capital sins, besides presenting reproach and contempt as desirable, raises negative responses in some contemporary women. Imagine a single mother who has just recently earned a college degree and found a full-time job after being dependent on food stamps, living in her car and placing her children in a school for the homeless. Her asking for reproach, contempt and material poverty as a desirable path to spiritual growth is inconceivable. She will say, "There is nothing here of relevance to my life, nor does this type of language or imagery contribute anything positive to my spiritual path and desire."

Humility too, is an ambiguous virtue, especially if presented as the desirable result of reproaches and contempt. Often the expectations for humility reflect a gender bias with differing written and unwritten norms for women and men. Some women associate humility with patriarchal obedience and submission to father, husband or priest. Humility has frequently been equated with passivity, hiding, and low self-esteem, all of which have been detrimental to women's responsible adult development.

Women themselves note the contradictions that arise interiorly when they sense an authentic call to find voice, speak truth, claim and honor their good name and person, and assert themselves, particularly in situations of oppression and injustice. Often women do not see the call to humility as in their own best interests and understand how it has been used in the name of religion to silence and subordinate them. In addition, humility can show a false face for women: hiding the truth of one's own giftedness and contributions. A deeper understanding of "true" as opposed to "false" humility is necessary, as our culture itself is ambiguous on the topic.[8]

Yet humility carefully understood can open up possibilities for women and remind them of their power of choice. Humility means truth, both of one's strengths and gifts of God, as well as one's weakness and limitation, one's reality before God. This truth provides a strong foundation for authentic discernment. Ignatius's famous letter to Teresa Rejadell recognizes the temptation to false humility. He describes how the enemy tries to get the person not to talk about the good things she has received from God so that fruit will not be produced in others, "for to cultivate awareness of what one has already received is always a help toward even greater things" (Ganss 1991, 334). Women themselves attest to the power and encouragement to do greater things that emerge out of an awareness of their gifts. For example in her *Dialogue,* Catherine of Siena has God speak:

> No virtue can have life in it except from charity, and charity is
> nursed and mothered by humility. You will find humility in the
> knowledge of yourself when you see that even your own exis-
> tence comes not from yourself but from me, for I loved you
> before you came into being. (Noffke 1980, 29)

A woman cannot have true humility unless she has a strong sense of self. Only then is she capable of self-transcendence.

In some cases, though, women find that their oppressive life situation gives them few options. Humiliations, poverty, insults and contempt are their daily lot. They have little choice and few opportunities to change their condition. Other women, from Ignatius's time to the present, receive insults and contempt as a result of a strong and faithful commitment freely chosen. This is not a poverty and humiliation imposed by culture, class or economic situation, but one arising from freely identifying with the poor out of love for Christ. It is the poverty and humility that emerges out of simplifying one's life to sustainable proportions for the sake of all. Likewise, words such as *riches, honor* and *pride* may reveal meaning and challenge for contemporary women by uncovering deeper questions: "Where does my treasure really lie? Do I accumulate and hoard? Do I worry what people will think of me? What are the sources of my security? How much do I equate self-worth with possessions, status and power?"

A first impression of the Two Standards may suggest rejecting this meditation as an historical oddity, but a second glance may reveal new and personal standards and standard bearers, drawing attention to women's gifts and leadership in the community. For example, Marge Piercy's contemporary novel about the French Revolution, *City of Darkness, City of Light* (1996), captures the struggle for liberation by the people, especially the women, and links it to the contemporary passion for human dignity and global freedom. The character of Claire, actress and revolutionary, who cries out for food for the children and elderly, could help reexamine the Two Standards. Like Claire, women and men today gather others of like mind to work for a common task and values. Standards still give identity and direction to expressions of community, whether the opening pageantry of the Olympics or civic parades and religious processions. Standards still have meaning; to raise a standard and follow it means publicly claiming identity and commitment.

The deeper reality of the Two Standards raises issues about when and how women take a stand and when and for what reasons they may risk alienating those standing somewhere else. Taking a stand raises an inherent question: "If rupturing a relationship results, is it worth it?" Likewise, pondering the Two Standards leads to other questions: "Where and with whom do I stand? What communities of resistance and solidarity am I aligned with?" Women may discover not only new ways of following but new ways of leading. The Standard of Christ is a sign of inclusion, equality and freedom, a vision for a new humanity.

Meditating on the Two Standards may also open up new areas of self-knowledge, understanding the divided places within. The struggles for "standing" may move from exterior causes to interior realities: "Who or what represents Lucifer and Christ in my particular struggle?" Delving into issues of truth and power touches people deeply, for this meditation focuses on conflict within themselves as well as outside. It concerns doubt and fear and denial. It means exploring what pulls people apart.

This meditation not only touches individual struggles and stands, but it can also lead to forming communities of solidarity and commitment where persons and groups live dedicated lives. God's reign of peace and justice, community and responsible relationships is a dream to which many women willingly commit themselves even through a long and taxing struggle.

## Three Classes of Persons

This meditation follows the notes on the Two Standards in the text and precedes the section on the public life of Jesus. The subtitle gives a clue about its purpose: "An aid toward embracing what is better" [149]. Whereas the meditations on Call of the King elicited commitment and the section on the Two Standards clarified the strategies of movement toward and away from God, this meditation and the one following, Three Degrees of Humility, illuminate the degree of potential response to Christ's call. The issue here concerns detachment from anything impeding movement toward God. The seeker desires a depth of indifference so as to ensure that nothing deafens her to the authentic voice of God.

Ganss's translation uses the familiar word "attachment" in this meditation about good persons who have received a sum of money and are considering how best to dispense of it [153–55]. Attachment comes from the old French *attaché,* which means "nailed to." Attachment nails desire to specific objects and creates addiction. Addiction, a more contemporary term, attaches desire and enslaves its energy to certain specific behaviors, things or people. One can be addicted to ideas, relationships, substances, being liked, work, power or powerlessness, self-image, or any other thing. Even "small" addictions stand in the way of freedom and love by sapping the energy of our desires. Psychiatrist Gerald May calls addiction "the most powerful psychic enemy of humanity's desire for God" (May 1988, 3). Ignatius's Three Classes of Persons pinpoints one of the most difficult tendencies to uproot in the human heart: nailing desires to something less than God.

Ignatius's case study presents "the postponers, the compromisers and the wholeheartedly indifferent" (Ganss 1991, 407). All three "desire to get rid of the attachment," the addiction. The first type talks and talks. Multiple words substitute for action and wishful thinking surfaces frequently in the form of "if only" dreaming. The second person tries to "have it all," to persuade or manipulate in order to have the best of both worlds. This person will go to great lengths to do many things, except the one thing really necessary. Finally, the third type of person roots her decision in love and her desire for true freedom, to choose with "indifference" that which God most desires.

## Problems and Possibilities for Three Classes

Emphasizing indifference achieved by will power alone downplays the seeker's need to cooperate with God's Spirit. Too much stress on diffidence can imply that the self-surrender is equated with loss of identity, choice and even oneself. However, this meditation can provide real possibilities for gaining clarity about both desires and addictions. It poses the questions: "What is the one thing I refuse to turn over to God's care? What is my "no" point? What do I find myself playing mind games around rather than letting go and trusting in God's love?"

Grappling with these questions can help the one making the Exercises learn an interior way of love integrated with greater intentionality and freedom. In consciously giving over her life to God, she receives life in surprising ways. The writings of Teresa of Avila illustrate that conscious self-surrender provides the only true antidote to attachment or addiction.

> One day while I was anxiously desiring to help the [O]rder, the Lord told me: "Do what lies in your power; surrender yourself to me, and do not be disturbed about anything; rejoice in the good that has been given you, for it is very great; my Father takes His delight in you, and the Holy Spirit loves you." (Kavanaugh and Rodriguez 1976, 324)

Both Teresa and Ignatius realized that self-knowledge and awareness, coupled with prayer and waiting on God, provided the only means of moving beyond attachment or addiction and into greater interior freedom.

The language of "detachment," paradoxically deals with finding oneself. Not only must an individual possess a self in order to give it away, but the Gospel also insists that she has to lose herself to find herself. Authentic self-donation, prompted by the Spirit of God, can be recognized by the fruits of strength, the building up of oneself and others rather than depletion and depression. Teresa became more herself, stronger, more effective for mission as she gave herself over to God.

The contemporary phenomenon of burnout often reveals an addiction and an attitude of drivenness: earning God or others' approval, a warped self-image, or doing things "my" way. An addicted person needs to uncover the addiction and deal with it in a balanced manner. She must learn to create boundaries of self-care that lead to reflection and renewal. Only with these boundaries in place will renewal occur and yield an energized self for mission. Discernment provides the crucial direction to any choice: one puts trust in God's creative power at work.

## Three Ways of Being Humble

This exercise is not presented as a formal meditation but as a subject to ponder prior to making an "election," a subject for further reflection on human and spiritual development. Ganss calls this exercise neither a meditation nor a contemplation, but a "consideration" permeating the days of the Exercises devoted to Election (1991, 410). The text first uses sin as a criterion for choosing, employing the "mortal/venial" language typical of the time. The exercise presents three ways a person decides a course of action. The first and most fundamental assumes obedience to God's law as the basic choice for salvation. The second way stresses "indifference" when faced with equally desirable options. The third and "most perfect" way imitates Christ by preferring poverty and contempt. This last way only makes sense when it emerges freely from solidarity with the poor Jesus and his friends.

## Problems and Possibilities for Humility

The major problem facing a seeker as she ponders this exercise lies in paralysis by her "I." "*I* don't have or even want this kind of humility. *I* can't do this. *I* can't reach this high level three," she says to her guide. "*I'm* not good enough to go the whole way of discipleship. *I'm* not as generous as others. *I* guess *I* don't have what it takes to really do the Exercises." This woman interprets this exercise in terms of levels of perfection, and she grades herself low, believing only the elite can ascend to the highest, or third, level. In this instance, the emphasis subtly shifts and attention transfers to self. Personal achievement and competition or their opposites, defeat and driving will power, become the dominant motivations. Rigid self-consciousness and determination can replace the desired freedom of spirit and spontaneity before God.

In spite of these potential pitfalls, this consideration can open on to humility, greater generosity, deeper self-knowledge. Prayer over each section leads to an integration and recognition that humility, understood as gift of God and God's work, does not ultimately depend on personal effort but on openness to God's power. This consideration invites persons of good will and those who desire God to be more like Christ.

From the beginning of the Exercises, indifference—the second way of humility—invites the seeker to follow God's ways, wherever they lead. The third way of humility, transcending even indifference, is a radical choice to give over all of one's life to be with Jesus no matter what the consequence. Jesus is the model of humility, who washes the feet of his disciples and ultimately "empties himself" (Phil 2:6–8). From the beginning, Christian tradition has recognized the humility of Jesus as model for believers.

> The value of humility as a willing dependence on and obedience
> to the saving mysterious God, taught by Jesus and embodied in
> the "way" that led to his death on the cross, was so deeply
> ingrained in the Scriptures that early Christian writers could not
> help but see it as close to the heart of the Church's spirituality.
> (Daley 1995, 9)

Unfortunately humility became distorted and distanced from its original biblical basis, but the three ways of being humble retrieve this basic meaning. They speak to a growing capacity for love, freedom and magnanimity rather than subservience. As long as the seeker desires to develop a healthy, balanced sense of self, this consideration can challenge her to become "more." The seeker who prays for the "desire for the desire" of the fullness of humility realizes that its achievement is gift, not the fruit of her striving.

## Contemplations and Scripture

To know, love and follow Jesus Christ presumes both a call to discipleship and a personal response. The Contemplations on the life of Christ invite the one making the Exercises to enter into the Gospel events and grow as a more mature and committed disciple. The material for the Contemplations introduces the Trinity's view of the world and the annunciation of the angel Gabriel to Mary [101–9], the major events of the hidden life, the nativity [110–17], the presentation and flight into Egypt [132–33], Jesus' obedience at Nazareth and his encounter in the Jerusalem temple [134]. Ganss notes that these initial contemplations intend to create "affective attachment to Christ in his poverty and humility" (1991, 403).

After the interlude of the Two Standards and Three Classes of Persons, the seeker moves into the events of the public life. At the same time, the seeker becomes more aware of the disposition needed for Election, an aspect treated extensively in chapter 11. The contemplations about the public life of Christ include the journey from Nazareth to the Jordan and the baptism of Christ [158–60], the desert temptations, the following of Christ by Andrew and others, the sermon on the mount, Jesus walking on the water, his preaching in the temple, and the raising of Lazarus to the events of Palm Sunday [161]. Ignatius encouraged blending the contemplations of the life of Christ with the meditations. The formative process of the Exercises depends on their reciprocal interaction.

Besides the biblical events mentioned above, Ignatius suggests additional mysteries in the life of Our Lord as further resources for prayer. Eleven options exist for the section on the "hidden life." The "public life" includes sixteen additional mysteries, some mentioned earlier in the Second Week section. The use of these "mysteries" of the life of Christ suggests that the events or episodes in his life include theological themes worth pondering more deeply, such as mysteries of trinitarian life, incarnation and redemption. The seeker reflects not only on what happened to Jesus but also on why and what it means for discipleship today. Ignatius expected that the movement of God, so real in his own life, would be replicated uniquely in each person's life. Pondering the action of God in human history brings a deeper awareness of God active and present in history.

## Problems and Possibilities for Second Week Contemplations

Did Jesus call any women? The "Call" events begin exclusively with men who then tell other men. Even the "come and see" passages in the Fourth Gospel involve "men only." The majority of the selections suggested in the text of the *Spiritual Exercises* include no women except Mary Magdalene. Ignatius's description of her as a public sinner, however, reflects a common characterization now repudiated by Scripture scholars. As with Second Week contemplations, women are often hard to find, frequently nameless and marginal.

Yet the Spiritual Exercises also provide a welcome opportunity to recover the long neglected stories of Jesus and women. The discovery of numerous "hidden" women help answer the lingering question, "What was it like for a woman to follow Jesus?" Strong and courageous women take center stage during the hidden life: Elizabeth, Mary and Anna. The women of the public life provide many and diverse encounters with Jesus. In addition, many scriptural examples show Jesus as free from patriarchal standards of male behavior, sometimes causing scandal to his male disciples. Even a cursory examination reveals that Jesus related to women in a human way, demonstrating empathy with their plight as poor and marginalized.

As Jesus called women to discipleship, he invited them too into a deepening knowledge and commitment. Women often served as the catalyst for Jesus breaking boundaries and stereotypes. Jesus associated with the oppressed, the poor and the most destitute; he interacted with those most despised, the prostitutes, and he broke taboos involving women. He included among his closest friends Martha and Mary, sisters of Lazarus. Jesus included and empowered women; he noticed women in their world and in his; he saw, heard, felt their various emotions; and he was moved and acted in response to his own "contemplative awareness." Women witnessed both the birth and death of

Jesus and found themselves sent to evangelize and be recipients of the Spirit's transforming power.

These biblical women model a process valid and fruitful for women today. Women's narratives in response to the Second Week prayer experiences often reflect the common human experience of getting to know somebody more and more deeply. Friendship begins through simple conversation, "Tell me about yourself." All stories are important: stories of growing-up years, family life, neighborhood, school and church and the larger social and cultural milieu. Women are naturally associated with the childhood of Jesus, but they also appear in his public life as active and caring disciples. He had an amazing ability to create and sustain relationships, exhibiting mutual care with a variety of persons. Perhaps the traditional expectations about knowing, loving and serving Christ the Lord has been based on experience more typical of men moving toward autonomy and achievement. Women's development, on the other hand, usually flourishes in attachment, intimacy and relationships. Jesus serves as a model of integrated humanity, exhibiting the values of care and connection more typical of women, as much as those traditionally associated with him—autonomy, justice and independence.

## Wisdom for the One Giving the Exercises

At this point, the one giving the Exercises needs to pay attention to how one living the Exercises responds. The dynamic of the Second Week leads to a gradual personalizing of commitment, moving from an objective sense of a "Call of the King" to a profound personal commitment to know, love and follow Christ and to accept the concrete implications for her life. A wise companion will emphasize the grace desired, namely, openness to really hear the call of Christ, even more than the content of the story. The deeper issue for the meditation is crucial: "Do I really want to hear God's voice, knowing I will be changed by what I hear? Can I trust that God may speak even in ancient and unfamiliar ways, as well as in those more compatible with contemporary idiom?"

In guiding another through this Week, certain signs indicate how one's personal story and the story of Jesus converge. The process need not be linear, with each "exercise" following on the other, step by step. It may just as readily be cyclic, with themes appearing and disappearing, then surfacing again later. Various responses, such as thinking about, pondering and feeling, may surface at unexpected times. Biblical stories may raise reflections on theological themes, such as Jesus' humanity or divinity or one's personal degree of freedom.

The guide needs to be aware of the various movements that particular Gospel stories may suggest. Some women may be attracted to and familiar with the Jesus of the Gospels, preferring consoling passages that deepen the relationship, but avoiding conflict or hard sayings. These difficult sayings might provide opportunities to probe more deeply the call to discipleship. Yet the guide should note what disturbs or does not ring true, such as militarism, male stereotyped characters and events in Gospel passages and simplistic or stereotyped understandings of humility and pride. Both attraction and resistance need attentive discernment.

The one giving the Exercises occasionally needs to stand back and examine the selection of material. First, notice why one text is included and another left out. Why select this material? Is this passage congruent with the grace of the week? Is it consistent with the seeker's own dynamic movement through the Week? When is changing direction necessary? The material of prayer will influence how one responds to the Christ who calls.

Each person needs to articulate a personal Christology as a means of greater self-knowledge about her relationship to Jesus Christ. Some leading questions may prove helpful: "What have been your most significant sources of knowledge about Jesus? How have your images of or relationship with Jesus changed through the years? Who is the Jesus you are looking for? What draws you into the mystery of Jesus and what characteristics do you most admire and desire to emulate?" Christology is an important component of the Second Week—as it will be in the Weeks following. The call to imitate Christ moves beyond gender stereotypes; Christ is—and invites all to be—faith-filled, strong, gentle, compassionate, confrontative, wise, loving, peaceful and relational.

The guide will often find specific issues arising in relationship to prayer and decision making, whether related to the Two Standards, Three Kinds of Persons or Three Degrees of Humility. One main responsibility, then, consists of assisting the persons to a deeper level of insight by providing helpful questions: "Where do you stand? With whom will you work? What are you willing to struggle for, to die/live for?" Thus, a discerning guide identifies issues associated with significant choices along with the inner movements they raise.

What if God asks one to do the hardest thing possible? Facing choices and making priorities and commitments can create fear and anxiety. One question focuses the guide's work—How is generosity manifested or blocked? The guide looks for clues, listens attentively to what holds the seeker back or impedes a fuller donation of self. Guiding the Exercises includes being with the person in discernment. The guide uses intuition and experience to reflect back how the seeker may be invited to greater generosity. A helpful guide will listen for how she makes decisions and what motivates her, carefully noting responses that seem too heady or emphasize will power alone, such as "I should be able to do this" or "I feel guilty because I can't do better." Discernment remains critical during this struggle, clarifying what attracts her and whether or not the attraction is of God.

Often the lives and commitments of others provide inspiration and encouragement during this Second Week. Ignatius suggested reading lives of the saints, as they had been influential in his conversion process [100]. Today there is renewed interest in the "communion of saints," and those engaged in the Second Week can benefit from multiple resources currently available in books, articles and videos. Insights emerging from historical theology and women's history and spirituality also provide a rich source of reflection.[9]

## Conclusion

The grace of the Second Week consists in knowing, loving and following in the path of discipleship with renewed life and commitment, a discovery of being called by God to follow "the Way." The engagement demanded from those who walk this way is nothing less than the whole person—body, senses, imagination, intellect, will, memories, hopes—immersed in life here and now. Ignatius saw no difference between the Jesus of history and the Christ of faith, and the Second Week fosters an encounter with the Jesus of history through the mystery of the resurrected Christ living among us today.

Experienced guides, also disciples on the way, can profit from their own learning. By gradually becoming more free of the text, yet understanding the dynamics of each Week, they develop greater freedom to follow the movement of the Spirit in the seeker. Together, guide and seeker search for and verify the fruits of the Exercises, knowing there is a "call-waiting" that requires clear and open reception. The Exercises do not aim to replicate the God experience of Ignatius but to encounter the living God who communicates in many and diverse ways through the central mystery of the life, death and resurrection of Jesus.

# Notes

1. Ignatius's personal experience of Christ is deeply affected by his convalescence in the Loyola residence, continuing his pilgrim journey to Montserrat, his formation in the basics of the Exercises at Manresa and his interaction with persons along the way as he told his story and listened to theirs, and his vision at Loyola of Mary and the child Jesus [*Autobiog,* #10]. He notes also that while at prayer in Manresa he saw with his interior eyes the humanity of Jesus [*Autobiog,* #29] and describes his enlightenment at the river Cardoner that sustained him the rest of his life. His desire to go to Jerusalem and walk in the footsteps of Jesus propelled him into a pilgrim's mode.

Many sources formed his religious images: the art found in the churches he so often frequented, the preaching he listened to and eventually practiced, the spiritual conversations so important to him, especially in his early spiritual growth. Being conscious of this imaginative religious influence can assist us in interpreting Ignatius's images and references to Jesus Christ; his constant inclusion of Our Lady, reflecting the influence of Marian piety of his times; and his references to the saints with the kind of familiarity that considered them part of the family.

2. For a more extensive analysis of the use of Christology and the oppression of women, see Rosemary Radford Ruether's work on Christology and feminism in *To Change the World* (New York: Crossroad, 1990). She examines the scholasticism of Thomas Aquinas, who argues that male is normative and the fullness of human potential, thus concluding that women are defective. Therefore, the incarnation of the Logos of God into the male is not a historical accident but an ontological necessity (45).

3. Anne Carr (1996, 160–61) gives an example of this scholarly search: "Uses of the Christ symbol in theological anthropology, ecclesiology and ministerial theology to support political, social and ecclesiastical patriarchy are in fact a perversion of its positive religious content. These uses are a sobering reminder that no symbol, no tradition, is entirely pure but rather all are ambiguous, multivalent, open to both positive and negative human use." See

also Mary Hembrow Snyder, *The Christology of Rosemary Radford Ruether: A Critical Introduction* (Mystic, Conn.: Twenty-Third Publications, 1988).

4. See Caroline Walker Bynum, *Jesus as Mother: Studies in the Spirituality of the High Middle Ages* (Berkeley: University of California Press, 1982). Roger Haight extensively explores different holistic interpretations of Jesus in his chapter "Appropriating Jesus in Christology" in *Jesus, Symbol of God* (Maryknoll, N.Y.: Orbis, 1999).

5. The ideal set forth in Crusader spirituality bears a strong resemblance to the Kingdom meditation in the Spiritual Exercises. Hans Wolter, "Elements of Crusade Spirituality in St. Ignatius," in *Ignatius of Loyola: His Personality and Spiritual Heritage,* ed. Friedrich Wulf (St. Louis: Institute of Jesuit Sources, 1977), 101, notes: "In Christ he saw the true leader whom one must follow....The Crusader considered the exertions, deprivations and sufferings of the journey into foreign lands—he wished to be homeless with the homeless Lord—and especially the constant threat of death, to be a spiritual participation in the suffering and death of Christ. Beyond that, victory—granted but seldom—was experienced as a participation in the victory of Christ...."

6. Jaroslav Pelikan devoted a chapter in *Jesus Through the Centuries* (New Haven: Yale University Press, 1985) to illustrating various interpretations and emphases given to the image of King of Kings. Early Christian martyrs claimed Christ as their king, threatening the political stability of Caesar by refusing to acknowledge the emperor as divine. Constantine attributed his military success to Christ the "victor King," guaranteeing the title permanence and honor in the tradition. The cross became a kingly symbol, emblazoned on the royal crowns and banners of European monarchs. The eternal kingship of Christ evolved into the divine right of kings who waged holy wars justifying political sovereignty. All these images reinforced the belief that political authority was linked to ecclesiastical authority. "Christ was King, the Church was a monarchy, the Pope was a monarch, and it was by his authority that earthly monarchs exercised their authority" (56). Some today still claim this leadership model.

7. See Sallie McFague's groundbreaking and scholarly *The Body of God: An Ecological Theology* (1993) as well as *Models of God: Theology for an Ecological, Nuclear Age* (Philadelphia: Fortress Press, 1987).

8. We suggest two additional sources related to humility. G. Gilleman, "Humility," in the *New Catholic Encyclopedia,* vol. 7 (New York: McGraw-Hill, 1967), 234–36, defines humility as the "virtue by which a man attributes to God all the good he possesses" (234). The article explores the development of humility in the Bible, theological thought and human practice. A different approach is found in William J. Bennett, *The Book of Virtues* (New York: Simon and Schuster, 1993). This book is intended to aid the moral education of the young. Ten virtues are considered: self-discipline, compassion, responsibility, friendship, work, courage, perseverance, honesty, loyalty and faith. There is no mention of humility.

9. Updated historical information and spiritual writing can be found in Paulist Press's Classics of Western Spirituality series. We also recommend biographies of well-known saints of the tradition as well as accounts of modern saints. A recent collection by Robert Ellsberg, *All Saints: Daily Reflections on Saints, Prophets and Witnesses for our Time* (New York: Crossroad, 1997) could provide a rich resource for directors from Agnes and Anthony of Egypt to Pedro Arrupe and Thea Bowman. Ellsberg also suggests further resources. See also Elizabeth Johnson, *Friends of God and Prophets: A Feminist Theological Reading of the Communion of Saints* (New York: Continuum, 1998).

# Chapter 8

# Discovering the Depth of Commitment:
# Exercises of the Third Week

*...to ask for heartfelt sorrow and confusion, because the Lord is going to his Passion for my sins.*

—Spiritual Exercises [193]

*I cannot accept that the suffering and criminal death of Jesus was "God's will." What kind of God would desire such torture for a beloved son? I feel God must weep for the atrocities humans do to each other, most of all what happened to Jesus.*

—A Contemporary Woman

In the Third Week or Passion Week, the one making the Spiritual Exercises hears anew the invitation to walk the way of discipleship, this time moving ever more deeply into relationship with God. To know, love and follow Jesus gains new meaning in light of the Third Week: the call to compassion with Jesus' suffering. Following Jesus draws the seeker into the drama of the Cross, for she goes up to Jerusalem and engages in the conflict that leads to death. Being with Jesus means entering into *his* perspective, focusing not on personal experience of the passion, but willingly sharing his: his choices, his anguish, his truth, his desires, his aloneness, his sense of the absence of

God. The attentive guide will notice the readiness of the seeker to enter into this Week as her prayer becomes simpler and she moves toward a forgetfulness of self in growing union with Jesus.

Like those who accompanied Jesus in his ministry, the seekers have experienced his deeds of power and heard his words of life during the first two Weeks of the Exercises. They are now confronted, however, with the fearful choice of whether to follow him into the depths of powerlessness. In this desolation Ignatius says, "divinity hides itself" [196].

## Material and Dynamics of the Third Week

Who is the Christ of the Third Week? One commentator notes, "With Ignatius we are always before the Christ of majesty, the Creator and Lord, the eternal King of the Kingdom who fulfills his mission here on earth by passing through the painful death from which he delivers us" (Cusson 1988, 299). Others encounter Jesus in his ultimate humanity: pain, suffering, betrayal and death. They share Jesus' sense of failure, grief, loss and betrayal by his friends.

The contemplations of the Third Week [190–209] feature Jesus with his apostles in mortal conflict with powerful religious and political institutions of his time and culture. They begin with the last supper, harmonizing the paschal meal of the Synoptic Gospels and the foot washing and last discourse of the Fourth Gospel. The second contemplation considers "how Christ our Lord descended with his eleven disciples from Mt. Sion where the supper had been eaten into the valley," [201] and entered the garden of Gethsemane. The subsequent contemplations lead to the house of Annas, the house of Caiaphas and the house of Pilate and to Herod as well as Simon of Cyrene, the presence of two thieves and his followers Joseph and Nicodemus. These scenes trace Jesus going from house to house, encountering strong and powerful men and being betrayed by the very friends he had gathered around him. Ignatius briefly mentions Our Lady in her loneliness, grief and fatigue [208] as sorrowful mother [298].

Given the inevitable end of this journey with Jesus, why would anyone choose to enter the passion week? The answer lies in the mysterious and compelling call to the depths of discipleship. For some, the Third Week confirms the decisions made during the Second Week. For others, the call to share the totality of Jesus' human limits and abandonment becomes a time of transformation. Prayer during this week may be unpredictable. Some experience the dryness and distance of God so concretely that this state in itself becomes an experience of the passion. For others, the prayer of the Third Week offers an experience of great consolation. The entire paschal mystery grounds the Third Week. Followers, then and now, must chose their response to this encounter with mystery, an encounter that can lead to new depths of compassion, friendship and love. Whether one meets the suffering servant or the glorious Messiah in prayer, the invitation to plumb the depths of God's saving love remains the same.

## Problems and Possibilities for the Third Week

Some women feel reluctance as they anticipate the Third Week. Pain and powerlessness feel too familiar and a suffering God seems a contradiction. As always, careful discernment will help to determine whether hesitancy serves as a warning that proceeding may prove harmful or an opportunity for conversion, grace and greater intimacy. Several problems areas as well as possibilities may emerge during the Week.

## Christ Image

While Jesus is the central figure in all the passion narratives, each portrays him differently.[1] In addition to these biblical portrayals, the tradition has emphasized, in both doctrine and devotion, images of the suffering Christ that have become stumbling blocks for some contemporary women. The image of Christ as sacrificial lamb and victim, for example, caused one woman to respond in this way: "The all-knowing, all-powerful and all-good Father God sent his Son to earth to be killed. The Son went meekly as a lamb to the slaughter without complaint. This sounds to me like cosmic child abuse is the way of salvation." These suggestions of abuse and passivity seem to glorify suffering in silence as a holy victim prevails; women today reject this "victim" image as detrimental to their own self-development.

The servant image can likewise prove problematic for some women who see Christ as servant, reinforcing the idea that servitude—even slavery—is preferred for followers of Christ. Womanist theologians cite this servant image as an example of how some use Jesus to reinforce white male supremacy. Holding up Jesus as a model servant, directly or indirectly, can subtly encourage toleration of slavery or keeping marginalized persons "in their place" as servants, helpers, caretakers. The image often reinforces a romanticized concept of servanthood suggested by those with no firsthand knowledge of its realities. Systems of domination and subordination reflected in relationships between lords and servants do not provide appropriate models for contemporary emulation.

So how can the image of Christ as model "servant" open up new possibilities for contemporary women? Matthew's Gospel has Jesus reminding his disciples that "whoever wishes to be first among you must be your slave; just as the Son of Man came not to be served but to serve" (20:27). As Ruether comments, "The essence of servanthood is that it is possible only for liberated persons, not people in servitude. Also it exercises power and leadership, but in a new way, not to reduce others to dependency, but to empower and liberate others" (1990, 54). In this model, persons choose the model of servanthood initiated by Jesus and flowing from his free and independent choice; they are not coerced by another. Finally, Gospel servanthood transforms disciples into friends. "I do not call you servants any longer, because the servant does not know what the master is doing; but I have called you friends, because I have made known to you everything that I have heard from my Father" (John 15:15). Turning these Christ images around provides an opportunity to explore whether they still have meaning for women. Theologian Anne Carr, for example, reinterprets the image of "victim": Jesus was neither a passive victim nor did he acquiesce to a sacrificial death. Rather, Jesus died because of the way he lived, the fidelity and commitment of his life and his liberating message (Carr 1996, 174).

## The Cross

Just as some Christ images can become obstacles to entering the Third Week, the cross as sign and symbol of Christian discipleship can block some women's progress. "If any want to become my followers, let them deny themselves and take up their cross daily and follow me" (Luke 9:23). Walking the way of discipleship in the footsteps of Jesus is one thing, but uncritically accepting the "sign of the cross" as a devotional symbol when it has historically also been a sign of domination and violence on battlegrounds and in Jewish ghettos is another. Today many women feel increasingly sensitive to the interrelationship of all systems of domination and resist association with symbols and language that perpetuate any kind of oppression.

Yet the cross symbolizes not only domination and death but also life and liberation. Contemporary women theologians and artists provide new interpretations. For example, the sculpture of *Crucified Woman* has both shocked and inspired. It has stimulated theological reflection about the relationship of art, the female body and needless suffering of women. Themes of relationship, healing and justice emerge as life and death questions. Who is on the cross today? One woman on seeing the sculpture responded:

> The usual image of a man hung on a tree really imprisoned me
> to the idea of a male God. The image of a woman liberates me
> into the idea that my being a woman allows me to identify with
> God's act. Beautiful, powerful, a challenge to take up the cross
> and not be a passive bystander. (Dyke 1991, 26)

The cross can also represent significant relationships. At a symposium exploring the Christ symbol and women, those in attendance were invited to bring a cross that belonged to them and tell the stories associated with it.[2] Whether jewelry, symbols of covenant commitment, artistic representations, mementos of someone or something special, each cross and story represented a personal and meaningful relationship.

The sign of the cross remains a sign of contradiction for some women today. Seeker and guide will need to ponder its power for liberation and life in the contemporary context as women continue to face their "daily" crosses.

### Exclusion from the Story

"I know this story already," says one woman of her problems with the Third Week material. Familiarity with the passion narratives and their representations through art, music, poetry, film and liturgical celebrations may dissuade the one making the Exercises from going deeper in contemplating the passion. Past prejudices, theological misunderstanding and false expectations could lead one to satisfaction with the superficial. Even the selected texts in the Exercises reinforce the assumption that the drama of the passion has an almost exclusively male cast. Yet one can reread the passion and balance the actions of men who dominate the traditional telling with the women who are not represented, yet simultaneously offered care and compassion to Jesus in his suffering.

The Exercises begin with the story of a meal, Jesus eating the paschal meal with his apostles. An alternative reading also begins with a meal, this one a supper at the home of Simon the Leper. An unnamed woman (Mark 14:3–9, Matt 26:6–13) anoints Jesus prior to his death. Although a traditional action, she anoints not his feet but his head as a sign of royal commission. Thus, she takes on the "untraditional position of priest and/or prophet" (Levine 1992, 261). Jesus recognized the significance of her action by noting that what she had done would be recounted through the ages "in memory of her." But her name was lost and the pioneering work of biblical scholar Elisabeth Schüssler Fiorenza only recently reclaimed her story. In a similar scene in the Fourth Gospel, Mary of Bethany anoints Jesus' feet, a sign of extravagant love, shortly before he himself washes the feet of the disciples. The scene reminds us of the special friendship among Martha, Mary, Lazarus and Jesus.

Women's voices also emerge in the passion story. The maid of the high priest serves as a foil to Peter. Her probing questions demand a truthful answer and stand in sharp contrast to Peter's denial. Pilate's wife, a woman of power because of her husband, pays attention to the warning in her dream. Yet her warning, spoken on behalf of Jesus, was ignored. The daughters of Jerusalem, weeping and crying out, elicit attention for suffering women and children. The "voiceless" women in the passion narrative communicate eloquently by their faithful presence at the death and burial of Jesus. They remain nameless except for three: Mary Magdalene, Mary the mother of James and Joses, and Salome. Luke also adds Joanna to the list of women present at the cross. The Fourth Gospel vividly portrays Mary, the mother of Jesus, and the beloved disciple standing beneath the cross, exemplifying discipleship as a relationship transcending bloodlines. Jesus' words in death give life to a new community of mutuality and care, which finds its fulfillment in Pentecost.

The women of the passion stand at a distance, but share the powerlessness of the one who suffers—Jesus. In contrast, the men engage in a struggle marked by power, domination, fear, dishonesty, cowardice, lying and physical violence. The grace of the Third Week, to experience sorrow and confusion for the Lord's passion [93], opens a wider realm of possibility as one prays with Jesus in the midst of his experience with both the men and women who participate in his passion narrative.

## Suffering, Guilt and Compassion

The notion that Jesus suffers because of "my sins," as stated in the text of the *Exercises* ("...the Lord is going to his Passion for my sins" [193] and "consider how he suffers all this for my sins" [197]) can block some women from progressing further into the Third Week. The phrase can elicit a pervasive and debilitating guilt over being the cause of Jesus' death. Such guilt has had many centuries to embed itself in the psyche of women. In the third century, Tertullian's treatise *On the Dress of Women* announced this judgment: "God's judgment on this sex lives on in our age: the guilt necessarily lives on as well. *You* are the Devil's gateway;...because of *your* punishment, that is, death, even the Son of God had to die" (Clark 1983, 39). Internalizing this kind of guilt can lead to an unhealthy preoccupation: "How am I the cause of Christ's passion?

222

What did I do to him to make him suffer?" Or worse, "Because I did
_____, Jesus had to die."

This aspect of the Exercises elicits a strong response from women
who have been asked and expected to suffer for the wrong reasons, for
example, to offer up the actions of an abusive husband "for the sake
of the marriage." Certainly, suffering is part of the human condition,
but knowing the difference between redemptive suffering and abuse
proves especially critical for women. Even this sense of meaningless-
ness and futility can bring us back into the presence of Jesus in his passion and open up possibilities for deepening spiritual insight during
the Third Week.

For example, in his supplementary material, Ignatius suggests
contemplating the Seven Last Words of Christ [297]; contemporary
women might listen to these words as the women at the foot of the
cross might have heard them. In asking to share the dispositions of
Jesus on the cross and allowing his words in death to be words of life,
amazing possibilities present themselves. After being with Jesus in his
suffering, some experience a breakthrough: they see the passion of
Jesus in their experience of suffering. At the same time a poignant
question arises: "What needs to die in me in order to really live?"

Pain can be a portal leading to a richer life. Situations of physical,
psychological and/or spiritual pain provide occasions to discern directions. "What happens as a result of this suffering? How can I learn to
suffer for the right reasons and what are they? How can I see meaning in this suffering, leading me to greater faith, hope and love? How
do I identify the value of living with pain and how do I get out of pain
that is destructive?" Past interpretations of spirituality and theology
uncritically accepted the value of suffering. Today, however, the
insights of psychology and liberation theology demand the alleviation
of demeaning and unjust suffering and expose the ways people and
systems legitimate this kind of oppression.

Yet, a profound and intimate encounter with God is called forth as one faces one's suffering. Discovering personal meaning in suffering brings with it the realization that suffering defies human understanding. The daily deaths one experiences can signify Holy Presence in all aspects of human life. No one can ever totally understand the mystery of suffering and death, but presence to God and to those who suffer teaches compassion. These times—when few if any words are needed—remind one that presence alone suffices in the face of inevitable suffering. Suffering, as with other human experiences, moves the seeker into another dimension of the mystery of relationship, compassion or "suffering with."

Set against the backdrop of Christ's suffering, prayer of the Third Week can reveal new understandings of passion and compassion as the seeker connects her passion with that of the larger Body of Christ. Passionate women praying the passion of Jesus Christ can experience deep affective responses: guilt, consolation, fear of her own and Jesus' suffering, love and intimacy. Sharing in the passion of another leads to communion with them and praying the passion of Jesus will inevitably lead to compassion for those most in need. As one attends to the suffering of another, one cannot force or even predict one's own affective response. One simply knows that "If one member suffers, all suffer together with it" (1 Cor 12:26).

As one of the graces of the Third Week, empathy, identifying with the thoughts and feelings of another, leads to a self-transcendence that opens up to others. While more than a simple awareness of other persons and their experience, empathy stops short of total absorption in another. Empathy creates transformation through mutuality and fosters a hope for his or her well-being, which paradoxically benefits oneself. "Such a dynamic may well underlie the Christian interpretation of Christ on the Cross identifying with all sin and sinners, and therefore able to redeem all sinners from sin" (Suchocki 1995, 111).

## Wisdom for Those Giving the Exercises

The Third Week presents scripture's sacred passion stories, releasing ultimate questions and profound feelings. The material often leads to greater personal depth and a deeper level of solidarity in suffering with all human persons and with the earth. The situation of contemporary women around the world, so many of whom are poor or suffer from sexual oppression and violence, illumine the Third Week through their intimate experience of suffering and death. Perhaps women could begin their contemplations of the Third Week with experiences of passion and compassion for other women Identifying with the suffering of any aspect of creation can lead to compassion or a way of being with suffering.

Ultimately, this week raises questions about who and where God is and how humans and God are in relationship: "What in my world is suffering? How am I to be compassionate?" Thus, several themes emerge from women's experience of the Third Week.

First, the passion narratives are theological statements, not historical accounts, descriptions or documentary evidence. The Gospel writers were not primarily interested in what happened, but in what the event *meant* in the life of persons and the community. The same perspective has relevance today. In choosing Scripture reflections, the guide can use a single Gospel or weave together various events from different Gospels according to the disposition of the one making the Exercises. Even a single event leaves room for various emphasis. The last supper, for example, can be experienced as sacrifice, sacrament, sign of a new covenant, a meal with friends or a table at which one is denied a place.

Second, engaging the whole person in body, mind and will, feelings, ideas and imagination is crucial to the prayer of this Week. The disposition of the one praying the Exercises proves as important as the selection of content. No one can predict what type of experience the seeker will have. Since pain, suffering and death in the context of love comprise the prayer material for this Week, the guide must determine how the one making the Exercises enters into pain, her own and that of her family, society and world. Discernment is essential. Is the pain redemptive or debilitating? Does pain cause undue self-absorption? What represents authentic grieving? What rhythm and expression lead gradually to a new place of understanding and peace? The Scriptures refer to women weeping, and the women making the Exercises may also weep. Let them. Other awkward feelings may arise in difficult moments when she does not know how to respond to suffering or feels unable to connect her suffering with that of others.

Third, the guide needs to be alert to signs of unhealthy guilt and grief. Extreme pain, suffering and guilt can block prayer and increase isolation. One can also get stuck in the pain or develop habits of avoidance or distraction. Dealing with deep affective life makes up part of the process of Third Week contemplations. Unfamiliar or fearful emotions can surface and temptation to accept superficial responses to the passion can block the grace that leads to the affective depth. Nevertheless, when one has faced and accepted death, life takes on new meaning. One realizes a connection to the larger human community in its vulnerability and finitude. The experience of grief can become an opportunity to care for and connect with others, to reach out instead of withdrawing.

Fourth, if the passion narratives prove problematic, alternative Scripture passages may be used to elicit the graces of the Third Week. These passages include the story of the grain of wheat: "I tell you, unless a grain of wheat falls into the earth and dies, it remains just a single grain; but if it dies, it bears much fruit" (John 12:24), the Suffering Servant Songs from Isaiah, the predictions of the cross at the transfiguration, or situations of death in which Jesus related to women (the stories of the widow of Naim, Jairus's daughter and Martha, Mary and Lazarus).

Finally, art, literature, film, music and even dreams can stimulate and enrich reflection on the passion. Liturgical resources provide prayer, music, Scripture and gestures that enhance the Third Week exercises. Cultural diversity marks the various observances of Lent and rituals expressing beliefs about death and ancestors. Devotions centered on the passion fill the Christian tradition with many examples of piety: the stations of the cross,[3] the Sorrowful Mysteries of the rosary or dramatic representations of the passion, for example.

Death is not final for Jesus, his disciples or the contemporary woman praying the Exercises. Who knows the moment when the sorrow and confusion of the Third Week, when "his divinity hides itself," [196] will become transformed into the gladness and joy of resurrection? But the fruits of the Third Week will manifest themselves in the seeker's deeper identification with Jesus in freedom and gratitude. For the guide, the task continues to recognize and support the movements of the Third Week in the unique experience of the individual seeker.

# Notes

1. See Raymond Brown, *A Crucified Christ in Holy Week* (Collegeville, Minn.: Liturgical Press), 1986. This small, insightful book of essays on the Gospel passion narratives provides an invaluable resource for anyone pondering the passion.

2. Elizabeth Johnson describes this event in greater detail in "Redeeming the Name of Christ" in *Freeing Theology: The Essentials of Theology in Feminist Perspective,* ed. Catherine Mowry LaCugna (Harper San Francisco 1993), 115–16.

3. Our readers may be interested in a publication of the Intercommunity Peace and Justice Center in Seattle, Washington. Their 1999 "Stations of the Cross in the Lives of Women" illustrates an effective adaptation of a traditional religious practice by incorporating the experience of women's lives in their prayers and reflection.

# Chapter 9

# Mission and Mutuality:
# Exercises of the Fourth Week

*Consider the office of consoler which Christ our Lord carries out, and
compare it with the way friends console one another.*

—Spiritual Exercises [224]

*I never imagined God could be so real and present in my life. I will
never be the same after making the Exercises.*

—A Contemporary Woman

Only a few pages of text indicate the direction for the Fourth
Week and the conclusion of the Exercises. At this point, the one living the Exercises moves into the fullness of the paschal mystery, the
mystery of the resurrection. Just as the Third Week draws the one
making the Exercises into the midst of the suffering and death of
"Christ the Lord," the Fourth Week inaugurates a time to "be glad
and to rejoice intensely because of the great glory and joy of Christ
our Lord" [221].

Ignatius encourages the one making the Exercises to "Consider
how the divinity, which seemed hidden during the Passion, now
appears and manifests itself so miraculously in this holy Resurrection" [223]. Likewise human experience can provide an entry place

for contemplation in the Fourth Week. Consolation of one kind or another becomes the touchstone. This week invites awareness of God's consoling presence. Just as the Gospel accounts reveal the risen Christ breaking through physical and psychological barriers in unexpected ways, so God is manifest in daily life—in gifts of joy, love, gratitude and peace. These moments are marked by pure surprise and giftedness, rejoicing in the resurrection.

## Material and Dynamics of the Fourth Week

The Fourth Week, like the Second, invites seekers to enter an imaginative nonbiblical scene, this time to share the intimacy of the reunion of mother and son, Christ our Lord appearing to Our Lady [218]. This model contemplation [218–25] is followed by the remainder of the Exercises found in "The Risen Life" [299–312]. Thirteen texts comprise the Easter stories. Some, such as those referring to the appearances to the women at the empty tomb, Peter, the disciples on their way to Emmaus, the disciples without Thomas and with Thomas, the disciples fishing and the commissioning on Mount Tabor, are quite familiar. Others are surprising: Jesus appearing to five hundred disciples, to James and to Paul (from 1 Cor 15), as well as an appearance to Joseph of Arimathea taken from the lives of the saints. The final contemplation of the ascension is from the Acts of the Apostles [299–312].

The disposition of the one making the Exercises changes significantly in the Third and Fourth Weeks of the Exercises; her perspective shifts from looking with her own eyes to viewing life through Jesus' eyes. While the process of the Second Week asks the person to consider her own call and response to discipleship, the Third and Fourth Weeks focus the contemplations on the experience of Jesus. Such emphasis presupposes that "being with" means letting go of one's personal agenda and taking up God's. This transformation entails intimacy and personal identification with the life, death and resurrection of Jesus. "Laboring with God" [236] in the world means being with him through contemplation of the paschal mystery in the Gospels and in the contemporary world.

The Fourth Week process notes continue to stress the engagement of the whole person and to emphasize embodiment, so that the total person experiences the prayer of the resurrection. Concrete suggestions include thinking about things that bring pleasure, happiness and spiritual joy, taking advantage of light and seasonal delights as well as whatever "will help me to rejoice in Christ my Creator and Redeemer" [229].

## Problems and Possibilities for Women

The church's selective memory about the resurrection raises problems for women during the Fourth Week. The tradition has too often forgotten the major role women have played as witnesses to the resurrection, and the text of the *Exercises* reflects this lack. Noticeably absent is Mary Magdalene's encounter with the risen Christ in the garden and her commission to tell the disciples that he is risen (John 20:1–18). Correcting this omission opens up rich ground. Images of women witnessing to the resurrection and being faithfully present to Jesus provide strong models for contemporary women. For example, one thinks of Mary Magdalene, reinstated as "apostle to the apostles," and her active leadership role in the early church. Women played a major role in the paschal mystery. They exemplified faithful presence at the cross and tomb and serve as a bridge to the resurrection. Even when discounted and trivialized (Luke 24:10–11), their voices proclaim truth for the believing community.[1]

Certain dispositions of contemporary women can raise obstacles to the liberating effect of the Fourth Week. Fear can paralyze women today, just as it did the women in Mark's Gospel (16:8) who fled from the resurrection. Change in their relational world challenges women's self-identity. Commitment can generate fear, for success and joy in one's accomplishments demands a response. Becoming an active player in the resurrection drama of daily life promises further engagement with the unknown. Often women desire to cling to the familiar, but the grace of the Fourth Week asks women to move out into the unfamiliar role of witness and public mission. In discovering God at work in the world, women must embrace all aspects of it.

The Fourth Week also calls for a recognition of moments of grace as postresurrection experiences: times when fear is transformed, times when relationships are renewed with God, with oneself, with the communities that have been present in prayer and life, and with the risen Christ in the world.

## Mary in the Exercises

Despite the general omission of women during this Week, Mary does hold a prominent place in the Fourth Week's first contemplation. Each of her brief but consistent appearances throughout the prior Weeks culminates in her presence here. Ignatius, appropriate to his times and culture, called her "Our Lady."

Mary is initially mentioned in the first prelude or composition of place in the first exercises of the First Week. Ignatius has those making the Exercises imagine a place "where Jesus Christ or Our Lady happen to be" [47]. In the third exercise she is the initial intercessor in the colloquies. "The first colloquy will be with Our Lady, that she may obtain for me from her Son and Lord three things...," which constitute interior knowledge and rejection of sin [63].

In the Second Week the contemplation on the incarnation asks seekers to visualize "Our Lady and the angel greeting her" [106].

The nativity segment asks those making the Exercises to recall "how our Lady and Joseph left Nazareth to go to Bethlehem....She was pregnant almost nine months and, as we may piously meditate, seated on a burro; and with her were Joseph and a servant girl, leading an ox" [111].

In the Third Week, Mary is present at the removal of the body of Jesus from the cross, and the *Exercises* refer to "the house where Our Lady went after the burial of her Son" [208]. "Consider, too, Our Lady's loneliness along with her deep grief and fatigue" [208]. In the Fourth Week we contemplate "How Christ Our Lord Appeared to Our Lady" [219].

Additional exercises at the end of the text place Mary in the contemplations of the infancy and hidden life, including the visitation to Elizabeth. In the public life, she appears at the wedding feast of Cana [276] and finally in the passion week, where Jesus speaks from the cross to Mary the sorrowful mother [297–8].

Problems can arise when people uncritically accept images and assumptions about Mary. Clarity about these prove both necessary and helpful. First, very little is known about the historical Mary of Nazareth, a first-century Jewish woman and mother of Jesus. Second, contemporary biblical scholars, both Catholic and Protestant, interpret Mary in the Gospels and Paul's singular reference (Gal 4:4) in the context of the faith of the early Christian communities. Third, the Mary of two thousand years of tradition in art and architecture, apocrypha, myth, saints' stories, doctrinal debates, devotions, apparitions and prayer staggers mind and imagination in its complexity. The question "Who is the 'real' Mary?" parallels the question posed about Jesus.

Mary's treatment in theological discussions raises a second problem. Until recently, Mary has been primarily interpreted in the dominant European and North American culture by clergymen and male theologians. They have stressed her femininity and unique virginal privilege and idealized maternity. One of the major critiques of Mary today rests on exaggerated attention to her titles of "virgin" and "mother," which emphasize her unique privilege and distances her from women who literally cannot be both at the same time. Such titles equate her value with her sexual role and stress her function more than her person. Others note that her characteristics of docility, humility and hiddenness often reinforce patriarchal ideals of women's passive and subordinate role. Thus understood, Mary perpetuates the patriarchal family as a model for church and an image of heaven. She reinforces such women's stereotypes as the "Eve-Mary syndrome," where one woman is demeaned as source of sin, the other idolized as without sin. Eve is rejected because she lived too close to the earth, Mary is inaccessible because she is too close to heaven.

However, today's climate offers opportunities to renew our understanding of Mary and her place in the spiritual lives of all believers. She hears the word of God and acts on it. The stages of her life reflect the recurring "Yes" of the annunciation. Some women have found rich prayer by reflecting on the many phases of Mary's life and how each reveals a special relationship with God. She is girl, child, daughter, woman, wife, mother, cousin, friend, teacher, middle-aged woman, widow.

In her relationship to Jesus, Mary provides a model for discipleship. Modern biblical scholarship, Vatican II's theological renewal and greater ecumenical awareness have provided more accurate information about her, while liberation theology and feminist theology critique and reclaim Mary from the perspectives of culture and gender. For example, the *Magnificat* (Luke 1:46–55), so long a part of the church's spiritual tradition, has been reinterpreted in light of women's and oppressed peoples' experience. Today, as a result of women's spirituality, Mary emerges with new vitality as friend, mentor and sister, thus making her more accessible to all.

## Wisdom for One Giving the Exercises

As with the other Weeks, the last Week demands that the one giving the Exercises be attuned to its particular dynamics. Here simplicity, quiet, confidence, wholeness and a sense of centered grounding in God continue to grow in the one living the Exercises. The recognizing, affirming and challenging role of the guide conforms to the desired graces of the Fourth Week. She or he, like the disciples after the resurrection, needs to recognize and name the resurrection moments present in the life of the seeker.

The guide also recognizes the signs of the resurrection in the seeker, who knows the risen Christ in his gifts and in the manifestations of his presence through peace, joy and consolation. She also has new eyes to see God's presence and action in different ways in her own life and in others and rejoices in the joy of resurrection. She realizes that all is gift and responds with gratitude, confident in relationship with the risen Christ who moves her to mission.

The seeker may experience a tendency to allow uncertainty to pull her back into the "old," forgetting that Christ is "new," but she must resist whatever pulls her back into her former and familiar self. Recognizing the postresurrection experiences in her life proves key. The risen Christ encounters her in her own experiences and their many, even contradictory, manifestations (so similar to the Gospel appearances to the disciples): feelings of fear and doubt, lack of recognizing God's presence, anxiety combined with joy, a sense of losing and finding, and a pervasive, consoling presence. Dealing with joy and peace does not always occur in the way a woman expects it, so she should be aware of "romance novel syndrome," which glamorizes emotions and expects one to live "happily ever after." Postresurrection appearances are not necessarily ecstatic, dramatic or highly emotional. Consolation has many, frequently subtle, manifestations. A seeker often needs a companion's assistance to recognize them.

Besides being sensitive to postresurrection appearances, the guide needs to remember and highlight the importance of women in the postresurrection communities. Praying over Pentecost and the events of the early church in the Acts of the Apostles can connect contemporary women to living out the resurrection event in the context of church communities today.

Finally, the Exercises can provide a significant opportunity to rediscover the richness of Mary as model disciple and God-bearer who crosses the threshold of Mystery. She can be a positive role model, showing how God desires all persons to be God-bearers, hearing the word of God, receiving it and allowing it to become fruitful in their lives. Knowing Mary, not only theologically and spiritually, but also with religious imagination and affectivity, becomes vitally important. The meaning of Mary for the life of the Christian community needs renewal in every generation, for Mary stands as model for all believers, women and men.[2]

## Contemplation to Attain Love

The culminating prayer of the Spiritual Exercises, the Contemplation to Attain Love, intimates Ignatius's own mystical awareness. Only here does he speak freely of love and the beloved.[3] Through contemplation one looks back at the graces of the Exercises and at God's gracious gifting in one's own life, savoring this intimate knowledge in gratitude and love. The wider vision gained at this point in the Exercises fosters "finding God in all things." Thus the prayer of daily living impels one to desire God in every aspect of life.

Ignatius gives two important pre-notes or observations. The first [230] highlights the necessity of deeds rather than words for expressing active love. This wise observation militates against any religious "high" and points to the criterion of authentic love, human or divine (Matt 7:21). The second pre-note [231] underscores mutuality. The lover and the beloved seek to share whatever they have or are. Experience uncovers the enormous difference between gifts given with little thought and those expressing wholehearted love, the very self of the giver.

The first prelude [232] or composition of place asks the one making the Exercises to see herself standing before God with the angels and saints who intercede. Deceased family members, mentors, dear friends, heroes and heroines might well be included, bringing a much stronger affective dimension. The second prelude ("what I desire" [233]) is a threefold plea for interior knowledge of the great good received, profound gratitude and an ability to love and serve God in *all* things. Finding God in all things means finding God's presence in rejection, betrayal, illness—the general craziness of life—as well as in great joy, faithful friends or good health. The "more" of the Second, Third and Fourth Weeks becomes the "all" of total self gift (Conroy 1995, 17).

The first point [234] offers the seeker an opportunity to reflect on all gifts received, pondering with "deep affection" not only the gifts, but the Giver who offers Self as well. The second [235] emphasizes God's immanence, in all of creation and specifically within the one making the Exercises. The third point [236] focuses on God laboring in all things, continually creating the universe. The fourth point highlights the source of all gifts as goodness itself. This Being empowers and shares divine life with the seeker, allowing her to find God not only in all things, but also to *be* God's presence toward all things.

Although much of the commentary suggests that these four points synthesize the corresponding week of the Exercises, the interrelationship of the points and graces is far more dynamic. Contemplation, repetition, application of the senses, colloquies and discernment lead the one making the Exercises to reflect on herself and respond to God's gifting in mutual love and deep affection. An implied "Take and Receive" [234] concludes each period of prayer, although Ignatius simply calls for a colloquy and recitation of the Our Father.

## Problems and Possibilities of the Contemplation

The Contemplation exemplifies the profound heights possible in the relationship between a person and God. The value of this culminating prayer of the Exercises, however, may be lost for some seekers. For some women, the Spiritual Exercises get rushed toward the end, and either they are not aware or are afraid to ask for the guidance needed to probe the potential of the Contemplation. Some women mistakenly consider the Contemplation the climax or high point of the Exercise and suffer a "letdown" at the conclusion of the retreat; they have not understood the Contemplation as a transition into daily life. And some women find it difficult to recognize, name, accept and take responsibility for their gifts, but gratitude constitutes the necessary prerequisite for the Contemplation and serves as the foundation for the service flowing from the Exercises.

Communicating to God who one is and has is a woman's dream, but the seeker might easily exclaim, "How can I give anything to God? I'm not worthy." Yielding in love to the action of the Spirit empowers God. This conscious awareness of God's mutual love and gift can nourish a woman through a lifetime of service and fidelity.

The admonition that love ought to manifest itself more in deeds than words can raise a problem with overgenerosity. Fear of intimacy may motivate some to unceasing action; overemphasized zeal can lead others to pour out their resources for others so that they have nothing left for themselves. They succumb to the cultural temptation that equates personal value with work and productivity.

Although problems with false expectations, feelings of unworthiness and over generosity may arise, the Contemplation to Attain Love offers many possibilities for women. In some ways, it is the most appealing exercise of the four Weeks. In response to the Contemplation, women will often exclaim, "This is the God I know!" The relational context, mutuality of love and tender intimacy create a climate in which women thrive.

The relational context of the Exercises also highlights the God who is ultimately relational. Within the contemplation, the Trinity is imagined as blessing the seeker, presenting Godself to her, laboring for her and energizing and empowering her. Contemporary feminist theology helps us reconceive a trinitarian theology that emphasizes relationship and mutuality among equals. God exists as the mystery of persons in communion. Only in communion can God be what God is and only in communion can God exist at all. In addition, the relational image of Trinity evokes the image of dance (LaCugna 1991, 270). No one "leads" in the divine dance: there exists only the eternal moment of giving and receiving. The ecstatic, relational actions of the persons of the Trinity toward one another constitute the unity.

The awareness of the Trinity then frames the reflection on the nature of human persons in themselves, the relationship between persons and between humankind and all other creatures as well as relationship with God. In the Contemplation to Attain Love, Ignatius notes that reverence, gratitude and self-gift must mark each relationship.

What is true with regard to the human community rings true also of all of creation, the household of God. The doctrine of the Trinity does not abstractly teach about God apart from the world, but about God's love in and with the world and each human being. Living trinitarian life means reverencing the earth, caring for it and seeing it as companion. "Living trinitarian faith means living together in harmony and communion with every other creature in the common household of God" (LaCugna 1991, 401).

## Wisdom about the Contemplation for the Director

Sometimes the one giving the Exercises minimizes this final exercise, giving it as a handout for use in the days that follow. Often the seeker expends so much time and energy in moving through the first three "Weeks" that time runs out. Regardless how far a seeker has progressed, the Contemplation to Attain Love should be offered as the concluding exercise. Here women especially connect with Ignatius's language and perception.

Because this is contemplation and not meditation, repetition and application of the senses prove extremely important in savoring each point. Some seekers may profit by writing their own "Take and Receive." In addition, in a kind of retroactive discernment, the one giving the Exercises can use the images for God-self-world of the Contemplation as a sort of touchstone determining the authenticity and wholeness of the retreatant's images from the beginning (English 1995, 252ff.).

Some women might use the Contemplation to Attain Love as a framework for examen. For example, the first point, which highlights continual gifting (including God's own Self), might suggest some of the following questions: " What is the lived depth of my gratitude? Love or obligation? How have I used these gifts for others? Do I see these gifts as signs of God's gratuitous love or as a measure of how effective I am? To what extent do I really believe in God's gift of Self to me? How does this impact my life, my self-identity, my ability to risk?"

The expressed progression of the dynamic of the Exercises develops in terms of relationship. The one making the Exercises begins by seeing her place in the universe, becoming a fallible but faithful follower of Jesus, rejoicing in Jesus' resurrection, and only after that, hearing the *language* of invitation to profound intimacy and mutuality with this God-in-Jesus. This progression moves from transcendence to immanence to intimacy. Since women usually develop by way of intimacy and relationship, the process of the Exercises can "work" for them provided relationship is continually stressed throughout the dynamic and the relationship with the one giving the Exercises is sensitive and freeing.

## Formation of Contemplatives in Action

The formation of contemplatives in action builds on the experience of the Exercises, culminating in the Contemplation to Attain Love. Contemplation in action invites seekers to discover new meanings in current reality, for God will transform and empower them to be with God and to act with God in the midst of the world. When desiring to live out the Ignatian Contemplation to Attain Love, love becomes the basis of all a seeker does and is, love expressed not only in words but also in deeds.

Attention to God's desires for humankind revealed in the desires and worlds of women is crucial: striving for personal integrity, autonomy and responsible relationships; developing opportunities for leadership and influence; and always sustaining concern for those most abandoned and vulnerable. Women expect to meet and labor with God as they express a deeper interiority and a global consciousness. They will develop a new faith-filled understanding and contemplative stance toward the mystery of God's presence in the world.

God's image, the world's image and personal image are transformed. God is revealed as God-with-us: God became human, dwelt with people, and still labors on behalf of all creation. This trinitarian God is a God-in-relationship at work in the world. In turn the world emerges as a place where God dwells and sustains life. This world, which humans can now view from the perspective of space, is seen as beautiful yet vulnerable, rich in resources and linked by a common destiny with all life on the planet.

All these things evoke an image of a contemporary contemplative in action. She welcomes the opportunity to be schooled in the ways of prayer and life. She manifests awareness, imagination, reflection and the ability to utilize "repetition," going deeper into the sources of God's reality in the world. She expresses the security of a contemplative stance that allows her to respect diversity and acknowledge various spiritual paths to God. She is aware of the bounty of spiritual gifts, faith, trust and love and their various manifestations through confirmation, challenge and courage. She is attentive, free, responsive, participative, relational and a person of great desires. She taps into life's rhythms of work and rest, giving and receiving, knowing and loving, sinning and being graced. She manifests the fruits of contemplation: integration, wholeness, peace, gratitude, desire for communion with God and with God's people, and all creation. Finally, she gathers together with others to create contemplative communities for transforming action in the world, realizing that personal growth flourishes in the midst of relationships.

This dynamic does not just refer to a "peak" experience, but to a passionate life spent growing toward the closeness of God in the continuity of each day. The contemplative in action sees with reverence, awe and appreciation. She desires to be in touch with the holiness of each moment and encounter.

Jesus as a contemplative in action models a way of life achieved through animation of the Spirit, not just through "the imitation of Christ." Jesus is the One who sees from God's perspective, acts in union with God and God's desires and is sensitized to all of life received in mystery and love. The contemplative in action desires God and, like Jesus, desires what God desires.

# Notes

1. See Pheme Perkins, "I Have Seen the Lord (John 20:18): Women Witnesses to the Resurrection" *Interpretation* 46:1 (January 1992): 31–61. Her thesis suggests that women were the first to hear the Easter message and played a crucial role in the founding of the earliest Christian community. She also cites the importance of the role of Mary of Magdala.

2. Some of the significant scholarship on Mary includes R. E. Brown, K. P. Donfried, J. A. Fitzmyer, J. Reumann, eds., *Mary in the New Testament* (Philadelphia: Fortress Press, 1978); Ivone Gebara and Maria C. Bingemer, *Mary, Mother of God, Mother of the Poor* (Maryknoll, N.Y.: Orbis Books, 1989); Hilda Graef, *Mary: A History of Doctrine and Devotion,* 2 vols. (New York: Sheed and Ward, 1965); Carol Frances Jegen, ed., *Mary According to Women* (Kansas City: Leaven Press, 1985); Elizabeth Johnson, "Blessed Virgin Mary," *Encyclopedia of Catholicism,* ed. Richard McBrien (San Francisco: HarperSanFrancisco, 1995), 832–38; Michael O'Carroll, *Theotokos: A Theological Encyclopedia of the Blessed Virgin Mary,* rev. ed. (Dublin: Dominican Publications, 1983); Rosemary Radford Ruether, *Mary, the Feminine Face of the Church* (Philadelphia: Westminster Press, 1977); and Maria Warner, *Alone of all Her Sex,* (New York: Vintage Books, 1983).

3. See Michael Buckley's classic article, "The Contemplation to Attain Love," *The Way Supplement* 24 (Spring 1975): 92–104, for discussion of placement and content.

# PART IV:

# Decision

# Chapter 10

# Developing a Single Eye: Rules for Discernment of Spirits

*In every good election insofar as it depends on us, the eye of our intention ought to be single.…In the case of those going from good to better, the good angel touches the soul gently, lightly, and sweetly, like a drop of water going into a sponge. The evil spirit touches it sharply, with noise and disturbance, like a drop of water falling onto a stone.*
—Spiritual Exercises [169, 335]

*I just don't know what to do. One day I think I am clear. I should go ahead with the divorce. I feel stuck and dead in the relationship, and I don't want to live the rest of my life this way. The next day I say to myself, "What we had was so good; if only I could get Robert to go to counseling, perhaps we could get to the bottom of it. If I just worked a little harder at it, it could happen." Another day I get overwhelmed with fear: How will I live? I'm nearly sixty and haven't worked outside our home for years.*
—A Contemporary Woman

Angels and evil spirits, sponges, rocks and single eyes—strange images from Ignatius's material on discernment of spirits and election. Discernment, the art of distinguishing what leads to God from what does not, plays an essential role in our choices; it also holds a central place in the interdependent content and process of the Spiritual Exercises. Discernment also charts the way toward increasing spiritual freedom, the goal of the Spiritual Exercises. The habit engenders continual self-reflection, which, in turn, helps women grow toward the fullness of their call. The significance of discernment can scarcely be overstated.

The Spiritual Exercises assume three levels to discernment. The most basic consists in a habitual discernment that flows from relationship with the Creative Holy One and comes to fruition in a "putting on the mind of Christ" (Phil 2:2). One learns and practices it continuously in all the contemplations and meditations and reinforces it through the particular examination. The second meaning appears in the Rules for Discernment of Spirits [313–36]. Here, the focus shifts to inner feelings and inclinations, as the one making the Exercises learns to assess them in light of this deepening relationship to God. The third meaning, found in the section on Making an Election [169–89], focuses on choices and actions. The seeker learns how to embody that relationship with the Holy in decisions and actions. These three senses of the term "discernment" are interrelated and cyclic. Each depends on the others.

Ignatius clearly intends that all three levels of discernment, especially discernment of spirits, be used both inside and outside the Spiritual Exercises. Since inner movements continually ebb and flow in response to all aspects of human life, discerning these movements and their causes has potentially unlimited usefulness. If discernment becomes a habitual skill for all of life, it will significantly affect one's relationship with God.

The Spiritual Exercises provide a training ground par excellence for learning discernment and growing into its habitual use. The full range of exercises, if entered into wholeheartedly, will evoke inner movements, frequently quite strong ones. In working with this flux, the one making the Exercises quite literally exercises her skills in noticing and interpreting her inner life and its exterior manifestations.

The Rules for Discernment of Spirits comprise the "how to" of discernment, its grammar, so to speak. Just as speaking is far more important than studying rules of grammar, discerning is far more important than studying the Rules for Discernment of Spirits. But grammar has its place in crafting careful speech, as understanding the Rules has in living a discerned life.

Discernment functions most explicitly in the material presented within the Second Week for choosing or "electing" a state in life [169–89]. To follow these exercises, one must have a working knowledge of the Rules for Discernment of Spirits.

## Women and Discernment

Before embarking on a treatment of the Rules for Discernment of Spirits, some observations about the general situation of women can frame this interpretation. Without intending to make universal statements, how might contemporary women approach discernment?

Central to all discernment is identity, who one is before God. Identity is not a fixed reality handed to a person at birth, but is created moment by moment as one responds to the choices presented in one's life. The first component of discernment, then, concerns listening to one's self, distinguishing the wisdom of the deepest self from other voices and learning to trust this deep inner wisdom. The one estranged from her own wisdom will have a difficult time with discernment. In this sense, identity and discernment act as partners, each reinforcing and clarifying the other.

Inner wisdom often reveals itself through one's body, intuition and feelings. They provide essential data for assessing choices.

Learning to value and "read" them will greatly enhance discernment. The closer one comes to the real, including insights about one's inner self, the closer one comes to God.

Many contemporary women need to balance the needs of others with their own needs. This issue may especially challenge those women who habitually interpret selflessness as a virtue and attending to one's own needs as a vice. The reality is far more complex. Some women may also need to distinguish passivity from "conformity to God's will." Learning these differences can free these women for appropriate, confident, focused action.

Important data for discernment also comes from the social and cultural forces influencing a situation. What systems and dynamics are present in social arrangements? When one's inner call conflicts with prevailing social structures, might it be that the social arrangements themselves contain unhealthy or sinful dynamics that require challenging and changing? Women may also need to interpret their affective experience in the light of social conditioning. Perhaps what seems "right," "proper" and "good" are actually social constructions concerning the role and "nature" of women. These social arrangements can exert enormous force, even dictating what one sees and what remains unconscious. Conflict, anger and sexual feelings may all be internalized as unacceptable and thus carefully censored from consciousness. Important tools for living are thereby ruled out of bounds.[1]

Women may need encouragement to generate alternatives when they feel trapped. Real choices, if only about the attitude with which one approaches the givens in one's life, do exist. Generating possibilities enhances the exercise of genuine inner freedom.

Finally, women will need to take into account the price of change. Qualitative change, the fruit of the Spiritual Exercises, comes gradually and frequently at considerable cost, especially when it involves structures. Mobilizing support systems and companions who help sustain hope during the time of "already but not yet" that comprises the majority of our days can make the difference between moving ahead and falling back into outworn patterns.

Theologian Kathleen Fischer (1988, 128), whose work is reflected in the points above, proposes an underlying principle: "Whatever promotes the full humanity of women as well as men is redemptive and holy; that is, it is of God. What denies and distorts that full humanity does not bear the power and authority of divine revelation." While this strong statement cannot be applied automatically to every concrete situation, it does state the goal of the Spiritual Exercises. One even needs to discern the norms for discernment.

## Rules for Discernment of Spirits

Explicating Ignatius's Rules for Discernment of Spirits resembles storytelling. Both ask for a suspension of disbelief and require analogical leaps from one reality to another. Ignatius clothes the dynamic forces that must be discerned with personalities of mythic proportions: God, God's angel and the bad angel. Ignatius portrays a cosmic struggle between the forces of good and the forces of evil and their increasingly subtle strategies. Surprisingly, this mythic literary form—here myth refers to cosmic scope, not falsity—suits this subject matter. But those who insist either on demythologizing the cosmic drama or on interpreting it literally find it loaded with potential stumbling blocks. Perhaps, as with C. S. Lewis's *Screwtape Letters,* the seeker would do best to allow the literary form to carry her beyond either interpretive extreme.

For some persons, a psychological perspective on good and evil provides a more fruitful approach to the Rules, viewing the "enemy" as intrapsychic rather than external. Gerald May, psychiatrist and spiritual director, posits four forces in human spirituality that need recognition: spiritual longing for God, God's reciprocated longing, internal fears and resistances to spiritual realization, and evil (1982a, 20–21).

The psyche can literally engage in intrapsychic warfare, as one aspect of the total personality longs for God while another longs for control. One need not look for principalities and powers to account for such interior movements. Although this psychological interpretation does not rule out the presence of evil or the demonic, it recognizes the capacity for this kind of drama within the self.

Theologian Walter Wink (1998) speaks about Powers (angels and demons) existing in the systems themselves: an intricate fabric of dominating power relationships that institutions and systems weave throughout society. Corporations and governments function like "creatures" with ambiguous and conflicted interests subject to discernment and action. His approach adds much to a larger view of social discernment.[2]

Allowing Ignatius the prerogative of his mythic literary form, some of his terminology still bears clarification. This section of the Spiritual Exercises speaks of "rules," "mortal sin," "consolation," "desolation," "good spirits," "evil spirits," and "angels."

## Ignatian Discernment Terminology

The term "motions," explained earlier in the book, is shorthand for the processes of thinking, feeling and imagining. It also covers the contents brought up by memory and the internal aspects of decision making. The dynamism implied by this term especially interested Ignatius and will likewise interest those giving and making the Exercises, because the origin, orientation and fruit of this flux will provide the material for discernment. These motions go on continually,[3] but frequently not consciously. Noticing them, naming them, assessing their origin and their direction, and finally encouraging some and discouraging others is precisely the goal of the Rules for Discernment of Spirits.

The points that Ignatius calls "rules" actually mix descriptions of spiritual experience with norms for discriminating among them. These descriptions discuss only a relatively small range of possible activities that might be called "discernment." He covers only inner events, prior to the actions that flow from them (Toner 1982, 11). "Rules," therefore, is a rather imprecise term as Ignatius uses it.

Furthermore, neither the title "Rules for Discernment of Spirits" nor references such as "Rules for the First and Second Weeks" are Ignatian. His much longer titles [313, 328] suggest at least two quite different kinds of discernment situations, each requiring different approaches and therefore different "rules." Note, however, that individual persons making the Exercises may not simply use the first set of Rules in the First Week and the second set in the Second and following Weeks; the determination about which set applies comes from the kinds of temptations occurring in the one making the Exercises, not the content of the Exercises themselves [9, 10]. Ignoring these distinctions risks misinterpreting Ignatius's wisdom on discernment of spirits.

"Mortal sin" [314] appears to mean something close to "capital sin," or a sinful tendency that increasingly hinders relationship with God (Toner 1982, 50). It functions like an Achilles' heel, expressing one's primary weakness and vulnerability to sin. It may not appear very significant at first: working overly long hours for the security of a substantial income, immersing one's identity in that of spouse or children, compulsive eating or shopping or other addictive behaviors, nursing a grudge for months. Yet each reflects a sense that one does not need God. Here, Ignatius describes the person who, without much thought or resistance, becomes more and more estranged from

God and her authentic self. The distinction is important because Ignatius excludes this person from further consideration in the subsequent Rules. Only the experience of one "advancing from good to better in the service of God" [315], even though she may have only recently set out on this journey, is under consideration in the subsequent comments. What this situation looks like concretely Ignatius does not say. Today's spiritual guide, as yesterday's, must assess this primary orientation in each discerner. What is it that each one most deeply desires?

The next terms, "consolation" and "desolation," have been the subject of extended discussion. As Ignatius describes them, each consists of three related parts. Consolation includes: (1) the consolation proper (affective feelings such as peace or gladness); (2) the causes or sources of consolation ("the soul sheds tears which move it to love for its Lord" [316]); and (3) the consequences of consolation properly speaking ("every increase in hope, faith and charity and every interior joy which calls and attracts one toward heavenly things...by bringing it tranquility and peace in its Creator and Lord" [316]) (Toner 1982, 86). That is, consolation comprises a rich complex of feelings, acts and consequences that have their origin in God and encourage and intensify the experience of moving Godward. Desolation, the opposite of consolation [317], demonstrates the same three related aspects.

Describing what consolation and desolation are *not* proves easier than describing exactly what they are. They are neither *simply* happiness and sadness, nor an "up" or "down" mood, though these feelings may play a role in spiritual consolation and desolation. Rather, consolation is the affective reverberation of the work of the Holy Spirit that draws toward God, and desolation is the affective reverberation of the antispiritual that pulls in the opposite direction. That is, consolation and desolation are *spiritual* realities.

Consolation encourages and intensifies experiences *of relationship to God.* Pleasant feelings alone do not necessarily qualify as spiritual consolation, a mistake beginning discerners often make. A feeling of euphoria after two martinis does not comprise a spiritual consolation. The Holy Spirit may use many means to promote spiritual growth, even difficult or painful feelings, the so-called "painful consolations." Consider, for example, the anger and frustration arising from injustice to others, or pain and sadness around areas in one's life that need healing. If such feelings draw one deeper into relationship with God, they are truly consolations, albeit painful ones (Lonsdale 1992, 81). Discernment of spirits involves not only the particular feeling but also its origin and direction. Nor should one confuse desolation with the experience of the various dark nights that John of the Cross describes. In this situation, God is at work, not antispiritual forces, gradually stripping away reliance on positive experiences in order to draw the seeker more deeply into God's own life.[4]

Finally, what did Ignatius mean when he referred to "evil spirits," "good spirits" and "angels"? In line with the cosmology and theology of his time, Ignatius assumed personal good and evil beings existed and acted on behalf of or against God. Ignatius thought of angels as God's messengers, and in the case of good angels, their activity need not be distinguished from God's—with one exception treated at the end of the second set of Rules. Not all angels, however, are good, and these evil spirits work continually and often subtly to deflect us from our true end (Toner 1982, 32–33).

One could dispense with a belief in angels, good or evil, and still profit from Ignatius's wisdom. It would be sufficient, as Toner notes (1982, 35–36), to recognize how the Holy Spirit works in one's life, how the opposite dynamic tendency toward evil functions within and around us and the difference, if any, between promptings arising solely from oneself and those arising from God working within. This latter point, however, brings the discussion immediately back to discernment. How does one determine what voice is speaking? Not infrequently do guides hear, "Is this from me or is this from God?"

Trusting God to work in and through one's own feelings comes harder for those women raised in theological systems that emphasize God's otherness and the total depravity of the human person; they tend to suspect anything arising from within themselves. The Ignatian wisdom on this question holds that good or evil spirits prompt good or evil interior motions, which issue in good or evil fruits. These fruits, in turn, give clues about which spirit is acting. One may, however, interpret the motions through their fruits without assigning the same ontological status to their origin as did Ignatius.

## Ignatian "Contraries"

Ignatius exhibits a penchant for dialectical opposites, especially in his treatment of discernment. Consolation and desolation act as mirror images of each other. Good and evil spirits also act contrary to each other. How does Ignatius develop this dialectical tension?

First, the orientation of the discerner's life plays a role. Is it habitually directed toward increasing intimacy with God or increasing estrangement from God? For those persons whose habitual disposition is increasingly *estranged* from God, the evil spirit will encourage more of the same, while the good spirit will oppose that tendency. The evil spirit will appeal to the *imagination,* while the good spirit will appeal to the *judgment* of conscience, causing remorse [314].

In the reverse situation, the players and their actions also reverse. For persons habitually growing in intimacy with God, the good spirit encourages this development by inspiring *feelings* of courage, strength, consolations, tears, inspirations and tranquility, but the evil spirit upsets the Godward tendency through *false reasonings,* causing anxiety, confusion and sadness [315]. The "spirit that matches the disposition" encourages that disposition, while the opposite spirit resists it.

Ignatius continues "working the opposites" in the second set of Rules. In the seventh rule [335], Ignatius offers an image for his "principle of contrariety": in the one advancing from good to better, the good angel works gently and lightly, like a drop of water going into a sponge, but the evil spirit touches it sharply like a drop of water falling onto a stone. Reverse the situation of the discerner, and the effects reverse, as well. Thus, once the seeker gets her bearings about basic orientation, she can begin to piece together what is going on and by the action of which spirit. But the matter will not remain quite so simple.

## Wisdom of the First Set of Rules

Knowing which spirit is operating requires a response. Ignatius concentrates the first set of Rules on the most difficult issue for those recently embarked on the spiritual life—how to survive the inevitable desolations that arise.

Since the evil spirit distracts one from God by any means possible, the seeker will want to act contrary to that spirit whenever it appears. Thus, experiencing desolation does not mean reversing decisions already made [318], but increasing resistance to the evil spirit by, for example, more prayer or penance [319]. Note, however, that "acting against" may consist in relaxing, taking more leisure or doing less, especially for those women who have internalized the belief that they can make things better by working harder. Furthermore, the one experiencing desolation can remember that God will always supply the necessary grace, even when it does not feel like it at the moment [320]. Eventually, consolation will return; meanwhile, waiting in patience comprises the counterattack against the present vexations [321].

As one would expect, Ignatius's suggestions for the time of consolation mirror his advice for the time of desolation, though more briefly: consolation provides an opportunity to consider how to act when the desolation returns, to store up new strength against that time [323] and to remain humble about consolation, for, after all, it came as God's gift [324].

Ignatius includes three theological rationales for the existence of desolation [322]; these points are suggestive rather than exhaustive. First, desolation may result from laziness or tepidity—not taking the relationship with God seriously will show up in the spirit. Second, desolation may serve to strengthen spirituality, causing it to mature beyond the need for constant consolation. Finally, desolation nurtures humility: only God initiates and sustains consolation.

Holding these three possible reasons in dialectical tension will help avoid a potential pitfall for women, who may say to themselves, "If I am not experiencing consolation, I must have not worked hard enough or done something right." Ignatius points out that individuals are not primarily responsible for consolation or desolation, but neither are they totally devoid of responsibility, puppets in the control either of inner movements or of their causal forces. The reality must allow both for God's sovereignty and human agency.

Ignatius closes the first set of Rules with three metaphors, each describing an aspect of the dynamic treated by this first set of Rules [325–27]. First, the enemy acts at times like a woman, attacking at signs of weakness but fleeing at signs of strength. Unfortunately, Ignatius puts no qualifier on "woman" here. The enemy also acts like a false lover, who threatens the one seduced if she "tells." Finally, the enemy is like a superior military strategist, who ferrets out the weakest point in the defenses in order to attack there. These metaphors teach three important things: face temptation boldly and unyieldingly; break the power of secrecy that perpetuates a negative dynamic; know one's weakest point and concentrate vigilance there.

These stark metaphors also invite examination of the negative repercussions Ignatius's formulation can raise among women. In choosing "woman" as a metaphor for the way the enemy works, Ignatius unwittingly employs a deadly stereotype of women, implying that they are vacillating, seductive, cowardly or, at best, weak. Against strong men they wilt, but they turn on weak men. A metaphor must work not only for the teller; it must also function for the receiver. Such a metaphor, reinforcing as it does the worst gender stereotypes, serves neither men nor women.

The second metaphor, that of the seducer, proves easier to disassociate from women as a class, perhaps because the evil one is not so directly and baldly associated with the entire sex. Yet this, too, portrays women in an unfortunate light as victims of an attempted seduction who, when they speak to their "heads," either father or husband, are freed from the power of the seducer. Again, the subliminal negative effects compromise the usefulness of this metaphor.

Since these metaphors carry negative baggage, a more useful pastoral alternative suggests not employing the metaphor as Ignatius originally wrote it. The Sisters of Providence offer a simple alternative:

> These points will help you *act against the bad spirits* which foster desolation:
>
> 12. Stand firm. Bad spirits attack where you show fear and flee when you demonstrate courage.
>
> 13. Be open with your director or another trustworthy person about what you are experiencing, since evil spirits flourish in secrecy and disappear in openness.

14. Do all you can to gain self-knowledge regarding your strengths and weaknesses, knowing that bad spirits attack where you are weakest. (1990, 233)[5]

This rewrite sacrifices metaphor in favor of simple imperatives. Others will develop alternative solutions appropriate for their contexts.

If not appropriately interpreted, Ignatius's counsel not to change one's circumstances when in desolation [318] poses a potential danger for women. Consider the following scenario illustrating one such misunderstanding: As a fruit of the Spiritual Exercises, Janet begins to pay more careful attention to what gives her life. She gradually becomes aware that her marriage is slowly strangling her. She realizes she has no separate existence as her husband increasingly demands total availability, acquiescence and loyalty. Cautiously she begins to assert herself, only to find her husband increasingly violent. Upon voicing her desire to complete her training as an early childhood educator, he explodes and hits her. She identifies this painful situation as desolation and remembers Ignatius's counsel not to change her circumstances during a time of desolation.

What about this situation, where difficult and painful situations are too easily equated with desolation? Should a woman like Janet make no move on her own behalf until she experiences consolation? Is physical or psychological danger, in fact, desolation? A surface reading of Ignatius suggests just this interpretation. However, common sense, a more nuanced understanding of consolation and desolation and earlier comments on women and discernment lead to a different conclusion.

When a person is in actual danger, either physical or psychological, one must *never* wait passively for circumstances to change. Not only should one generate alternatives when feeling trapped (Fischer

1988, 126), but one must actually remove oneself from danger—or in the situation of the woman unable to do that for herself, those who accompany her must help her marshal the resources to act for her own safety. The conditions for discernment do not exist until one may calmly and safely consider alternatives. Within such physically and psychologically neutral spaces, such as a shelter, safe house or foster home, discernment may eventually occur. But even arriving at the conditions for discernment may take weeks or months of painful struggle. Companions to such women have a moral responsibility to accompany them to safety.

## The Wisdom of the Second Set of Rules

This set of Rules assumes increasing sensitivity to one's own experience of the spiritual life and increasing skill in noticing, naming, judging and choosing. The more skillful one becomes in noticing the workings of the evil one, the more skillful the evil one must become in order to continue confusing the advancing person. In fact, the evil one is quite capable of counterfeiting authentic consolation [331].

In addition to greater sensitivity to spiritual experience, one's understanding of how God works also becomes more nuanced. Only God our Lord can give consolation without a preceding cause [330]. That is, God may directly touch any creature without relying on any mediating reality. Nothing causes such a consolation but God alone, no prayer, no beautiful sunset, no experience of being loved by another person, no victory over struggle, no success, no virtue. When it occurs, this consolation can be trusted. Ignatius here preserves God's sovereignty within a cosmology that believes in a realm of mediating forces and beings. Both good and evil angels, on the other hand, being themselves mediated created beings, can only work in a mediated fashion.

Two Rules will help here. One sketches out the modus operandi of the evil one, and the second suggests a tactic. The evil one will take on the appearance of the angel of light, and so clothed, will gain admission through "specious reasonings." With the unsuspecting or inattentive discerner, the evil one begins to subvert the consolation little by little. A little less vigor, a little diversion from the mark, a bit of an extreme, a hiding of one reality within its look-alike: these subtleties now confront the discerner. Is this patience or passivity? Is this pride really a sin or an invitation to true self-possession? Is this acting on one's own behalf selfish or virtuous? This alternative feels really freeing, but is it authentic liberty or just a disguised form of license? How can one know?

Ignatius advises seekers to pay attention to the whole progress of one's thought. Is it, from beginning to end, consoling? What is its fruit? Does it end up in something less good? Does it weaken or somehow disquiet? These distinctions are subtle, as vividly suggested by Ignatius's comparison between the drop of water on the sponge and the drop of water on the stone [335]. But just as one can notice the difference between these two qualities, one can always—eventually— distinguish the difference between the work of the evil one and the work of God's angel. And even what appears to be a mistake in discernment at a particular moment in time can be turned toward good [334]. Such struggles, paradoxically, can increase one's future ability to discern, another occasion for God's love and mercy. In the pedagogy of discernment, nothing need be wasted.

There is one last subtlety. God acting directly, which can be trusted, and the reverberations that echo in us after God's touch are different realities. Be careful, says Ignatius, not to confuse the two, as the latter reverberations are not always dependable. These look-alikes need to be discerned just like any consolation with cause [336]. How many persons have launched enthusiastically on a course of action at the end of a particularly consoling retreat, assuming it to arise from God, only to have it turn sour?[6]

## Problems and Possibilities for Women

Several problems inherent in the Rules for Discernment of Spirits, including aspects of the language of the text and the danger of too facilely invoking Ignatius's caution against making a change in time of desolation, have already been explored. A potentially serious pastoral issue, distinguishing between depression and desolation, remains to be examined. Despite these problem areas, though, the Ignatian material on discernment of spirits also holds significant possibilities for women. Two stand out for consideration. First, the Rules for Discernment of Spirits provide a pattern and discipline for continually appropriating one's life as it unfolds. Second, discernment of spirits helps rehabilitate the role of feelings in discriminating what is from God, a role many women have found ambiguous. Structural theories of women's psychological development prove helpful in illuminating these problems and possibilities for women's discernment by clarifying some aspects of the human ability to discern.

## Women's Sense of Self: A Developmental Perspective

The structural developmental perspective of such theorists as Carol Gilligan, Robert Kegan and James Fowler[7] sketch the successive patterns of meaning that govern one's life. These theories have proved especially helpful in illuminating women's development. Rather than concentrating on the tasks of each era of life, as did Erik Erikson, the structural developmental perspective focuses on the successive patterns in these underlying and largely unconscious meaning-systems and their possible and very gradual shifts over the course of a life time. These underlying structures change only when they no longer offer a worldview complex enough for dealing with life's challenges. Thus, an adult may go for long periods of time in the same meaning-structure. But when a structural change does occur, it revolutionizes the way a person conceives the whole of reality, transforming one's view of self, friends and associates, culture, creation and God.

Structural change is not directly tied to age. However, it requires sufficient life experience at each stage for deconstructing one's assumptions of "the way things are." Paradoxically, living fully one's present stage opens the possibly of a new stage. In the structural view of development, stage change is not inevitable. When it does occur, it truly represents a *metanoia*. Once a transition begins, the only course open lies in deconstructing the present meaning-structure and more or less painfully constructing a new and more complex view of "the way things are."

One transition in particular—if it occurs—is crucial for discernment of spirits: the transition from a Conformist or conventional perspective to a Conscientious or postconventional perspective. This shift may happen to a few women in their young adulthood, to many at midlife, but others may never experience this transition. What difference does it make for discernment of spirits?

The key organizing principle of the Conformist stage comes from the groups to which one belongs: conforming to the expectations of these groups defines one's identity. The conformist person usually thinks concretely and stereotypically, orders life around external norms, allows few exceptions to the categories of right and wrong, focuses on external behavior with little perception of internal motive or ability to introspect, experiences global and undifferentiated feelings, values external appearances and group status symbols, employs concrete forms of prayer such as rote recitation, follows rules faithfully, denies "negative" feelings such as anger, hatred or sexual attraction and lives in a personal world comprised of close-in and face-to-face groups.

The great development marking the Conscientious stage is the critical appropriation of one's formerly tacit value system. Because one can now create self-evaluated, long-term goals and values, a sense of responsibility for living up to goals also appears. One no longer leaves external authorities unquestioned; authority for one's life moves "inside." A person is truly reflexive with a rich and differentiated inner life.

This stage also includes greater conceptual complexity that allows one to see alternatives and contingencies, systems thinking, awareness of psychological causation and motive, a wider range of emotional experience and expression, awareness of relativity and contingency, a focus on self and self-identity, a sense of being the author of one's own destiny, increased objectivity with respect to other persons now seen as selves in their own right and increased potential for interpersonal relationships, including the relationship with God (Liebert 1992, 84–91, 102–11).

The importance of this shift for discernment of spirits cannot be underestimated. Prior to it, one has little access to the inner life, little sense of self as an actor responsible for one's own life, little sense of the real identity and autonomy of other persons and a concrete sense of human community comprised of the groups one belongs to personally. Once the momentous developmental shift occurs—if it does—"I" becomes rich and nuanced, but so do other persons, as they become more differentiated and less projected in one's own image. Mature conscience develops because one's motive is now accessible to self-reflection along with long-range plans and goals. Discernment of spirits becomes a real developmental possibility when the locus of authority moves from outside to inside oneself and access to one's inner life becomes habitual. This developmental stage is, in fact, a prerequisite to entering the Spiritual Exercises with the self-reflection they require.

This perspective highlights some of the discernment issues for women raised in this chapter. The certitudes held at the Conformist stage give way to ambiguities as one enters the transition. New questions appear in the place of former certainties: Who am I now that I am not defined by the groups I belong to? Who is God, whom I now can recognize working within me? What do I do with the range of feelings and thoughts cascading around within me? Which voices can I listen to? What do I do when they conflict with my old authorities? Is this new desire for self-fulfillment just selfish? How can I take care of myself and others?

The world is much bigger, not only because one's inner world has come alive, but also because one's social world now includes people whom one might not see face-to-face. New questions appear here, too: What is my obligation to these people, and they to me? What do I do with the complexity that they inject into life? The Rules for Discernment of Spirits offer a pattern for paying attention to this immense range of new data facing the person in the Conscientious stage, particularly concerning her inner life.

As with each developmental stage, however, the Conscientious stage has an inbuilt limitation that increasing focus on discernment of spirits may unwittingly exacerbate. Regularly turning attention to one's inner movements in discerning may enhance the Conscientious tendency to overvalue the "I." "I have discerned" can prevent one from listening to persons with needed wisdom. Such is the pitfall of the overvalued self, one not (yet) balanced by a sense of interdependence. Having both discernment of spirits and the discerner framed by a community of accountability helps prevent this potential overbalance. At the same time, women's sense of self, often gained at the price of great struggle, needs to be honored and affirmed. The balance may be delicate.

### Desolation or Depression?

The incidence of depression among women, already at epidemic level, continues to rise. Depression occurs two to six times more in women than in men. This reality affects many women making the Spiritual Exercises, begging the questions: Are depression and desolation related? If so, how?

Our thesis about the relationship of desolation and depression runs as follows: All depression has desolating reverberations, but depression and desolation may not be simply equated.

Comparing the phenomenological experiences of desolation and depression highlights striking similarities. Ignatius describes desolation as darkness and turmoil of soul, an impulsive movement toward base and earthly things, disquiet from various agitations and temptations, listlessness, tepidity and unhappiness. Symptoms of depression include a sense of moving in slow motion, fatigue, sad feelings, numbness, inability to concentrate, sleep disturbances, digestive difficulties, a lack of enjoyment in things that once brought pleasure, loss of interest in sexual activity, a sense of emptiness, guilt, self-blame, pessimism or hopelessness, a sense of hopelessness about ever feeling any different, isolation and inability to connect with God or one's true self or life-giving relationships (Neuger 1991, 156). Depression can be diffuse, paralyzing most or all aspects of a person's life, or it may be clearly connected to a particular trauma or loss that is consciously known, such as divorce, job loss or terminal illness. To the extent that depression interferes with one's growth in faith, hope and love, it could be considered desolation.

From the point of view of their causes, depression and desolation may also be related. Ignatius believes that the evil or antispiritual forces cause desolation and that God might permit short-term desolation for some remedial or pedagogical purpose [322]. Much discussion surrounds the causes of depression; theories include chemical imbalance, anger turned inward, a learned response to a frustrating environment, negative thinking or "self-critical tapes" and living out particular roles in the family system. It is only a small step from desolation as caused by the antispiritual to depression as caused by antiholistic forces, especially if one's understanding of *spiritual* contains within it the notion of wholeness and completeness. Both desolation and depression dampen a vigorous, hopeful, generous and enthusiastic "Yes!" to God's call.

Some of Ignatius's wisdom about responding to desolation proves useful in responding to depression as well. His admonition not to change the circumstances of one's life when in desolation [318], for example, parallels the common wisdom that making major changes while depressed is unwise. The caveat about always acting for the safety of women also applies in the case of depression. Severe or long-lasting depression needs professional treatment, and guides must be alert to its symptoms and make referrals to appropriate professionals.

Ignatius does encourage making changes in *oneself* designed to act against the desolation; given his understanding of the nature of the antispiritual, he suggests increased prayer and penance. The therapeutic community suggests analogous ways to "act against" depression: physical examination and appropriate treatment of physical conditions, chemical treatment of bipolar disorder, therapy, body work, meditation and guided imagery and sustained and direct action to change systems. Such actions help one take control and cease acting like a victim. Of course, such sustained action may require assistance from others.

The one guiding the Spiritual Exercises, however, should not become the primary caregiver for any serious depression. Those giving the Spiritual Exercises should remain spiritual directors, recognize their limits and act within them. But guides may well need to assess the situation in collaboration with the one making the Exercises. Is this desolation or depression? If depression, how debilitating and longstanding is it? If serious, postponing the Spiritual Exercises would probably be recommended. Thus, the seeker could focus all her energy on healing from the depression. The Spiritual Exercises can resume later.

Many depressions, though, are much milder and, though painful, are less seriously debilitating. Discovering the truth about themselves as valuable and loved in God's eyes, exposing the secrets that have burdened them, having their experience validated before God, letting go of destructive images, rigid spirituality and constricting relationships with the church—all these fruits of the Spiritual Exercises can serve as healing balm for women experiencing such depressions.

However, one should not draw too close a connection between desolation and depression. Hence the second part of our thesis states that depression and desolation cannot be simply equated. First, not all depression can be simply and completely subsumed under the rubric of desolation. For example, a woman, Patrice, who has been clinically depressed for many years, finds her relationship with God the one thing that keeps her going in the face of the "deep black hole." She clearly recognizes that her depression has been a vehicle for forging this hard-won deep relationship. Her depression, stubbornly unyielding to any treatment, has actually impelled her into deep and continual reliance upon God for the resources to face each day.

On the other hand, desolation is not always associated with depression. Sometimes experiences of God simply "dry up." Other aspects of one's life may be free of signs of depression, yet the old zest for the spiritual has vanished. The favorite images of God leave one cold and spiritual exercises seem distasteful or a waste of time. Similarly, prayer that had been easy and enjoyable is now dull and difficult. All these signs suggest classic experiences of desolation.[8]

From a developmental perspective, a transition from one stage to another shares many phenomenological characteristics of desolation, such as disorientation, loss of familiar images and certitudes, loss of the identity that locates one in the world and disruption of a sense of the future: "I don't know who I am anymore, or who God is." In a developmental transition, initial disorientation yields to a long time "between dreams," as William Bridges puts it. The experience is often marked by an emptiness in which "the old reality looks transparent and nothing feels solid any more" (Bridges 1980, 112, 117). In the structural view of development, such a transition is a lengthy affair.

Many persons seek out the Spiritual Exercises when in the midst of transition; indeed deconstructing old certitudes may motivate some persons to make the Spiritual Exercises. These transitions provide yet another cause for certain desolation-like inner experiences, and the one who gives the Spiritual Exercises is well advised to hold open this latter possibility. The chief ramification appears around Election. Making a significant election in the midst of a lengthy transition may not be best. The person making the Exercises will most likely signal this situation by her inability to move ahead with a major decision in the light of her shifting perspective. She may intuitively know that this is not the time for a major life decision.

Feminist researchers also offer theories that suggest refraining from a tight equation of depression and desolation. They propose that depression may stem from deep societal causes. In the wake of the societal changes concerning women's role and status, their optimistic perceptions about the options available to them and about their power to make choices concerning these options never match the reality. Having rising expectations without the means to fulfill them contribute to the frequency and severity of depression in women (Neuger 1993, 201; Liebert 1996, 260). Author Dana Crowley Jack (1991, 5, 16, 21) concludes that understanding depression requires an examination of systemic and interpersonal relationships that result in "loss of self." Depression, then, is more than one woman's personal problem; it has a structural and societal foundation in patriarchal institutional oppression. In this system, women never catch up no matter how their situation improves. It may be that the woman experiencing depression is well attuned to the psychological and social environment. Consequently, viewing and treating depression as *purely* intrapsychic while ignoring the overarching system that breeds the power differential does women a disservice.

Everyone experiences ups and downs, some severe, some transient. The "downs" have different etiologies requiring different responses, and it is not always immediately evident what is at issue. Yet, with appropriate ethical attention to the safety of those coming to the Spiritual Exercises, Ignatius's wisdom about desolations offers a way to remain steadfast during the inevitable discernment about the nature, cause and response to each individual's lived experience, even those times when God seems distant and unresponsive.

## Affirming and Grounding Women's Experience

For the woman just launching herself tentatively into a Conscientious developmental stage, consistent and disciplined attention to her inner movements provides one of the best means for consolidating this developmental transition. If the one giving the Exercises encourages her, the seeker will gradually learn to distinguish finer and finer nuances in her inner dispositions. Meanwhile the guide remains a consistent, encouraging and honest anchor with the external world, balancing the increasing sense of self with a loving community of accountability. Thus, discernment of spirits can provide a pattern and discipline in service of appropriating one's own life at increasingly deeper levels.

The overview of women's discernment issues alluded to the ambiguous position in which women may find themselves when they employ feelings to assess their surroundings and choices. Many people perceive feelings as "soft," "feminine," fickle," "unreliable," "fuzzy" and "sentimental," and the person who relies on them, by extension, also takes on all these characteristics. Contemporary culture assesses feelings negatively, stereotypically attributes them to women as a class, though perhaps not to an individual woman, who appears as an exception to the rule. Our culture connects the opposite characteristics, "tough," "masculine," "steadfast," "reliable," "clear" and "unromantic" with the thinking function, and stereotypically attributes them to men. Thus, when women pay attention to and make choices by means of their affections, they unwittingly strengthen this feminine stereotype. But the next chapter will show that Ignatius also encourages thinking and imagining in discernment. Women do not have to choose one to the exclusion of the other. Meanwhile, the Rules for Discernment of Spirits provide a pattern for making increasingly subtle distinctions about affectivity and assessing its significant role in responding with ever greater integrity to the circumstances and choices of life.

## Wisdom for the One Giving the Exercises

Turning our focus to the person who guides the Exercises focuses some of the perspectives presented above. How might the one giving the Exercises tailor discernment of spirits to the experiences of women in our culture? As always, the individual woman and her desires and circumstances suggest the manner of proceeding. However, those giving the Exercises might consider the following.

The guide can be sensitive to the underlying structural bases for the situation in which women find themselves. Here "structural" means the systemic, nonpersonal patterns that continue despite individuals coming or going. Thus, structural foundations exist for women's relative economic insecurity, incidence of single parenting, lack of advancement in employment and high incidence of depression. Abuse and violence directed against women in general, to say nothing of the abuse and violence perpetrated on individual women, as well as a pervading sense that one's environment is dangerous, have a definite deleterious effect. Attempts to vindicate individual women when they have been violated often get lost in these larger systemic dynamics. All these are among the "spirits" regarding discernment.

"Structural" can also apply to a way of looking at development. It can point to the transitional anomie and disintegration that must occur for stage change to take place. Desolation-like manifestations have different causes and different responses; some should be resisted and one, the deconstruction that occurs in developmental transition, should be encouraged. The one giving the Exercises, then, is invited to careful discernment of desolation-like symptoms.

The guide can also help women not blame themselves for inevitable spiritual desolations. They have not done something wrong. They are certainly not, somehow, "bad" or a failure. Spiritual desolations come and go, an inevitable manifestation of living a spiritual life. They serve, for one aware of them, as indicators of growing edges and what needs attention. The giver of the Exercises also needs to help women understand that "acting against" must also include self-care.

The one giving the Exercises should also pay careful attention to power arrangements, encouraging the autonomy and self-appropriation and personal naming of experience by each person making the Exercises. The seeker should literally make the Exercises her own; in particular, she should appropriate the Rules for Discernment of

Spirits to help her notice, name and choose the direction of her growing integrity.

Finally, the one giving the Exercises might consider ways to expand the community within which discernment occurs. These ways include group sharing within the context of an at-home version of the Spiritual Exercises, a regular liturgical and sacramental community or through group ministries of direct service. All these communities make their way into each woman's discernment of spirits.

# Notes

1. See Kathleen Fischer, *Transforming Fire: Women Using Anger Creatively* (New York: Paulist, 1999) for an excellent treatment of the constructive uses of women's anger.

2. Wink's 1998 work, *The Powers That Be: Theology for a New Millennium,* summarizes his trilogy on the Powers. For further detail, see the third volume, *Engaging the Powers: Discernment and Resistance in a World of Domination* (Minneapolis: Fortress, 1992).

3. We will prescind from the mental activity that occurs when we sleep, although such an investigation could yield interesting implications for discernment of spirits.

4. For a thorough discussion of this distinction, see Jules Toner (1982), appendix 2, 271–79. For the relationship between depression and desolation see Mary Jo Meadow, "The Dark Side of Mysticism: Depression and 'The Dark Night,'" *Pastoral Psychology* 33 (Winter 1984): 105–25; Joann Wolski Conn, *Spirituality and Personal Maturity* (New York: Paulist, 1989), chapter 6; and Gerald May (1982a), 84–92. For a treatment of Dark Night from the perspective of contemporary women's experience see Constance FitzGerald, "Impasse and Dark Night," in *Living with Apocalypse: Spiritual Resources for Social Compassion,* ed. Tilden Edwards, reprinted in *Women's Spirituality: Resources for Development,* 2nd ed., ed. Joann Wolski Conn (New York: Paulist), 410–35.

5. This retreat in daily life developed by the Sisters of Providence contains a rewriting of the first set of rules for discernment that is strikingly simple. It provides another pastoral option for those giving the Exercises; however, its very simplicity may need elaboration.

> 1. If I'm stuck in a sinful pattern, I GO WITH thoughts of change and GO WITH feelings of remorse; and I LET GO of imaginary satisfactions that keep me stuck in what feels good but isn't.

2. If I'm breaking loose from a sinful pattern, I GO WITH inspiring ideas and GO WITH feelings of courage, strength, and hope; and I LET GO of imaginary obstacles and feelings of discouragement.

3. I know I am in desolation when I sink into feelings that are hopeless, lukewarm, and separated or into thoughts that are despairing, selfish, or put-downs.

4. When I am in desolation, I make no decisions.

5. When I am in desolation, I act against my feelings by prayer, self-knowledge, and penance.

6. When I am in desolation, I put myself in God's care.

7. When I am in desolation, I persevere by thinking of future consolation.

8. When I am in desolation, I look for the cause.

9. When I am in desolation, I pray my own "Psalm 63."

10. I know I am in consolation when I rejoice in feelings of union with God and thoughts of giving myself to God.

11. When I am in consolation, I gather strength for future challenges.

12. When I am in consolation, I'll pray my own "Magnificat."

13. When I sense an evil spirit, I act with courage.

14. When I sense an evil spirit, I am open about my experience.

15. To avoid an evil spirit, I learn my own strengths and weaknesses. (1990, 246–47)

6. Again, the Sisters of Providence have created an elegantly simple rendition of the second set of rules:

1. I expect joy and spiritual gladness from the good spirit.

2. I reject sadness and turmoil from the evil spirit.

3. I recognize the creative power and Providence of God in surprise consolations.

4. I am aware that I may be consoled by good spirits leading me toward action that is better or by bad spirits leading me toward action that is worse.

5. I am alert to recognize a deceitful train of thought which starts out good but ends up less good.

6. I observe the direction of my thoughts; where they begin, continue, and end.

I recognize a good spirit when the whole process is good.

I recognize an evil spirit when I end up where I didn't intend to go or lose my peace.

7. By reviewing how I got where I did in my thought or action I avoid repeating the pattern.

8. I expect a gentle touch from a good spirit but a harsh touch from an evil spirit when I am going from good to better.

9. I experience a strong touch from a good spirit and a soft one from the evil spirit when I am going from good to less good.

10. I trust the consolation which comes as a surprise from God; but I discern carefully before I act on what follows. (1990, 248–49)

7. James Fowler's major works include *Stages of Faith: The Psychology of Human Development and the Quest for Meaning* (New York: Harper and Row, 1981); *Faith Development and Pastoral Care* (Philadelphia, Fortress Press, 1987); *Weaving the New Creation: Stages of Faith and the Public Church* (San Francisco: Harper, 1991); and *Faithful Change: The Personal and Public Challenges of Postmodern Life* (Nashville: Abingdon, 1996). Robert Kegan's two seminal works are *The Evolving Self: Problem and Process in Human Development* (Cambridge: Harvard University Press, 1982) and *In Over Our Heads: The Mental Demands of Modern Life* (Cambridge: Harvard University Press, 1994). See also Gilligan (1982) and Jane Loevinger's *Ego Development: Conceptions and Theories* (San Francisco: Jossey-Bass, 1976).

8. John of the Cross may also be helpful here, as he examines a similar phenomenological experience from a different set of presuppositions. For a comparison of John and Ignatius on this point, see Jules Toner (1982), 271–82.

# Chapter 11

# Dancing toward the Light: Election

*Friday, February 8, 1544*
*In the afternoon for an hour and a half or more, I went through the*
*elections in the same way. I made the election to have no fixed income*
*and found myself experiencing devotion and a certain elevation of*
*spirit, with great tranquility and without any contradictory thought*
*of possessing anything. I no longer desired to continue the delibera-*
*tions for as long as I had thought of doing a few days before.*

—Spiritual Diary, [10]

*You know what is so interesting? I learned a decision-making process*
*in one of my management courses where you line up all the pros and*
*cons and weigh the lists to come to a decision. Now I find that*
*Ignatius suggested just such a process more than four hundred years*
*ago. But it makes such a difference to set everything into a prayer*
*context.*

—A Contemporary Woman

In Ignatius's spiritual diary, he works through the decision about
the degree of poverty the new Society should hold. It was one of many
decisions that affected not only Ignatius, but the whole group of his

colleagues. What has he to say to contemporary women regarding their own decisions?

Election is surely one of the most useful aspects of the Spiritual Exercises. Everyone makes decisions every day. Many are of little consequence, some have more obvious implications for self and others, but all reflect and hone the person one is always becoming. The wisdom of Election transcends the Spiritual Exercises. It offers accessible spiritual practice to bring to the heart of life, decision making. For women, this spiritual practice can be pure gift.

## What, When, Where and Why?

The most focused and intense application of discernment within the Spiritual Exercises appears toward the conclusion of the Second Week. Here, Ignatius proposes that the person who has not yet chosen a state of life make this choice and offers a systematic process to do so. Ignatius's suggestions contain much that can transfer to other decision-making contexts. Yet the Spiritual Exercises provide a privileged context for decisions so basic that they literally form one's identity—vocation in its deepest sense.

One specialized term appears in this section, "election." This word summarizes the process by which one chooses the state of life, the judgment about what that should be and the actual choice itself (Toner 1991, 103). As long as one understands all the nuances involved in *election,* one might substitute *choice* as a reasonably acceptable synonym.

Although Ignatius generally uses "election" for a particular choice, one's state of life, he also uses both the word and the method for other significant choices [189]. Following Ignatius's lead, some use this material at other times than the Spiritual Exercises.

Election weaves throughout the Second Week and forms its climax. The Week opens with the meditations on the kingdom and the contemplations on the early life of Christ from the incarnation through the presentation in the Temple. At this point, Ignatius introduces the notion of choosing a state in life [135]. The one making the Exercises begins reflecting on her call in the midst of her contemplation of the public life of Jesus, whose disciple she is becoming. To prepare for this journey, Ignatius proposes two more dialectical meditations: the Two Standards [136–48] and the Three Classes of Persons [149–57]. Several days of intense contemplation later, the one making the Exercises has arrived with Jesus at the events of Palm Sunday. One last preparation for the election material remains: the Three Ways (Degrees) of Being Humble [165–68]. All these exercises have been discussed in chapter 7.

The placement of election is no accident. As she begins the process, the one making the Exercises not only becomes more intimately acquainted with the person of Jesus, but also more acquainted with the workings of her own spirit. She has experienced the dynamics of consolation and desolation and become more skillful in distinguishing the subtle ways the evil one might deflect her from her deepest call. Now she takes time to consider that call.

The first consideration [169] involves setting priorities: Why, ultimately, am I here? Ignatius, speaking from within the worldview of the Spiritual Exercises, summarizes: "...the praise of God our Lord and the salvation of my soul." But each person making the Exercises will have to frame her ultimate purpose: How do I understand myself before God? How can I live that call most deeply? Developing this "single eye" is crucial, otherwise one readily confuses the means (one's state in life) with the end (one's very reason for being). Ignatius's example remains relevant. How often does someone choose marriage (a means) and only long after the fact consider how life as a married person can help fulfill her final purpose. Ignatius wants to put first things first—clarity about means and ends is the "hinge" around which election turns (Ganss 1991, 412 n. 83).

Confusing the means with the end easily happens. One woman, after a concentrated and successful struggle with cancer, realized that, in order to marshal her energy to fight the cancer, she had blocked out everything else, including her husband's expressions of affection and love. She had unwittingly let the cancer create a breach between them. Election for her became a reaffirmation of the centrality of her marriage, and she began searching for new behaviors to replace the old habits that no longer served her healing.

Without clarity of intention about means and end, does Ignatian election exist? The whole point of both discernment of spirits and election consists of the gradual ordering of all aspects of life to one's ultimate identity and purpose. Ultimate purpose as a dynamic reality and integrity is both the product of decisions and the basis for decision making; this realization grounds our reading of Ignatius's wisdom on election. Election is not simply an expedient method for making an important choice; it is nothing less than seeking one's ultimate call from God. Each of Ignatius's suggested methods for making a good election begins and concludes with this central focus.

About what might an election be made? Ignatius proposes several points. First, the moral status of the choice matters: it must be either indifferent or good. Anything clearly involving evil lies outside the realm of appropriate matter for election because it could never lead to the greater glory of God. The difficulty lies in ascertaining whether a specific decision is morally evil, indifferent or positively good. Ignatius determined what was either indifferent or good by whether it functioned constructively within the institutional church. What might that mean for contemporary women? How does it function for persons not in union with the Roman Catholic Church, Ignatius's context? This point [170] connects the election material with the Rules for Thinking with the Church, the subject of the next chapter.

Even if one were to accept Ignatius's counsel at face value, it would still not necessarily offer sufficient guidance in deciding about what an election can be made. In significant decisions, the mature moral agent may not totally abrogate, even to the church, the responsibility for decision making. The person is morally obliged to follow a well-informed conscience.

Second, Ignatius assumes that some choices, once made, cannot be undone. In this situation, the only option he sees is "the full-hearted gift of self to this state in life" (Fleming 1978, 105). But what should be done if one later recognizes that in making this major decision she confused the ends and the means? One could express sorrow and make an attempt to amend by putting efforts into living now as fully as possible within this choice. Today's dynamic understanding of the human person recognizes that one's experience or lack of it, one's knowledge or ignorance, one's options or lack of them, all play a part in decision making. Decisions may be flawed according to Ignatius's abstract criteria and yet still occasion great grace, growth and insight and serve as steps toward greater personal integrity. One can respond to Ignatius's core insight while holding a more developmental sense of divine call. Responding with integrity to the best lights at the time is all God requires, as *Lumen Gentium* (#16) notes (Flannery 1996, 21–22).

Ignatius's examples of irreversible elections include ordination and marriage. But even these "unchangeable" elections are sometimes reversed. Many women, for example, find themselves in a position of discerning whether their marriage ever existed, or whether it is wholesome or even safe to remain in a lifeless or abusive situation. Thus, the notion of an "unchangeable election" may itself need discernment.

Most persons making the Spiritual Exercises today, however, will have already chosen a state in life. Ignatius addresses their situation under the heading "To Amend and Reform One's Life and State" [189]. The decisions he imagines still have parallels within many women's lives. Today's women might consider if or when parents or in-laws should live with the family, the most appropriate values to instill in their children and the best means to do so, or how to use their material resources so that greater justice comes about. In other words, many decisions, large and not so large, are occasions to use the methods offered under the rubric of Election. The attitude of discernment brought to decision making is one of the primary fruits one can take from the Spiritual Exercises into daily life.

The final introductory point concerns looking back at elections made earlier in life from the point of view of the Spiritual Exercises. In reviewing these important life decisions, it may become clear that important yet changeable elections were made with the ends and means in right relationship; if so, there is no need to change them now. But if some were made in a "disordered" fashion, the person making the Exercises may wish to return to them, renewing them from the perspective of the glory and service of God [173–74]. Remembering a past decision that was not well made in this Ignatian sense might initiate a profound healing process.

## The Three Times for Making an Election

Ignatius next considers three appropriate contexts for making an election, which he calls "Times," each defined by a particular spiritual state. The first two are terse almost to the point of ambiguity. Ignatius divides the third into two processes. Examples given below concerning three women, each of whom faces a similar choice, illustrate the Times by their differing inner processes.

The First Time, or spiritual context, for making an election occurs when God attracts us to an option so clearly the uncertainty evaporates [175]. How often God might work this directly Ignatius does not say. Practically speaking, any claim to such an experience would require discernment. One might discern by examining the sense of direction according to either the suggestions for the Second or Third Times, or both. This First-Time experience need not be extraordinary. For example, one woman announced with certainty:

> I've spent the past twenty years putting my husband through school, and then the kids. I was happy to be taking the kids to Little League, but now it's time for *me*. There is a community college close, and my son just got his driver's license, so there is no need to be carting him to after-school sports. I'm going to school now. It's the right time and the right thing to do. I just know it.

The Second Time for election, which Ignatius thinks the most typical, concerns the situation in which the discerner experiences consolation and desolation and receives clarity through discerning these various movements [176]. The one making the Exercises has been noticing, naming, discriminating and choosing with respect to various spirits throughout the Exercises. She has gained experience in even somewhat subtle situations covered in the second set of Rules. This example of another woman's process has quite a different feel:

> I've been having a real strong sense that I need to investigate something new. The kids are all in school. I've thought about going back to school myself. But I'm afraid that I couldn't do it after all the years I've been out of school. Sometimes it seems like it would be selfish, at my age, because we will be having college

expenses for the kids in a few years. But it really would be satisfying to focus some time on my own mind after all these years. When I think about it, I get excited—and really scared.

The Second Time raises questions: How certain should one be? How does one proceed in the case of desolation? Does the appearance of any desolation, or a lot of desolation, rule out the option? Fortunately, Ignatius gives a bit more help in the *Autograph Directory*:

> [18] Among the three modes [times] of making an election, if God does not move him in the first he ought to dwell on the second, that of recognizing his vocation by the experience of consolations and desolations. Then, as he continues with his meditations on Christ our Lord, he should examine, when he finds himself in consolation, in which direction God is moving him; similarly in desolation…. (Palmer 1996, 9)

In the Second Time, then, the seeker proceeds indirectly, returning to the contemplations of the Second Week rather than intensively working on the decision to be made. Then, in the context of a growing relationship with Jesus, she examines the decision.

From the perspective of the Rules for Discernment of Spirits, the seeker watches for fruits in the Second Time process: Does the consolation arise from God or is it counterfeit? Does it remain oriented to good from beginning to end? Is there sufficient evidence from accumulated instances of discernment of spirits that this direction ultimately honors one's deepest call? This Time takes time.[1]

The Third Time for making an election is "one of tranquility," by which Ignatius means that no alternating consolation and desolations are present around the choice being considered. If these and other affects are quiet, intellect becomes the means to a decision. A

third woman facing a decision about returning to school relates the
following:

> I am about to begin a new chapter in my life. There are a num-
> ber of things I can do, all of which have some appeal. I could
> enroll in the School of Social Work, which I've always been
> interested in. I could return to early childhood education, which
> I was doing before we had our kids and really liked at the time.
> I'd have to go in as an aide, not a lead teacher, until I picked up
> some more classes but I could do that in maybe one or two sum-
> mers. Either one is possible for us financially, so I really am free
> to do either. By the end of the year I will probably have reached
> my decision. I'm still checking out a few things.

The first *process* that Ignatius elaborates in the Third Time looks
enough like contemporary strategies for good decision making that
one might miss the critical distinctions between Ignatian election
and decision-making strategies taught in management seminars.
The first point [178] asks for clarity about the alternatives and what
each involves. It may require several attempts to clearly formulate
the choice.

The second, third and sixth points highlight the difference
between election and other contemporary decision-making processes.
In the second point [170], the crucial "hinge" appears: one places oneself and the whole decision within the ultimate purpose of life. One
then seeks the grace of being disposed to either option, so long as it
serves this ultimate end. This "indifference" appeared earlier in the
Principle and Foundation. Election is, inescapably, a faith process.

As in the First and Second Weeks, the third point [180] concerns
asking for the grace desired: here, that God will work through one's
reasoning to accomplish the greater glory of God through this concrete

life decision. Asking for this grace reinforces the purity of intention sought in the preceding point. The fourth point [181] sets out the reasoning process itself: consideration of the advantages and disadvantages first of one alternative and then of the other, all framed by the goal of election, the greater glory of God. After setting out the pros and cons of these alternatives, one reasons to the decision.

But the election does not end here; the final point also distinguishes election from other kinds of decision making. One brings the tentative decision arrived at through reasoning to God for confirmation [183].[2] Ignatius's text is sufficiently ambiguous about what confirmation entails and thus this question has evoked considerable discussion. Fortunately, a vivid example of one of Ignatius's own elections is preserved in a fragment of his spiritual diary, covering the period from February 2, 1544, to February 27, 1545 (Ganss 1991, 215–70). A partial entry from February 8, in which Ignatius considers the degree of poverty that will characterize the Society of Jesus, opens this chapter.

Examining this and other instances of election in Ignatius's own experience communicates several things about confirmation. First, seeking confirmation is, in Ignatius's mind, essential. Second, actually receiving it depends upon the weightiness of the matter for discernment, the time given to the process, the time frame in which the decision must be made and so on. The faith perspective underlying election holds that God would, one way or another, give some *disconfirmation*. In its absence one might proceed. Third, confirmation might consist in any or all of the following: spiritual consolations such as courage to proceed, increasing energy and enthusiasm, new reasons for the choice, intensification of the reasons already named or of desire for the choice itself, and a sense of having done everything possible to find God's will in the choice at hand. Fourth, seeking confirmation entails waiting, actively reviewing the process and outcome, offering the decision to God and asking that the outcome be disconfirmed if not in line with one's ultimate call. A final aspect comes after the completed election: appropriate authorities confirm the decision (Toner 1991, 201–32).

Ignatius realized that imagination also offers powerful ways for making an election and included three exercises of imagination. Each, using a slightly different perspective, creates some objective distance on the discerner's situation. The first directs her to imagine what she might say to a stranger who proposes the same alternatives. The second asks her to consider what she would wish to have done from the perspective of her deathbed. The third asks her to consider what she would wish to have done on the final judgment day. Given Ignatius's penchant for imaginal prayer, these scenarios need not be in the least dry or predictable in their outcome. In addition, one need not restrict oneself to these three considerations, though they all have precedents in the tradition.

Not surprisingly, Ignatius begins these considerations with the "hinge" upon which election turns, asking the one making the election to set the deliberations, once again, within the ultimate purpose of her life [184]. In the other critical dimension in Ignatian election [188], the one making the election again brings the results to God for confirmation.

Although some interpreters of the Spiritual Exercises believe that the Second and Third Times treat separate processes and should remain distinct, the Second and Third time processes naturally complement each other. Using one's whole self, reason, affects and imagination creates a more holistic process and allows for a fuller devotion of oneself in prayerful decision making.

All this Election material can feel terribly heavy, ponderous or rigid. Yet it need not. That which gives God greater glory generally brings great satisfaction and fulfillment.

## Problems and Possibilities for Women

Everyone makes choices daily, and life-changing decisions once in a while. How can this "coming-to-be-who-I-am" be woman-friendly? What attitudes and adaptations would free women to make the best possible decisions? These questions obviously move beyond the scope of this work. Restricting the discussion to the Spiritual Exercises, however, reveals several potential difficulties in the processes proposed by Ignatius, including the notion of "God's will," the action women might take when faced with "disordered" choices or decisions opposed by various communities of authority, and some of the tensions women might experience when faced with any serious decision.

Election inevitably raises the concept of God's will, even though the phrases "God's will" and "discernment of God's will" never appear in the *Spiritual Exercises*. For many persons, a notion of God's will flows from a medieval cosmology; these persons see God's will as an unchanging reality "out there" where God "dwells in unapproachable light." Their task as Christian moral persons entails discovering what that will is and then conforming themselves to it, whether easily or tortuously.

This theological assumption may exist in quite subtle forms. For example, one woman, experiencing a deep and generous attraction to discipleship with Jesus, found herself praying, "O Lord, just show me your will, and I will do it." When she reported this prayer to the one guiding her through the Exercises, she added, "As soon as I get a sense from Jesus about how he wants me to serve, I will do it." Her guide gently responded, "Did it ever occur to you that perhaps Jesus might be waiting for you to decide what *you* want to do and then he will join you there?" "Oh! she replied, "I hadn't thought of that." They went on to explore the seeds of her call planted in her heart, recognizing her attractions, desires and gifts, the possibilities open to her and so on. Her subsequent prayer was no less generous, but she also began to recognize her own freedom and unavoidable responsibility in setting the directions of her life within the scope of God's love and mercy for her and all creation. She began to see *herself* as a creative act of God.

Although the concept of "God's will" does not appear in the *Spiritual Exercises,* a statement that the end of the human person is "to praise, reverence and serve God," frequently does. This framing of one's ultimate end leaves open an immense range of possibilities about particular decisions, actions and lifestyles that could embody it. No "blueprint in the sky" exists. This insight can be either frightening or freeing—or both at the same time. To be fully herself, each person must take up her own destiny.

That prospect, especially to one who sees herself as innocent and childlike, can evoke great resistance and even terror. Embracing the feelings and accepting the responsibility for one's life eventually leads to the birth of the adult moral person. But this growth in moral personhood does not take place in isolation from others. The mature conscience is formed in dialogue and exercised in community (Gula 1989, 124).

Women often find it difficult to trust their own experience. To the degree that it has either been actively denied and suppressed or, more subtly, left unnoticed and therefore invisible by those whose power names the world—parents, spouses, educational system, the culture itself—women's own experience can seem strange and even foreign to themselves. And to the degree that their experience and trust have been abused, women may deny what their experience tells them. Humans have such a need for meaning-making and coherence that if the world does not make sense—for example, if those who should provide safety violate it—they will deny what has happened to them in the interests of a cohesive worldview. "I must have asked for it," we might hear one say, or another, "God must be punishing me now for having sex with my boyfriend." The methods for election and skillful accompaniment may offer individual women a graced opportunity to commit to their own identity.

Second, what of so-called "disordered" choices? What of earlier choices that, in hindsight and from the vantage point of the First and Second Weeks of the Exercises, seem to reflect poor discernment? Take, for example, the woman who married her high school sweetheart soon after graduation, realizing later that she chose the only life she could then imagine and the only way she could find to "leave home" in her small town. What does she do in light of Ignatian election exercises? What about situations where apparently well-made decisions have gone sour? Generous women can feel especially grieved by and feel greatly responsible for such decisions. Has bad discernment led to bad outcome?

These situations do not necessarily indicate bad discernment. They point to limited discernment, perhaps, or small horizons, inadequate life experience, limited perceived options or invincible ignorance. But, in keeping with an understanding that one's final "end" is a process rather than a product, these decisions may have been necessary and appropriate steps toward a developing personal integrity, subsequently honed in the face of life's inevitable blows and blessings. Freeing someone from negative judgment on early decisions may also free her to face the difficult decision currently before her.

What of those women facing decisions about something opposed by their communities of moral authority? What about the evangelical woman who files for divorce, the divorced Roman Catholic woman contemplating remarriage, the woman who gives up custody of her children to attend school and launch herself professionally, the parent of a twelve-year old considering an abortion or the woman who relinquishes her faith community or her vows? A literal interpretation of

Ignatius's qualifying factors in [170–73] would eliminate several of these decisions. But such existential decisions face real women who have definite limits to their supportive communities, economic and educational means and autonomy. These decisions make an impact beyond the women themselves that will ripple down through the years. Women who face such momentous and complex situations especially need to examine their concrete experience, gather data and explore the ramifications of their decisions. And they need to do all this within the context of the faith community if they are to develop the greatest possible degree of interior freedom and integrity in these difficult choices. The election methods suggested by Ignatius, coupled with skillful accompaniment, provide a privileged context for their prayerful, discerned decision making.

## Decisions and Commitments: Making, Keeping, Changing

Decisions both express identity and provide the vehicle for further developing it. Decisions have religious import too, even when made and executed without adverting to God at all. They constitute a vantage point for understanding both God's commitment to us and the reciprocal desire on God's part for our commitment. In a real sense, decisions express relationship to God. For this reason, decision making lies at the center of the Spiritual Exercises.

At the beginning of her study of personal commitments, theologian Margaret Farley (1986, 4–8) suggests why women may have difficulty with decision making:

> Who, overall, have known better than women the deep needs of the human spirit for commitment? Yet who, overall, through the centuries, have experienced more sharply the bitter pain of being deserted in commitments that were believed to be mutual? Who

have learned with untimely grace that promises can rise from a personal freedom that transcends purely cultural roles? Who struggle now so desperately to balance multiple commitments, to forestall guilt in compromise, to accept limitations without abandoning trust and hope? Who press now so consistently to distinguish servile fidelity from a fidelity that is both liberated and responsible? (1986, 8)

Some needed perspective comes from examining what constitutes commitment, how commitment is an outgrowth of love and the basic considerations around release from obligation.

Commitments are certain kinds of decisions in which a person "places" a part of herself or something that belongs to her into another person's "keeping." It gives the other person a claim over her. In making a promise, she does not give *herself* away, except in the sense that another holds her pledge. In that sense, she binds her future freedom. If she betrays her word, she stands to lose a part of herself (Farley 1986, 16–18).

But why make commitments? Commitments and the trust they engender assure others that one will be consistent. But one also assures oneself in the face of personal unpredictability. Commitments facilitate important aspects of human community: personal relationships, political life and human communication all depend on promise making and keeping. All stand to gain mutual protection, companionship and love. Furthermore, while commitments do cut off some options, they give freedom to act. Without commitments, all things are possible, but nothing is actualized. As the old adage says: "It is impossible to run in all directions at once" (Farley 1986, 19–22, 44). No one is so paralyzed as the person who tries to keep all options open indefinitely.

Fundamental to making a commitment or promise is free choice—no free choice, no binding promise. Choice moves toward some kind of action, but the difficulty often centers around letting go of other kinds of actions. Reflective decision making, which occurs in the methods of election, encourages one to weigh and sift the possible actions, trying to understand and evaluate them.

Below the free choice and the action, however, lie several layers of desire, the deepest of which is desire for love. As Farley (1986, 29) puts it, "every free choice includes a choice of what and how to love." The methods for election and the entire dynamic of the Spiritual Exercises allow seekers to enact the belief that their deepest desire and ultimate good, and that of other persons as well, are the same. God's preferential love grounds all finite expressions of love, making them possible and completing them. In this sense, love wants commitment because it wants to express itself as fully as it can to assure its completion.

Women may need some general guidelines for making loving commitments. They ought, for example, to have reasonable grounds for trusting themselves to another, and for hope that they can fulfill that promise. They ought to have some evidence that the human relationships constituted by this commitment are subject to the norms of justice, such as respect for persons, equality and mutuality and equitable sharing, as well as some means to redress grievances (Farley 1986, 36). With these parameters in place, a woman can turn to the loves of her heart. What does she most deeply desire? These loves require decisions and commitments as their natural completion and expression (Frankl 1959, 157–58).

The often difficult question about terminating a major commitment still remains. Women who have internalized the responsibility for relationships—for example, women care for aging in-laws and parents as well as dependent children much more frequently than men—can be particularly distressed when relationships are strained to the point of collapse.

While each situation has its own particulars, several generalizations can help provide the framework for examination. One might begin by seeing if the conditions for a commitment and the capacities for a choice are present and whether the choice is freely entered into. One can ask whether there is enough knowledge of the parameters and consequences of the choice that it can be competently made? Is the commitment desired by the recipient? Is the sacrifice wholly disproportionate to the value to be gained? In a mutual commitment, does the other party also understand and agree to essentially the same commitment? In addition, the limits of the commitment, both in time and terms need exploration.

Margaret Farley proposes three conditions in which commitments, even serious ones, may be released: (1) when it truly becomes impossible for either party to sustain the commitment-relationship; (2) when a specific commitment-obligation no longer fulfills the purposes of the larger commitment it was meant to serve; and (3) when another obligation comes into conflict with and supersedes the commitment in question (1986, 75–84). Careful reflection, usually with the assistance of one or more compassionate companions, helps determine if these conditions are present.

These considerations presuppose commitment grounded in relationship. The commitments made within the Spiritual Exercises ideally flow from vision of a certain kind of world and the call to assist its birth. This vision also rests on relationship with the Holy, the Creative One. This relationship, unlike human ones, is unfailingly characterized by truth, justice and mercy.

Finally, the reality of self-sacrifice can prove very problematic to contemporary women, as theorist Carol Gilligan (1982) so vividly illustrated. While self-sacrifice is required of all parties in all commitments of any substance, is there a limit to it? Farley offers the following ethical guidelines. First, one may not relate to others in a way that ultimately destroys either the other or the self. In essence, one may sacrifice everything one *has* for the sake of the other or the commitment, but not everything one *is*. One may never sacrifice the capability for union with God and other human persons. Thus, demands that violate personhood or that rest upon false needs in the other or that envision sacrifice as an end in itself carry no obligation for a truly just love to fulfill. Furthermore, all this must be examined within an analysis of the power arrangements: When a disproportionate burden of sacrifice is laid upon the less-powerful person, then the less powerful person's duty to self-sacrifice needs to be critiqued (Farley 1986, 105–7).

But—and here the presence and action of grace often breaks in—restoration may still be possible. Sometimes situations can be restructured, even radically. Sometimes changing one's interpretation of the situation can make all the difference. And sometimes the grace of forgiveness is given to one or both parties. Forgiveness, an act freely offered, can never be rushed. When forgiveness is present, at least the one forgiving, and possibly the one forgiven, is freed to reenter the commitment or to move on.

This matter of decisions and commitments, so essential to election, is complex and often problematic for women. It asks them to take their own experience seriously, to learn to recognize the deep desires of their own hearts and to accept responsibility for stepping out in loving commitments that grow out of their personal experiences of being loved and returning love. The methods for election invite each woman to make or reappropriate her identity in the very lifestyle she will embody. That this identity is essentially apostolic and mission oriented is one of the great graces of the Spiritual Exercises.

## Wisdom for the One Giving the Exercises

The opportunity to facilitate the seeker's bringing together her identity with its lived vocational expression is a privileged one. It may also be difficult, as it requires a delicate balance not only of interest and affirmation but also of objectivity and dispassion. Ignatius thought Election so central to the Spiritual Exercises that he dedicates two of fifteen preliminary notes specifically to the director: The one giving the Exercises is to caution against hasty or ill-considered promises and may not influence the seeker toward one or another decision. The Creator alone must be allowed to deal directly with the seeker. Self-knowledge and indifference on the part of the guide are essential.

The one giving the Exercises can especially help the seeker by broadening the options that she can imagine, focusing them into a clear discernment questions, facilitating the healing of old wounds so as to be free to move on, and selecting and attending to the outcome of the various methods. The guide may also offer additional methods complementing those Ignatius has suggested, especially ones tapping the wisdom of the body.

It may seem strange to broaden the imagined possibilities when the ultimate task is choosing a life direction, but many women can imagine only a restricted range of options. Unless real options exist and unless women *experience* them as real options, election will not be as free and true as it might.

Enriching the imagination entails a much larger process than is possible during the Spiritual Exercises. Such education of the imagination may involve art, literature, travel and education. Some kinds of enrichment fit best in a pre-Exercises time of preparation. These could involve encouraging the one making the Exercises to let herself dream about what she really wants to do before the "voices" of reason, economics and commitments crash in on fragile new images of possibility or helping her name and feel comfortable with her gifts and voice, both literally and figuratively. Other avenues may involve awakening the imagination or learning to pay attention to dreams. The one giving the Exercises can lend authority to taking this enrichment seriously.

One can also find many ways to continue the enrichment appropriately within the scope of the Exercises, especially in strengthening the imagination through the meditations and contemplations and encouraging the seeker to voice the graces she desires. A fully alive person will respond more to the Holy Spirit as she approaches important decisions within the Spiritual Exercises and afterwards.

At the appropriate time, a carefully framed discernment question can greatly facilitate the election. However, sometimes a question may be too focused, or the process too intense. Persons are often encouraged to make the Exercises before important decisions, in part because of the election aspect of the Exercises. In such cases, the question may loom too large over the dynamics of the Exercises, and the one making the Exercises may need to set the decision aside for the time being. Putting "brackets" around the decision and letting it move from the center of one's consciousness over to the margins allows the one making the Exercises to immerse herself in the dynamics of the First and Second Weeks. These dynamics cultivate the necessary dispositions for election. When the time comes to return to the pending decision, the one making the Exercises will be changed.

In contrast to being too focused, sometimes the matter for election will be diffuse and vague. In some cases, simply encouraging the shift from an open question like "What am I going to do?" to a more specific yes or no question such as "Should I go back to school?" will help bring the appropriate matter into focus. The seeker can try out a number of these questions until she comes as close as possible to the real issue for discernment. Noticing what she desires, what gives her energy and where her gifts point help refine the discernment question.

For some, the question changes during the course of either the election exercises or the subsequent Weeks. This development should cause neither distress nor discouragement; it is simply a version of confirmation—the first question was not confirmed as the most appropriate one. One simply frames the new question and returns to the election exercises. The guide may need to encourage this movement back and forth, helping to avoid premature closure.

As the one making the Exercises begins to work with the election processes, she may uncover an old wound or blockage that requires attention. This healing work may need to precede the election. If its scope falls within the competence of the one giving the Exercises and its duration seems proportional to the dynamic of the Exercises, it is perfectly appropriate to focus on the healing. But if immense and complex, as, for example, surfacing of memories of early sexual abuse, the one giving the Exercises will have to adjust the process of the Exercises accordingly. The greatest grace of the Exercises might be the courage to attend to one's healing through the necessary means outside the context of the Spiritual Exercises.

The primary function of the one giving the Exercises, however, will consist of introducing the methods for election as appropriate and helping the seeker to notice and interpret the data she receives. Ignatius implies a priority of methods: infused clarity, if given; alternating consolation and desolation; and finally, in the absence of the first two, using the rational processes of thinking and imagining. The one giving the Exercises today may wish to work from the strength of the discerner. How has she made important decisions in the past? How, for example, did she come to the decision to make the Spiritual Exercises? Beginning with the woman's own experience of decision making allows her to claim it as part of discerned decisions in the future. Thus the graces of the Exercises may more easily spill over into daily life.

If she begins with the processes that employ her natural ways of making decisions and her personality strengths, the seeker can complement this discernment with an alternate process. A highly imaginative person, for example, might look at her decision using the rational means of listing the reasons for and against. The data elicited will differ, and sometimes crucial insights emerge when employing a less dominant personality function.

The one giving the Exercises might also encourage the seeker not to skip over "negative" data, but to stay with it as attentively as one would with "positive" data. He or she may also sometimes notice resistances on the part of the seeker, of which she is unaware, and help her gently but fearlessly face them.

The processes Ignatius gives can also be elaborated and adapted. The "hinge" of Ignatian election does not lie in the processes, but the indifference with which one approaches election and the confirmation that one receives about the specific decision. Therefore, any decision-making process placed inside these all-important "hinges" may prove useful for election. The imagination-based exercises can expand to include others derived from the woman's own story. She herself may come up with the scenario. Ignatius does not suggest processes based on intuition, though it is quite possible to understand the First Time as God working directly through intuition. A simple guided meditation that facilitates the emergence of a direction may prove invaluable. The Quaker discernment tradition is based on the premise that wisdom and direction is already planted by God deep within the individual, and the task of discernment consists in removing any obstacles that stifle that inner wisdom. Around intuition the Quaker and Ignatian traditions fruitfully meet.[3]

Human beings are embodied creatures, a theological assertion frequently overlooked in discernment. Thus, the body constitutes another entry point for discerning decisions. Eugene Gendlin (1981) has developed a simple process called Focusing, based upon the assertion that the body and the brain know far more than is usually available to the conscious mind. The six-step process takes seriously the wisdom of the body. Anyone can learn it.[4]

Focusing can assist with discerning decisions at several levels. The discernment question might take the place of the "problem." Or the "problem" might reveal the things that the body says must be dealt with before one is free enough to consider the discernment question. Focusing can also be a part of the confirmation process: does the body itself say Yes! to the outcome of discernment?

Of course, many other ways of working with the body enhance discernment: forms of embodied prayer such as Zen walking, prayer based on data of the various senses, massage and dance, both spontaneous and liturgical. These embodied prayer forms may offer powerful pathways to divine presence, and thus to discernment.

The process of election has immense significance. As women make important decisions, they embody their ever-forming identity with a particular way of living it out. In the context of the Spiritual Exercises, the election process elicits a generous response to the call of God in the person of Jesus. The decision gains depth and clarity throughout the remainder of the Exercises and of their lives. An apostolic identity takes concrete form. Discernment and Election are truly precious gifts shaping all of life.

# Notes

1. For an alternative method, see Karl Rahner, "The Ignatian Process for Discovering the Will of God in an Existential Situation, Epitomized by Harold E. Weidman," in *Ignatius of Loyola: His Personality and Spiritual Heritage,* 1556–1956, ed. by Friedrich Wulf (St. Louis: Institute of Jesuit Sources, 1977), 288. For a simple process based on the Second Time, see Sisters of Providence, *The Love of Christ Impels Us* (Spokane: Sisters of Providence Provincial Administration, 1991): 237–38.

2. For a simple method for making a personal election based on the Spiritual Exercises [178–83] but free from Ignatian jargon, see Sisters of Providence, *The Love of Christ Impels Us* (Spokane: Sisters of Providence Provincial Administration, 1991): 241–45.

3. Helpful resources on the Quaker Clearness Committee include Suzanne Farnham, Joseph P. Gill and Taylor McLean, *Listening Hearts: Discerning Call in Community* (Harrisburg, Pa.: Morehouse, 1991); Parker Palmer, "The Clearness Committee," *Weavings* 3 (July/August 1988):37–40; and Parker J. Palmer, *The Courage to Teach* (San Francisco: Jossey-Bass, 1998).

4. Focusing, as developed by Eugene Gendlin, can be summarized in six steps. Of course, much more can be said about each step, but even this outline can provide sufficient structure for experiencing profound inner wisdom.

# Focusing: A Short Form

*1. Clear a space (inside of you)*
    How are you? What's between you and feeling fine? Don't answer; let what comes in your body do the answering.
    Don't go into anything. Greet each concern that comes. Put each aside for a while, next to you. Except for that, are you fine?

*2. Felt sense*
    Pick one problem to focus on. Don't go into the problem. What do you sense in your body when you recall the whole of that problem? Sense all of

that, the sense of the whole thing, the murky discomfort or the unclear body-sense of it.

### 3. Get a handle

What is the quality of the felt sense? What one word, phrase or image comes out of this felt sense? What quality word would fit it best?

### 4. Resonate

Go back and forth between word (or image) and the felt sense. Is that right? If they match, have the sensation of matching several times. If the felt sense changes, follow it with your attention.

### 5. Ask

"What is it about the whole problem, that makes me so_____?"

When stuck, ask questions: What is the worst of this feeling? What's really so bad about this? What does it need? What should happen? Don't answer; wait for the feeling to stir and give you an answer.

What would it feel like if it was all OK? Let the body answer: What is in the way of that?

### 6. Receive

Welcome what came. Be glad it spoke. It is only one step on this problem, not the last. Now that you know where it is, you can leave it and come back to it later. Protect it from critical voices that interrupt.

Does your body want another round of focusing, or is this a good stopping place? (1981, 177–78)

# Chapter 12

# Black Appearing White: Rules for Thinking with the Church

*Salamanca, August, 1527. A small man with a decided limp, dressed in rough, poorly dyed black clothing, emerges from the local prison. As he comes through the low stone door, he shields his eyes from the bright sunlight. A few moments later, he is joined by several companions, also emerging from the door of the prison. Together they walk toward the town plaza, conversing among themselves: "Now what? We can't do what we are called to do. They have not condemned us, but they have silenced us all the same."*

*A medium-sized city in the United States, Easter Vigil, 2000. A woman sits in the pew, watching the new pastor baptize the adults and children she has catechized. Two weeks later, she is summoned to his office and told her contract will not be renewed. The staff is to be reorganized. She emerges from the office into the bright sunlight, blinks rapidly and sighs to herself: "Now what? Do I have the energy to start again somewhere else?"*

Ignatius of Loyola, following his call and using his unique gifts, encounters church authorities who imprison and silence him. A contemporary woman, using her gifts, is dismissed and effectively silenced. Who or what is this church? What characterizes the relationship between the one making the Exercises and the church in which she or he feels called to serve?

## Rules for Thinking with the Church

The final and most problematic section in the *Spiritual Exercises* is a set of directives that has come to be called the Rules for Thinking with the Church. More than any other portion of the Spiritual Exercises, this section must be understood in light of the historical context, particularly the theological controversies of the time. Much of its specific advice is dated, and its usefulness to contemporary women appears so compromised that many recommend eliminating this section from the Spiritual Exercises. Understanding the Rules in their historical context, however, opens the possibility that even this difficult section of the Spiritual Exercises may hold something useful for contemporary women.

The fact that the *Spiritual Exercises* do contain a section entitled Rules for Thinking with the Church raises several crucial and inescapable issues for women's participation. First, it highlights a number of questions about the relationship between the church and the Spiritual Exercises: "Are the *Spiritual Exercises* emphatically institutional or totally individualistic or somewhere in between (Buckley 1995, 441)?" Can one make the Exercises without relationship to any faith community? Or are they, at root, an instrument of evangelization and church renewal? What does it mean that women disenfranchised from the institutional church increasingly present themselves to make the Spiritual Exercises? Whether one resists or assents to including the Rules for Thinking with the Church, the mystery of church requires examination, if only because one's personal spirituality is consciously or unconsciously informed by the larger reality called church.

Second, what is the significance of "church" for those who make the Spiritual Exercises and for those who give them? Contemporary women approach the Exercises with a variety of passions and emotions toward church, from anger to indifference to appreciation, and with a variety of ecclesiologies, including Roman Catholic, Anglican and Protestant. These experiences, feelings and ecclesiologies inevitably color their relationship to the Spiritual Exercises. The relationship between the one making the Exercises and the church also creates a dynamic context in which election occurs. It will be impossible to ignore the reality of church as one proceeds through the Spiritual Exercises.

## Context of the Rules

The sixteenth century held complex and dynamic challenges for the Roman Catholic Church from both the outside and inside. Within the church, some persons practiced a mysticism that ignored dogmatic accuracy and theological precision, such as the Spanish *alumbrados*, with whom Ignatius was several times confused. Others, such as Luther and Calvin, openly split from the orthodox Roman positions. In the sometimes heated rhetoric of the era, many elements of Roman Catholic piety came under attack. A third group made up of disgruntled or critical Catholics, undermined church morale from within with their sarcasm. The ironic and satirical writings of Erasmus come to mind here (Ganss 1973, 73–77). The church today, now split into various denominations more or less suspicious of one another, faces equally challenging issues. To these historic rivalries one must add modern atheism and a pervasive secularism unknown in Ignatius's day.

Ignatius's own life brought him happy and unhappy contacts with the church. Soon after his conversion, he sought out a spiritual director, began conversing with whomever would discuss religion and set about publicly catechizing. He grew to love the Mass and the sacraments, especially the Eucharist, which he received as often as possible. However, these innocent-appearing contacts with the church yielded no fewer than eight legal processes directed at Ignatius by church authorities between 1526 and 1538. They concerned matters ranging from the clothing he and his early companions wore, the education upon which he based his catechizing, his teaching about mortal and venial sin, his relationships with youth, the Spiritual Exercises themselves, the content and fruit of his spiritual conversations and his orthodoxy and that of his companions. Several of these investigations entailed his arrest and imprisonment, once for as long as twenty-two days (Padberg 1993, 10–17).

In his later years, Ignatius worked directly with various popes over issues related to the Society of Jesus, relationships both profitable and conflictual. On the one hand, his collaboration with Paul III and Julius III established and strengthened the Society in its fledgling years. On the other, he struggled especially with Paul III and Paul IV over attempts to make members of the Society cardinals or bishops, a practice Ignatius adamantly opposed (Padberg 1993, 10–17).

When Cardinal Gian Carafa was elected Pope Paul IV in 1555, Ignatius feared what the new pope might do to the Society. He is said to have quaked in his bones before he could repair to the chapel to regain his composure (Tellechea Idígoras 1994, 558). Yet the dying Ignatius asks of that same pope a blessing, reflecting the traditional Roman Catholic understanding that the grace of God is transmitted regardless of the disposition of the minister. Clearly, Ignatius was no stranger to the process of reflecting on both consolations and desolations arising at the hand of the institutional church and its leaders.

Contemporary women likewise recount enlivening and disillusioning experiences with the church. The circumstances eliciting consolation for many contemporary women include a new affirmation of a rich variety of spiritualities by Vatican II's universal call to holiness; access to theological and biblical studies and to the fruits of a rich theological and biblical heritage; the ordination of women in most Protestant denominations; and the reclaimed memory of interesting, complex and effective women within the Christian heritage. Women also struggle with experiences of the church and its ministers. Abuse of power, sexual abuse or harassment, job stratification, unjust salary differentials, lack of access to decision making, exclusive language and the loss of traditional and cherished images of God wear down even the most determined and focused church women. The experience of the unnamed woman at the beginning of this chapter is far from unique.

## Contents of the Rules

Ignatius probably composed the Rules for Thinking with the Church during his student days in Paris, though he may have completed some points after his arrival in Rome. The Rules bear some resemblance to decrees of the Council of Sens (1528), held just after Ignatius arrived in Paris. The highly public profile of Ignatius and his companions compelled him to formulate an approach not only to the private conscience, but also to the public conscience (Boyle 1983, 256). He created a series of counsels about a constructive attitude within which to form concrete pastoral responses to the conflicts of his time.

The usual title, "Rules for Thinking with the Church," is not Ignatius's own, but an attempt to summarize his much longer title.[1] *Sentido,* the word usually summarized by "thinking," actually includes both affect and praxis. With *sentido,* Ignatius wished to convey a habitual way of acting that springs from a loving, reverential yet critical relationship to the church.

*Rules,* though Ignatian in origin, is also a misnomer. The points actually represent a collection of guidelines to be used with flexibility. The early directories suggest they be given only to those whose ministries will plunge them publicly into the complex dynamics of the ecclesial situation of the time.

Although the Rules may appear to be a rather haphazard collection of points, Ignatius states his fundamental principle in the first Rule [353], and then he develops this proposition in three groups of directives. The first set, Rules 2 through 9 [354–61], involves suggestions for an attitude about aspects of the devotional life of sixteenth-century Catholics, under attack either from within or from outside the church of Ignatius's time. The second group, Rules 10 through 12 [362–64], builds up a positive attitude toward authority in the church regarding jurisdiction, learning and holiness. The third group, Rules 13 through 18 [365–70], treats complex doctrinal truths under heated discussion in Ignatius's day, setting out a positive pastoral strategy for dealing with them. The first Rule in each section, namely the first, tenth and thirteenth, grounds the subsequent points in that section (Ganss 1973, 77–80).

The first Rule [353] asks those making the Exercises to develop a loving and deeply reverent and obedient attitude toward the church, even with its weak and human leaders, and to let that attitude color all dealings with it.[2] In a climate in which both friends and foes of the church make light of its teachings or actively tear down its leadership, organization and its very spirit, this Rule exhorts all to speak positively of these same realities. In a climate of cynicism about the church, spontaneous and simple affirmations can speak volumes. This reverential love, Ignatius's own life shows, will be more than our own doing; it will spring from God's grace at work in all parties. Blows suffered at the hands of the church will often be quite sufficient, naturally speaking, to change sympathy to bitterness, friendship to enmity, good will to disillusionment. Just as one would give a long-time friend loyalty, so one tries to develop a habitual reverence and loyalty to the church, which is no less mother and friend.

The tenth Rule [362] echoes the basic attitude with which Ignatius began the Spiritual Exercises [22]. It advises one to be more inclined to praise than to blame the personal and public actions of those who hold positions of authority in the church. Even if their actions are blameworthy, dragging down their reputations serves only to tear down the faith of all. On the other hand, one can and should deal directly and privately with those in a position to do something about the person or problem facing the church. But, this avenue presumes access to persons of power, something for which women have had to continually struggle.

In the thirteenth Rule [365], the most controversial from today's perspective, Ignatius proposes a difficult principle. "What I see as white, I will believe to be black if the hierarchical Church thus determines it." In Ignatius's time, the statement simply reiterated the commonly accepted belief that, in certain cases, what the church defined could contradict the senses. For example, the Roman Catholic position toward the Eucharist holds that the consecrated elements, which appear as bread and wine, are actually the body and blood of Christ. Therefore, the strong reaction against the thirteenth Rule quite possibly arises either from misunderstanding what Ignatius actually meant or from changing philosophical, theological and ecclesiastical circumstances. It would have passed as a noncontroversial statement to Roman Catholics of his era.[3]

The thirteenth Rule encourages a suspension of disbelief out of a spirit of faith when perceptions and judgments appear to contradict the church's position. In a sense, Ignatius proposes an attitude that totally reverses the so-called "Protestant principle," which holds that the divine transcends any created reality, including the church

(Tillich 1957, xvi–xvii).[4] In other words, God's will transcends any church. Both perspectives, without the balance of its opposite, can lead to extremes: Ignatius's exhortation seems to ask for "blind obedience," while the Protestant principle appears to glorify hanging onto one's version of the truth at the expense of unity. The mystery of the church in its fullness requires an integrity that respects both ends of the continuum.

## Problems and Possibilities for Women

Are the Rules for Thinking with the Church essential to the Exercises? How many persons have even heard of them? Should they be quietly relegated to the back of the text where they will remain relatively invisible?

### How Important Are the Rules for Thinking with the Church?

Why not just quietly relegate the Rules for Thinking with the Church to the end of the Exercises and hope that no one notices them? Are they too central to ignore? Well-respected interpreters of the Exercises hold opposite positions on this question.

Some, such as Juan Polanco, believe that because of their lateness of composition and appendix-like nature, the Rules for Thinking with the Church remain peripheral to the integral dynamic of the Exercises. His *Directory,* composed between 1573 and 1575, suggests that the group of Rules, including those for almsgiving, scruples and the use of food, should "be proposed not to everybody, but only to persons who seem to need them and for whom it is worth the effort" (cited in O'Malley 1993, 50). John Futrell (Cowan and Futrell 1993, 169), however, claims that the Rules for Thinking with the Church provide the criterion of individual discernment. This challenge is somewhat more difficult to address. The thirteenth Rule, Ignatius's stated norm for certainty, allows a test of Futrell's claim.

Ignatius believed that every good impulse, whether personal or ecclesial, came from the same Spirit. Therefore, in submitting one's personal perceptions and discernment to the public discernment of the hierarchical church, there should be no conflict between one's properly discerned experience and institutional faith. Relinquishing final judgment to the hierarchical church, however, avoids a crucial question. Many contemporary women, both Roman Catholic and Protestant, have difficulty accepting such an unequivocal position on the institutional church's role in confirming individual discernment (O'Connell 1990, 117). What if the hierarchical church itself was prompted by an evil spirit, under the appearance of light, that distorted its perception (Boyle 1983, 255)? The feminist hermeneutic—whatever promotes the full humanity of women as well as men is redemptive and holy and is therefore of God; what denies and distorts that full humanity does not bear the power and authority of divine revelation (Fischer 1988, 128)—too often contradicts the institutional church's positions and its treatment of women. This possibility leaves women with a considerably less certain position than Ignatius asserts.

No absolutely certain norms for evaluating concrete and specific discernments exist; the best outcome is more or less relative human certitude. As much as one might wish, discernment does not abrogate the necessity of faith. Thus, neither the position that one can ignore the Rules for Thinking with the Church nor the position that they serve as the norm for all discernment expresses a sufficiently nuanced perspective. They are, in fact, both more radical and more relative.

## Potential Usefulness

Objections to the Rules for Thinking with the Church are varied. Their imagery is distasteful, even repulsive; they seem to demand unthinking obedience; they grow out of and support a narrow and pre–Vatican II ecclesiology; they are so time-bound as to be irrelevant to the contemporary context; they only apply to the Jesuits who by vow have placed themselves at the disposal of the pope for mission; they are not, strictly speaking, part of the Spiritual Exercises.

Yet properly understood, the Rules for Thinking with the Church hold possibilities to move seekers toward a new perspective. The first centers around the notion of a profound affective attitude of love for the church, a sense of ecclesial commitment in response to the issues facing it at a given time (Cowan and Futrell 1993, 170). Ignatius calls for a basic existential love for the church that causes one spontaneously to support and defend it out of this heartfelt connection. This felt-experience of love for the church is one of the fruits of the Fourth Week; here the church is the primary vehicle through which Christ carries on his work in the world. Imagine what a difference such a felt-love could make inside church institutions and within the wider society.

The tenth Rule also strikes this irenic note: One should be more inclined to praise than blame superiors. This rule proposes a basic good will grounding relationships in the Spiritual Exercises and extends it to one of the most neuralgic issues of his day and perhaps ours, the relationship to the persons in church structures who hold legitimate authority. But note that Ignatius also counsels bringing "bad conduct" to the attention of the appropriate authority, a counsel Ignatius himself frequently carried out.[5]

Ignatius's praxis in regard to his ecclesiastical superiors illumines what otherwise could come across as naive support of unworthy and corrupt leaders. He did not hesitate to pray ceaselessly, convince politically powerful friends to intervene on his behalf, create a paper trail or visit the pope personally—Ignatius did whatever it took to hold off or reverse a papal decision he felt was wrong. Scholar John Padberg calls Ignatius's relationships with popes one of "realistic reverence," noting, "Obviously Ignatius supposes that Church authority has the final say, but clearly only when it was really final" (1993, 26, 31–32).

## The View of the Church in the Spiritual Exercises and Now

The underlying issue has to do with the nature of the church, its relationship to the Spiritual Exercises and consequently to those making and giving them. What did *church* signify to Ignatius? What does the contemporary church look like on these same issues?

Perhaps the most problematic of Ignatius's images is "hierarchical." The "hierarchical" church is inescapably an earthly reality, incarnated in a human community with a human authority structure. This description reminds us of the need to deal with the concrete manifestations of power and authority; one cannot spiritualize these human aspects of the church out of existence (Cowan and Futrell 1993, 175). By speaking of the hierarchical church, Ignatius signaled that he wanted to serve that church through the direction of the pope. He felt convinced that the pope, for all the faults he might have, had the most all-embracing view of the needs of the church. Ignatius's church is always relational, and the relationships are human as well as divine.

In Ignatius's time and up to Vatican Council II, the metaphor of "the church militant" signified the living members of the church continually struggling to bring about the kingdom of Christ. Together with the "glorified members," they comprise the whole communion of saints. In exploring this image, it helps to recall that Ignatius's fundamental worldview was one of conflict. In living out its essential call, the church inevitably participates in this conflict and must struggle actively against evil. The Rules for Discernment of Spirits indicate the cosmic nature of this struggle in Ignatius's mind. He names that against which the church struggles the "enemy of human nature." For Ignatius, anything antihuman or humanly destructive is diabolical. Asking the one making the Exercises to develop a positive attitude toward and act in harmony with the church militant, then, means asking that person to commit herself constructively and consistently to this struggle against the antihuman wherever it is found (Buckley 1995, 444–46). Struggle is part of obedience today, especially for women, who may capitulate too easily in the face of conflict.

Within the first Rule [352], Ignatius also offers two important balancing images for the church, "Spouse of Christ" and "our Holy Mother." These two metaphors suggest an intimate unity of Christ and the church and provide an antidote to the imagery of the church militant. The images of the church as spouse and mother illumine the immediacy and intensity of the love with which Christ communicates himself to the one making the Exercises (Buckley 1995, 462). The image of the church as mother evokes one totally taken by God, who brings to birth in Love. This reciprocal love allows one to follow the guidance of God. Held together, Ignatius's images create a rich and complex view of the church that invite a response of realistic reverence.

Four hundred years later, a renewed ecclesiology brings new ideas to the Rules for Thinking with the Church. The fruits of Vatican II have affected all contemporary persons, Christian and non-Christian alike. In calling the Council, Pope John XXIII hoped to update the church, to renew it interiorly but also to increase its relevance to the contemporary world. If the church were to be a sacrament of unity in the world, it would first have to confront the scandal of division among the Christian denominations. The very notion of church must undergo conversion.

The vision of church projected by Vatican II is rooted in the mystery of God revealed in Jesus Christ, light of nations. The Council used various biblical images to represent the church, offering a wider palette than did Ignatius: sheepfold, farm, building, temple, as well as mother and spouse (*LG*, #6). In this church, persons are called not just as individuals, but "[a]ll are called to this catholic unity of the people of God....[T]o it belong, or are related in different ways: the catholic faithful, others who believe in Christ, and finally all of humankind, called by God's grace to salvation" (*LG*, #13). The universal call to holiness means loving God and neighbor and thereby fostering a more human manner of life on this earth. The church of Vatican II claims the name "pilgrim," identifying a people on the way, in process, in relationship to the community of saints who have walked this way before us and share humanity's struggles and success.

However, the church envisioned by Vatican II not only looks within, but also outward to the world, desiring solidarity with all people, particularly the poor and afflicted in their joys and hopes, griefs and anxieties. The church recognizes the profound dignity of human persons, yet it is not blind to the reality of sin. It recognizes the essential reality of human community, the value of human activity in the world, and the significance of dialogue as the means of transforming the world into a more just society. In this outward focus, the church remains faithful to its mission to facilitate the coming of the reign of God.

A renewed ecclesiology sees the church in process, continually trying to live out its mission. For Vatican II, church is mystery, the people of God gifted with charisms of lifestyle and ministries of ordained, lay and religious. All are called to holiness on their pilgrim way. This church recognizes its past and continuing role in "the theater of human history," and its credibility today depends as much on what it does as what it says.

The church envisioned by Vatican II is also a community of service, both to the world and to the reign of God. This community follows the servant Jesus Christ, whose life calls all to fullness. This servant church must concern itself with every aspect of the human journey toward life in Christ: economic, political, artistic, scientific as well as moral and spiritual. Jesus told his disciples, "the kingdom of God is very near you" (Mark 1:5); thus the servant church seeks to call attention to this reign of God and to enable its coming into all parts of creation. This reign can be promoted in an infinite number of ways, both far-reaching and down-to-earth: in the feeding, clothing and housing of refugees, including the economic refugees in our own inner cities; in teaching young and old and researching all areas of the arts and sciences; in giving care in the most ordinary of human situations to our children and elders; in struggling with the medical, social, political and environmental causes of lack of well-being; and in caring reverently for life and all that sustains it. Each person has a particular gift to offer on behalf of this reign (Lonsdale 1990, 153–55).

The church is also the ordinary community of support for expressing discipleship and mission; the church sends individuals and groups for apostolic service. This aspect of a Vatican II ecclesiology has particularly strong resonances in the Spiritual Exercises, which conclude with a mission to apostolic service. As God labors on our behalf [236], so we labor on behalf of others. In this context, discernment may be seen as an effective means for continuously putting on the mind and heart of Christ and election as a similarly effective means for choosing a particular embodiment of discipleship. Discernment and election take place in the context of church, and our choices stand in harmony with the history and faith experience of the individual's or group's faith community (Lonsdale 1990, 156). Discernment and church need each other for their completion.

Vatican II has been called the council of the laity, a significant number of whom are women. For this reason, special issues arise concerning the relationships of women and the church. Many women today, Protestant as well as Roman Catholic, recognize that one area of stress and tension in their lives concerns their relationship with a church that professes to hold women in highest esteem while at the same time prohibiting them from full participation. Church tradition and structures have historically been androcentric, patriarchal and hierarchical. Many see specific changes in current practice as only cosmetic and pragmatic, not transformative. Roman Catholic documents continue to legitimize the exclusion of women from full participation in church life and mission while affirming their dignity, gifts and the importance of their participation and leadership. Women in other church structures experience their own versions of alienation and marginalization.

Women making the Spiritual Exercises reflect the rich diversity of the church catholic. Some women's church experience leads to discouragement, alienation and anger; others' experience of church structures and leadership leads them to such despair that they believe they have no alternative but to leave. On the other hand, numerous women commit themselves to stay with the institutional church and work for change from within. Women with theological and ministerial training provide leadership in the church at local, regional and national levels, in rural and urban settings, and in traditional and new ministries. Many women's religious orders have, through chapter acts and priorities, publicly placed themselves in solidarity with women in ecumenical, interfaith and justice networks working for development and liberation. Historically, Protestant women's missionary groups have been rich and effective vehicles for addressing the broader needs of the world's people (Bass 1979); new structures today channel this same energy into solidarity with the human community.

Other women find themselves taking a long perspective, noting that in the big picture women have come a long way and have accomplished as much as is possible in the current situation. These women patiently yet actively wait for change. Others deny that any issues specific to women deserve this much attention in the church, that issues of global scale and widespread moral decline demand priority. Wherever one finds oneself on this broad spectrum, issues of women in the church touch a wide range of the people of God.

## Implications for the Spiritual Exercises

The starting point for the Spiritual Exercises is the Principle and Foundation, which asks the one making the Exercises to situate herself in the context formative for her life, to desire to get in touch with areas of unfreedom and to order her life in God. Although this language emphasizes a person's individual experience, the mystery of God and the life and ministry of Jesus are mediated for the Christian through the church in its various expressions. The past experience and current attitudes of the one making the Exercises will affect her liturgical participation, her election orientation and her sense of call to service in context of the community of faith.

The Exercises move from an individual's consciousness of her own relationship with God to her ability to find God in all things. "All things" includes the church, where increasingly she will be able to identify and distinguish movements of divine breakthrough as well as the reality of sinful human condition. The Rules for Thinking with the Church suggest that, for a contemporary person engaged in the Exercises, the relationship with the church as a community of faith includes critiquing the past, living gracefully in the present with hope and imagining a future that will more adequately express the mystery of the church in its fullness.

By faith, these relationships are animated by the Spirit promised by Jesus. The Spirit discovered through personal discernment in the Spiritual Exercises is the Spirit active in the daily life of the church and its people. This same Spirit asks for a renunciation of power, understood as "power over," replacing it with "power with." The quality of relationships constituting the church in its many manifestations must also reflect the intricate interdependence that marks all of creation under the power of the Spirit.

Ignatius intended the Rules for Thinking with the Church for use by public church persons, primarily Jesuits, but also influential clergy and laymen. Today, however, women also teach and preach and enjoy other leadership roles in the church. The call to prophetic consciousness and action are inherent in the Exercises, so women making them are bound both to critique the domination and to celebrate the evolving liberation of women's experience of church.

Women making the Exercises may find that their experience leads them to discern and to dissent. Anthropologist Gerald Arbuckle (1993, 9) cautions against a narrow and highly restrictive understanding of the word *dissent* that interprets it only as pejorative, a sign of disrespect and repudiation of authoritative teaching. He understands dissent as "the prophetic move by people who genuinely love the gospel and the church to offer reasonable alternative ways of preaching the good news to the world of our time." When understood in this way, dissent signifies a healthy organization or society. Although women may have been socialized to acquiescence, understanding agreement and approval as more in harmony with "true womanhood," the experience of the Exercises may lead more women to this broad understanding of dissent by raising disagreement, objection and protest. These women will cause conflict and opposition as well as pose alternatives. They will combine invaluable prophetic critique and loving service.

## Wisdom for the One Giving the Exercises

The Rules for Thinking with the Church have not been given to all those completing the Spiritual Exercises, even in its enclosed form. Thus, the decision about whether to use the Rules for Thinking with the Church for reflection and prayer can flow from the same criterion Ignatius apparently used: Will this person be dealing with the church in any public way? If so, some version of Rules for Thinking with the Church may invite and challenge her to a positive, irenic, though still demanding and lovingly critical perspective on the church and its visible manifestations in structure and personnel.

The deeper issue, however, concerns each person's relationship to the mystery of church as the very human and limited persons and structures struggling to make Christ more fully present. This mystery seems essential to the dynamic of the Spiritual Exercises, for each person making the Exercises has some understanding and relationship to church. Questions may help facilitate this exploration of Church: What words, images and metaphors would she use to express her vision and experience of church? How has the vision of church emerged from her family and community history? How might her vision deepen as she becomes more and more a disciple of Christ Jesus today? How will that mystery unfold within her and be expressed in her life? As always, the Exercises guide takes his or her cue from the one making the Exercises and her dynamic interaction with the Holy Spirit. Discernment and election in their far-reaching effects become instruments in service to this larger mystery of church.

Similarly, what sense of ministry does the one making the Exercises possess? How might this call be deepened? How will election embody the call to ministry offered to her and to each member of the church through baptism? How has she received the fruits of God's labor and extended that labor in response? What ebb and flow of giving and receiving marks her call at this moment?

To achieve the positive end of the Rules for Thinking with the Church, namely a realistic love for the church in all its human frailty and divine call, those who give the Exercises will need to reframe them for today's women. This is no easy task. Ignatius suggested pertinent answers to precise problems; today's pastoral and theological issues are vastly more diverse and complex and the cultural context much expanded.

Thinking with the church today, theologian Ladislas Orsy believes, must be ecumenical, precisely if it is to be catholic. It must value internal inspiration and the primacy of individual conscience, while at the same time recognizing the importance of participation in a visible manifestation of the church. Contemporary thinking with the church must oppose disintegrating forces within the church and encourage trends that build the community. Finally, thinking with the church today will recognize the Spirit at work in the secular as well as in the sacred (Orsy 1975, 28–31).

Pastorally, seven conclusions follow: (1) The fundamental attitude of a Christian desiring union with the church consists in an interior alertness to the movements of grace that come from the Spirit of God. This Spirit will bear witness about the church. (2) Being one with the church means being one with a mystery, existing in human form in space and in time. "Blessed," says Orsy, "are those who are not shocked by God's unfolding plan and can recognize a divine presence behind a human reality" (1975, 32). (3) Aware of the church, one must proclaim it, but at the same time seek increasing understanding of this mystery. (4) Those who hold authority in the church hold it in trust and *must* use it according to the mind and heart of God; for the rest, the right attitude toward authority entails recognizing it truthfully, giving it neither too little nor too much power. (5) All charisms given by the Holy Spirit for the good of the church must be honored. Likewise, weaknesses in the church call for compassion and healing action. (6) The greater good may sometimes ask one to sacrifice human respect, personal plans or institutional expressions. (7) To be one with the church is to hear and respond to the cry of the poor, and of those who hunger and thirst for justice, and to work for the healing of the divisions among Christians (Orsy 1975, 31–40).

In light of the contemporary ecclesiology thus sketched, the following rereading of the Rules for Thinking with the Church may prove helpful. Alternately, the one making the Exercises may wish to find her own contemporary analogies, metaphors and images.

## A Contemporary Reading of the Rules for Thinking with the Church

The first Rule speaks about putting personal judgment aside and keeping minds disposed and ready to be obedient to the church. A rereading suggests the indifference of the Principle and Foundation and openness and obedience to a contemporary vision of the church, such as that of Vatican II.

The second Rule praises confession and Eucharist. A rereading names the church as sacrament of unity and affirms a wide understanding of liturgical renewal, so that the sacramental life can be accessible to all.

The third Rule praises the prayer of the church for all occasions. A rereading notes the need for church renewal based on faith, individual and communal spirituality and a holiness that transforms the world.

The fourth Rule praises religious life and marriage in a hierarchical order. A rereading affirms the many charisms in the church where holiness is lived out in a variety of lifestyles, while rejecting the former concepts of higher and lower states of life.

The fifth Rule praises the religious vows as a way to perfection. A rereading would affirm the worth of various states of life in order to highlight the deeper value of intentional Christian living and discipleship rooted in baptismal commitment.

The sixth Rule praises the saints and devotional practices. A rereading confirms the importance of the community of saints in a pilgrim church and values the diversity of their religious expression.

The seventh Rule praises fasting and interior and exterior penances. A rereading affirms the value of spiritual disciplines as formative for Christian life.

The eighth Rule praises church architecture and decoration as well as religious signs and symbols that produce prayer and devotion. A rereading values the sacramental and symbolic aspect of worship, recognizing the whole person at prayer.

The ninth Rule praises the teaching of the church and encourages defense rather than attack. A rereading affirms Vatican II and other contemporary statements of faith as human articulations of a search for truth and life in the process of dialogue between the church and the world.

The tenth Rule speaks of approval of superiors and prudence in the manner of criticism. A rereading encourages leadership in the church and reminds all of the responsibility to represent their needs and concerns to persons responsible.

The eleventh Rule speaks of theology and its role in understanding the mystery of God's person and work among God's people. A rereading encourages a variety of theological voices from both the center and the margins—all remaining in creative tension with one another and thereby illuminating the dynamic mystery of God, ever at work among us.

The twelfth Rule concerns comparing the living with the saints. A contemporary rereading discourages holding up present day persons and practices for adulation in such a way as to disparage past peoples and traditions.

The thirteenth Rule concerns the willing suspension of belief in sense data when it conflicts with the mystery of God's revelation. A contemporary rereading stresses the ability of the Holy Spirit to work with even discordant and discrepant perceptions, drawing deeper unity and expressing deeper truth, and trusts that the Holy Spirit works in the church beyond individual perceptions and constructions.

The fourteenth Rule names the tension between God's prevenient grace and human free will. A contemporary rereading encourages speaking and writing of these two mysteries in a way that upholds both.

The fifteenth Rule speaks of the pastoral problems involved in the doctrine of predestination. A contemporary rereading suggests avoiding either pessimism to the point of despair or presumption that one can become transformed purely through personal efforts.

The sixteenth Rule speaks about the paradox of faith and good works. A contemporary rereading stresses that both are gifts of God and one completes the other.

The seventeenth Rule addresses the paradox of grace and free will. A contemporary rereading underscores using freedom of choice to select, from among the various means of development available, those most suitable while recognizing that the Holy Spirit empowers our very desire to choose.

The eighteenth Rule speaks of the motivations involved in serving God. A contemporary rereading encourages the recognition that motives for serving God are always mixed and gratefulness that God brings good out of our confused and conflicted desires.

# Conclusion

From this somewhat extensive investigation of the images and dynamic role of the church in Ignatius's life, in the text and in the experience of contemporary women, one may draw some tentative conclusions about the place of church in discernment, election and ultimately the whole experience of the Spiritual Exercises.

First, plural ecclesiologies suggest that the church is a rich and dynamic mystery that resists being reduced either to one ecclesiology or one metaphor. This variety of images and ecclesiologies itself creates a dynamic tension in which all inescapably live out their spiritual lives.

Second, encountering the mystery of church is inevitable in the one making the Exercises, as church is integrally associated with bringing about the reign of Christ, the apostolic dynamism nourished by the Exercises.

Third, the impulse of contemporary times, and a positive sign in personal discernment, is toward widening the circle of dialogue, attentiveness and affection. Discernment is deepened and enriched as it includes more persons. In this way, one comes closer to the mystery of church, though how that is embodied in an institutional form may vary widely.

Fourth, the Rules for Thinking with the Church, conditioned by time and particular controversies, challenge women and men today more by the positive, committed, faithful attitude they call for than by any particular doctrinal or devotional perspectives.

Finally, this dynamic and faithful attitude coexists with a continuing struggle for the integrity of the church in all its manifestations. A critique issuing from love and commitment to the church empowers each person to work for its renewal and transformation. We are the church.

# Notes

1. The literal translation, according to Buckley (1995, 452, n 39), is: "For the true sense of things which we should maintain in the Church militant, the following rules are to be observed."

2. Vatican Council II calls for this same attitude in *Gaudium et Spes*, #92.

3. According to O'Malley (1993, 49–50), the Rule most likely to cause controversy in Ignatius's time was the fourteenth [366], which advised great caution in preaching about predestination.

4. The principle of justification by faith alone is tied to the Protestant principle because, in our relation to God, it holds that we are dependent on God alone, and in no way on ourselves. We are thus grasped by grace, which is another way of saying that we have faith. The Protestant principle was frequently at work in the theological struggles of Ignatius's time. The 1999 document "Joint Declaration on the Doctrine of Justification by Faith," signed by the Roman Catholic Church and the Lutheran World Federation, marked a historic moment in the reunion of Christian churches and a striking reversal of earlier entrenched positions about the meaning of church.

5. John W. Padberg, "Ignatius, the Popes, and Realistic Reverence," *Studies in the Spirituality of Jesuits* 25 (May 1993): 3–9 gives an overview of the eleven popes during Ignatius's lifetime. Even such a brief sketch reveals the substance of the saying of the time: "Everything is for sale in Rome" (8).

# Appendix

# *AnyWoman:*
# An Imaginative Reappropriation
# of the Spiritual Exercises

Ignatius says: "Imagine the place." Countless persons following his direction have encountered the holy through sensory imagination: seeing, hearing, smelling, tasting and touching the memory of biblical and personal stories. This application of the senses provides strong and vivid summary contemplations for each week of the Spiritual Exercises.

We say: "Imagine any woman's experience of the Spiritual Exercises." Our feminist consciousness challenged us not only to critique and reclaim the Spiritual Exercises for contemporary women, but also to offer something new and creative for the profit of all. So we explored ways to re-create, reenvision, and reimagine alternative means of sensing the mystery of God contained in the Spiritual Exercises. By imagining a woman, pilgrim and seeker living the dynamics of the Exercises, using her own language and familiar symbols from her world, we discovered AnyWoman. We offer a creative summary, our "application of the senses," a way of repetition and reviewing the Exercises through the lens of women's experience.

*AnyWoman* is a modern morality play inspired by medieval drama. The medieval style allows us to personify abstract qualities through imagined characters in action and to tighten and condense mythic realities into a simple text and familiar characters. Conflict resides not so much in external action and events as in the interior struggle of making life choices. Although the language and style may appear unfamiliar, even jarring, compared to contemporary conversation, we hope our readers will engage in this dramatic piece as a way to discover the dynamics of the Spiritual Exercises. An imaginative perspective breaks out of the language of the text and uncovers meaning deeper than words; imagination suggests rather than literally describes. What is left unsaid may be far more important than the actual words of the script.

Our drama is best read aloud, in community. We hope that the characters and their qualities, AnyWoman, Wise Woman, Discernment, Senses, Examen, Principle and Foundation, Grace, Eve, Memory, Intellect, Imagination, Will, Election and Joy will enliven contemporary seekers and deepen their spiritual practices. We trust the reader will recognize AnyWoman's journey converging with her own. We have found that to be true already as we share our recent experience.

## What We Did and Why

Imagine a group of forty persons (women and men) making or directing the Spiritual Exercises. These persons have been together for nine months as participants in the adaptation of the Spiritual Exercises called Retreat in Daily Life. Both directors and those making the retreat gathered at year's end for a day's retreat to deepen and integrate the experience of the Exercises in a communal context. In previous years the culminating activity of the program included four talks on each of the four weeks followed by personal and group reflection and sharing. This time we offered the play *AnyWoman* to assist retreatants in reviewing and deepening the graces of the year. Each of the four scenes from the play stimulated the "memory" of each week. The actors in this reader's theater presentation were the directors of the Spiritual Exercises. They assumed the roles with scripts in hand and a few significant props strategically placed. They read aloud with feeling and understanding while emphasizing those aspects of the play having special meaning for this particular group of retreatants.

The staging was simple and flexible in a large space with various "stations" for each scene. The journey image came to life as main characters AnyWoman and Wise Woman, moved from one space to another gathering characters, "friends," who joined them along the way. Thus the exterior journey became a metaphor for the interior spiritual journey of each retreatant during the year.

At the beginning of the morning, we prepared the group for the drama as a unique way of experiencing the Spiritual Exercises. First, we introduced the cast of characters and the various settings, encouraging the retreatants to be open to the portrayal of each character. Then they were invited to recall their own personal experience of the Exercises: their journey, their spiritual guide/director, their graces and significant movements, their struggles, their choices and their joys. Thus their own experience of the Spiritual Exercises provided the background and disposition for watching the drama unfold on stage.

The retreatants were then encouraged to activate their imaginations by the following suggestions: "See the characters on their journey, imagine the place and its environment. Hear the variety of sounds in the voices of each character. Smell the odors and fragrances in the air and atmosphere. Taste the foods mentioned in the dialogue. Feel what it would be like to walk in the shoes of each character. Allow yourself to respond as you walk through the Exercises with these characters, utilizing your memory and imagination, letting this moment lead you to prayer, the Ignatian colloquy."

The retreatants gathered in movable chairs that allowed them to follow as the actors progressed to various "stations." After each scene the retreatants were invited to take some personal quiet time to reflect on questions related to each week and draw on the memory of their own prayer, naming their own personal graces of that particular week. This process of repetition through imaginative re-creation culminated in a deeper level of knowing and claiming their own experience.

The final activity of the retreat day was a eucharistic celebration. The Jesuit presider (who read the role of Imagination in the play) reminded us all at the beginning of liturgy that "Imagination is the heart of the Exercises." Symbols from each of the characters and the four weeks provided the environment for the Eucharist as we all circled the altar.

## What Happened as a Result

At the conclusion of the day both retreatants and directors were enthusiastic and affirming in their responses. Some said it brought together their whole year's experience in an integrated and deeper way. Another noted that, as a young person coming from a visual culture, it helped her to see the characters in action. Seeing the dynamics of the Exercises enacted made them even more real for the retreatants and directors.

Directors particularly noted the deepening and refreshing values of the drama experience. One noted: "Acting out this very simple but powerful play was more meaningful than any closure dialogue we could have had. *AnyWoman* provided a timely, prayerful and playful way to conclude the retreat." Another noted that her retreatants were able to remember and articulate their own personal prayer experiences: "As they watched and felt along with AnyWoman they were reliving their own experience." Others described their experience as: "Powerful, emotional, spiritual, awesome." Another realized that terms such as "discernment" and "imagination" took on new meaning as well as revealing something missed earlier in the retreat. One director commented afterward: "I saw before me not just the memory of the Four Weeks but I envisioned the Exercises becoming a whole unified tapestry displayed before us. I felt a deep sense of gratitude to be part of the drama, for we (directors and retreatants) can all recognize AnyWoman in ourselves."

Somebody asked us, "What would Ignatius say about all this?" We think Ignatius would approve, for he knew that truth is deeper than words. He was a visionary who knew the power of imagination, a man unafraid to be moved to tears, a man who valued reason, will and imagination, a man who knew the reality of human embodiment for felt knowledge leads to great desires, and a man who desired freedom for people that they might do great things for God.

Now we invite you to cross the threshold into the world of the imagination and *AnyWoman* and see for yourself.

## AnyWoman

### Scene One

STORYTELLER: Good day and welcome. Here begins a story of God and AnyWoman, who is precious in God's sight. On their journey together, God gifts AnyWoman with many friends, each a messenger and unique reflection of Godself. One day AnyWoman sets out on a quest, following her questions: "How do I name and claim my true self? How and with whom am I in relationship? How deeply can I commit myself? How can I live a life of love and service more fully?"

Carrying her questions, she first followed a sign called "Faith" although she felt waves of strange uncertainty as she became more conscious of the weight of her questions. Before long, she saw a figure walking ahead of her. She ran to catch up, seeking company. She soon discovered her companion was an old woman whose strong, peaceful presence calmed her. They walked in silence for a while.

ANYWOMAN: Who are you? Where are you going?

WISE WOMAN: Why do you ask?

ANYWOMAN: I am seeking someone wise enough to show me how to care for my questions as I carry them.

WISE WOMAN: How far are you willing to walk and how sturdy are your sandals?

ANYWOMAN: I am willing to walk as long and as far as my questions take me to discover the true meaning of my life. My sandals are new; see how sturdy they are. You look as though you have walked many pathways and pondered many of life's questions. I need someone to walk and talk with me. Will you accompany me, guide me, be a friend and mentor, a companion on the way?

WISE WOMAN: I will walk with you, but you must let your own questions and desires direct you. You will also need some other companions for your journey. They will appear when you need them. Each has something special to offer you. None is more important than she who is behind us now. How frequently we forget her and what wisdom she has to offer if we but call upon her and patiently wait for her. Her name is Memory.

MEMORY: Good day, AnyWoman. I will serve you as you call upon me. In my book I hold your story, all the experiences of your life 'til now, the brokenness and the blessings, the happy and the sad, the wise and the foolish, the finished and the incomplete. I also hold the treasured stories of all the people of your family, by blood and faith, the sacred stories told from generation to generation, those remembered and those forgotten. I will walk as your companion and you can call upon me as you need me.

ANYWOMAN: Thank you, Memory. Sometimes I do forget what is important. I must remember to remember.

WISE WOMAN: In order to know what is important in all life experiences past and present, you need another companion to assist you, a precious one, Discernment.

DISCERNMENT: Greetings, AnyWoman! I will walk with you and help you choose pathways leading you to what you most desire. Yet, to walk with me demands that you pay attention. You need to note all that moves you toward joy or sadness and all that draws you toward goodness and light—or the appearance of light. To profit from my companionship you must learn to be attentive to every moment of your life. Here are more companions who will aid you in this task.

SENSES: I can see, I can hear, I can smell, I can taste, I can touch. What a great gift your senses are for you! What a gift your body is for you: a way of life for communicating with all creation, other persons and God. AnyWoman, how can you taste and see the goodness of God if you haven't enjoyed the color and delicious sweetness of strawberries or the mellowness of a fine wine?

EXAMEN: Wait, don't forget me! I'm here to remind you, AnyWoman, of those moments and movements of everyday that have meaning for you, more than you realize. Each day of your life is like a book, to reveal to you the truth of the mystery of your own life, the blessings and challenges of each day, the sources of your own truth and temptations of falsehood, the lies of your life. But most of all I am your reminder of the graciousness of God, sometimes hidden, sometimes revealed, but always present in the dailyness of life.

WISE WOMAN: Now, AnyWoman, with these companions to assist you, you must continue your journey by standing still. You must plant your feet firmly on the ground, feeling the earth between your toes, casting your eyes to the boundless sky above your head. You must claim your own perspective—where you stand determines what you see. An infant crawling on the ground has a different view of the world than a child sitting in the high branches of a tree beside a river. You must place before your mind's eye the questions with which you began your journey. "How do I name and claim my true self, my relationships, my commitment, my future?" Take time to ponder: What does life mean to you? How do you see your life in relationship to creation: to all the earth and its life, including human persons, female and male? How do you see your relationship with God? Who is God for you? And how is all this life interconnected?

ANYWOMAN: But how do I begin to do this?

WISE WOMAN: Well, let me introduce you to the twins, Principle and Foundation. They are identical. You can't tell them apart except that one carries a shovel and the other a watering can. You see, wherever they go they are trying to plant and nourish seeds of truth and life, helping the roots to grow strong and deep. They will most often appear when anxiety or doubt or fear plague you. Their job is always to see that you are grounded in the truth of who you are and who God is.

PRINCIPLE AND FOUNDATION: Good travels to you, AnyWoman! Here is a gift for your journey. It is a walking staff called Indifference. This staff will support you as you weigh your decisions and allow you to walk with energy and purpose toward your goal.

WISE WOMAN: Now, AnyWoman, to set out on this journey you must compose yourself with the help of these companions and know clearly what you desire.

ANYWOMAN: Oh, Wise Woman, now I feel confused and uncertain. How can I know what I want?

GRACE: Perhaps I can help you, AnyWoman. My name is Grace and I will help you ask for what you truly need. Here is a bracelet for you to wear with beads of various shapes and colors. You will find that each bead holds a gift for you. Just let me know when you are ready.

ANYWOMAN: Thank you, Grace; all of a sudden I hardly feel like myself. In the company of so much goodness and so many friends to help me, I feel ashamed and confused. This journey seems too hard and asks too much. And I don't find God in any of this. Perhaps I should turn back. I wonder if I really want to set out on this journey, and besides my feet are hurting.

WISE WOMAN: Ah! I feel the movement of the enemy of human nature close by, perhaps in those shadows by the side of the road. And where is God? Pay attention, AnyWoman, to the desires deep in your heart; you will discover God. Now you must trust me. Your journey is already underway. Trust that your questions will lead you. But it is getting dark and it is time to rest. I bless you AnyWoman. Be attentive to God's visitations this evening.

STORYTELLER: The night passes and the day dawns.

ANYWOMAN: Wise one, awake! I must tell you of a dream I had last night. I saw a struggle, a cosmic conflict between the angels, beings of such beauty and power. I watched in awe and felt within myself that I was being drawn right into their struggle. Before the Holy One of such light and love, each had to choose and name its allegiance. I felt a force within me drawn first to one then to the other. At a final moment I found myself surrounded by those whose "No" to light and love thrust them into darkness and a terrible abyss. I too was falling, falling....Then I awakened. What does this dream mean?

WISE WOMAN: That is for you to discover. Walk a while with Memory and Discernment; perhaps they can help you understand.

STORYTELLER: So AnyWoman walks on ahead, talking, listening, pondering in the company of her new friends. A little later their conversation is interrupted as they pass a fruit stand and a pleasant middle-aged woman calls out.

EVE: Apples, fresh apples for your journey! Red, yellow and green, many colors for many tastes. Stop a while and refresh yourselves! This fruit of the earth captures the sunlight in its shiny skin and delicious taste, while its juice will quench your thirst.

ANYWOMAN: Let's stop here and try some. Where did you come from?

EVE: My name is Eve, and this is Eve's Stand. Now, don't jump to conclusions and run away. Others may have told you about me; but let me speak for myself. I am a woman, mother of the living, created in God's image along with my partner Adam. The two of us were equal in God's eyes, from the beginning. I made a mistake—that's evidence of being human, isn't it? But I am not my mistake. The real mistake, the original sin, is whatever destroys the equal balance of relationships. God's original plan intended partnership: humans with the earth, women with men, persons with God. I am Eve, and the God I know who created and loves me understands that human beings make mistakes. And God is gracious and forgiving. What is most important is God's love, not my mistake. Don't blame me for the whole world's sin.

ANYWOMAN: Sin! Maybe that was what my dream was about. Maybe sin is about struggle for power, dominion and deception. Maybe sin blinds me to who I am really meant to be. There are times in my life when I feel as if all I am doing is playing a role, sometimes to fit another person's expectations of me and other times to take the easy way out: roles of niceness, passivity, silence, helper, manipulator, victim, peacemaker, beauty queen, superwoman. It's painful to remember how the power of these roles can take over my life. It feels like…hell. I used to say I didn't believe in hell. But if I'm honest, there are moments in my life I'd call "hell." These are only tiny glimpses of the "hells" human beings have created for one another. The story of humankind can be read as a cycle of dominating and deceiving one another expressed in all kinds of violence. How can there be a God when life can be such hell?

WISE WOMAN: Look at the sun, it can warm or burn you; taste the water, it can refresh or poison you; breathe the air, it can strengthen or strangle you; feel the earth, it can nurture or starve you. Human freedom, it can liberate or destroy you! AnyWoman, your only choice is how you live your life right now. At this moment you are *here*.

SENSES: Open your eyes to look around at the beauty of creation. Open your ears to sounds and silence. Feel your heart beat and the air in your lungs…you are ALIVE.

MEMORY: Remember all the people in your life who have cared for you, who are important to you…you are LOVED.

EVE: You are a woman, created, loved and forgiven by God.

WISE WOMAN: All is gift. You can choose how you wish to respond. What is your deepest desire?

ANYWOMAN: Where are you, God, and who are you? An apple falls and the earth's cushion breaks the fall. A small bird's melody is answered from a distant treetop. The stream rushes by filled with glistening fish. A mother gives birth and holds her tiny infant to her breast. All creation praises you for the gift of life, and so do I. I who am AnyWoman. All these gifts of creation are signs of your love and presence to me. O God, who am I to be surrounded by such love? I have ignored you, doubted you and forgotten the stories of your faithful love for all creation. I have looked by myself for answers to my questions and forgotten you, the source of truth and love. You have called me by name, "AnyWoman." I am precious, and you love me—thank you!

**Scene Two**

STORYTELLER: Scene two—It is midday the next day. AnyWoman and Wise Woman are continuing their journey together and they come to a crossroads.

WISE WOMAN: Well, AnyWoman, now you need to choose what direction to take. The path to the right will return home, and you can conclude your journey. Or you may continue down the road we are on.

ANYWOMAN: I've learned a lot about myself and my questions. It would be easier to return to where I've come from. This might be a good place to conclude our journey. But there is a restlessness within me, an unfinished feeling, a sense that there is more to this journey. (Pause) Look, by the side of the road up ahead. There is something glittering, caught between the stones of that old wall. Let's continue down this road to see what is there. Look, it's an old locket...

WISE WOMAN:...with an inscription of an ancient royal crest still visible. It reminds me of the story from long ago about a mighty king and queen and their royal partnership. This royal couple, so the story goes, were kind and generous, leaders for their people, brave and wise. They called forth those to serve and struggle with them to establish a reign of peace and justice for all people. Among the most courageous and committed of their followers was a woman who defied the customs of her times by leaving her comfortable and secure life to join the royal supporters. She was revered for her intelligence and compassionate heart. She gave all her energy and passion to the struggle to bring about the vision they shared, royalty and commoner together.

ANYWOMAN: Oh, how I too would like to live life like that! I want to live with courage. I want to make a difference. I want to join others bringing it about. I want to give my life to someone or something I really believe in.

STORYTELLER: As they continue, Wise Woman begins to sing a chant under her breath:

WISE WOMAN: Mary, Theotokos, we remember you, be with us.
Miriam, we remember you, be with us
Mary of Magdala, we remember you, be with us
Phoebe, we remember you, be with us
Thecla, we remember you, be with us
Macrina, we remember you, be with us
Egeria, we remember you, be with us
Helena, we remember you, be with us
Lioba, we remember you, be with us
Hildegard, we remember you, be with us
Julian, we remember you, be with us
Elizabeth, we remember you, be with us
Catherine, we remember you, be with us
Teresa, we remember you, be with us
Mary Ward, we remember you, be with us
Ann Lee, we remember you, be with us
Kateri Tekakwitha, we remember you, be with us
Sojourner Truth, we remember you, be with us
Dorothy Day, we remember you, be with us

ANYWOMAN: What are you mumbling along the way?

WISE WOMAN: It is my litany of courageous women, women who lived and struggled for a vision: I call them our mothers in faith. They all followed a "King," the Messiah, the Prince of Peace, Emmanuel, Jesus, son of Mary of Nazareth.

ANYWOMAN: I know the stories of Jesus, but they seem so long ago, so distant. What could they contribute to my search now?

STORYTELLER: As AnyWoman fingers the beads on her bracelet, Grace appears.

GRACE: All you need to ask for is that the stories of Jesus will lead you to know him more deeply and follow him more closely.

WISE WOMAN: Look ahead, an old church. Let's go inside and sit down. At this time of day the colors of the sun will shine right through the stained glass.

ANYWOMAN: Who are those figures moving about in the front of the church?

WISE WOMAN: Those are the craftspersons and artisans waiting to serve you. Their names are Intellect, Imagination and Will. Their job is to assist you to see and understand the mystery hidden in the stained-glass windows. Then you can choose the part you want to play in the continuing story.

ANYWOMAN: I don't understand. None of this makes sense to me.

INTELLECT: Sit down here by the first window and think about what you see.

ANYWOMAN: It reminds me of a scene on a Christmas card.

MEMORY: And when you were a little girl…

ANYWOMAN: I had forgotten; I played a shepherd in the Christmas play. I remember it was just as though I were really there. And what is that next window?…Up there next to you, Imagination.

IMAGINATION: With my eye I see Mary, Elizabeth, Anna, Martha, Mary, Mary of Magdala, Widow of Naim, bent over woman, woman with the hemorrhage, daughter of Jairus, Samaritan woman…

ANYWOMAN: Where do you see them? I've looked all around this church. I didn't see any of those women in the windows. Where are they?

IMAGINATION: They are hidden in the glass. You must imagine them into the scene with Jesus, for they are also his friends and disciples. Their stories are part of your story; you must continue to look for them everywhere.

WILL: And when you discover them, let them speak to you, in ways that touch your heart.

STORYTELLER: So AnyWoman engages Intellect, Imagination and Will in an animated and lengthy conversation. Time passes as the sun begins to set and the color of the windows changes in the shadows.

WISE WOMAN: AnyWoman, it is getting late in the day. We must move on.

ANYWOMAN: Oh! Can't we stay longer? It's so peaceful and quiet here. There are so many untold stories of Jesus: by the lake and walking through the fields, talking with people, healing them. We haven't seen them all. And Intellect, Imagination, Will and I were talking about building a new church with women's windows, too.

WISE WOMAN: But even Jesus had to move on. There came a moment when Jesus needed to decide. When he did, he turned to walk toward Jerusalem.

ANYWOMAN: Oh, how I hate to make decisions. It always means giving up something. It's always risky. Suppose I make a mistake? How can I be sure what God is calling me to? Sometimes I feel I should move in one direction; other times I feel pulled in the opposite direction. It makes me dizzy.

WISE WOMAN: What you need is balance, a way to measure your steps as your learn to walk in God's ways. But now, judging from who is standing at the door of the church, God is calling you to dance. Look who just arrived; it's Election, the dancing teacher.

ELECTION: I am the one who is the interpreter of movement and the teacher of various steps. You will need your staff of Indifference at all times. But I will teach you various steps for each partner: one type for Intellect, another for Will, a specific step for Memory and yet another for Senses and Imagination. Whatever the movement, I, Election, will be there to assist you to learn the steps you need for the dance that will move you toward God who calls you.

WISE WOMAN: You didn't think this journey would just involve walking, did you?

## Scene Three

STORYTELLER: Scene three takes place late in the day and AnyWoman and Wise Woman are crossing a bridge.

ANYWOMAN: Can't we rest awhile? I'm tired and it's getting dark.

WISE WOMAN: I, too, would like to pause and let this night pass, but it is the darkness that we must enter. Come walk by my side. Here it is important that we journey together.

ANYWOMAN: Your voice is serious and sad; it makes me feel afraid.

WISE WOMAN: It is a time for fear, the kind of fear that only love can overcome. But listen. I hear the sound of water. Look, there is a stream. Let us pause and let the water refresh us. Here, AnyWoman, drink from this cup, and then take off your sandals and let me wash your feet.

ANYWOMAN: Oh, no, I can't let you do that. I should be washing yours.

WISE WOMAN: Just rest and receive; your time of service will come soon enough.

ANYWOMAN: It's getting so dark. I can hardly see you now. Where are you? Are you still close by?

WISE WOMAN: Yes, don't be afraid. Can you come and pray one hour with me?

ANYWOMAN: Of course, but my eyes are heavy, the night is so dark, I haven't eaten, and the travel today has tired me. Oh, I almost stumbled over this mound of earth. I can't see, but it feels like something is buried underneath. It feels like a mask, only part of it is burned. How curious. I wonder whose masks these were and what they mean?

WISE WOMAN: This discovery of yours, AnyWoman, reminds me that masks invite us to cross a threshold into mystery, for masks reveal a special kind of story. When one puts on a mask, the wearer shares the power of the story it represents, whatever its sentiments. Masks make visible the inner creative spirit of the human mind and heart. Are you ready? Here put this one on.

STORYTELLER: Wise Woman hands her the Jesus mask to put on.

ANYWOMAN: My Father, if it is possible, let this cup pass from me; yet not as I will, but as you will.

STORYTELLER: Immediately she pulls off the mask and places it at her feet.

ANYWOMAN: No, it's too much. You can't ask that of me. Let me try on another.

STORYTELLER: The old woman offers her many masks: Peter, the serving girl, Pilate's wife, Pilate, soldier. Tentatively AnyWoman chooses the mask of the crowd and places it over her face.

ANYWOMAN: Hail King of the Jews! Crucify Him!

STORYTELLER: She quickly takes off the mask and cries aloud:

ANYWOMAN: How could they? He was so good. I don't know what to do. I need the grace to go on, to enter the mystery of this mask.

STORYTELLER: As she fingers a bead on her bracelet, Grace appears again.

GRACE: If you hold the bead of Compassion, AnyWoman, you will have the ability to feel with, to just be with, the pain and the suffering. Here is your mask.

STORYTELLER: She hands AnyWoman the Jesus mask again.

WISE WOMAN: What do you see, AnyWoman, through the eyes of this mask?

ANYWOMAN: I see the homeless, the starving, refugees, abused women and children. I see people killing other people. I see the land dying from drought and the forests burning. The people, the whole planet is suffering and crying out to God in pain: "My God, my God, why have you forsaken me? O God, into your hands I commend my spirit."

STORYTELLER: The wise woman watches and waits at a distance.

## Scene Four

STORYTELLER: Scene four: The sun is rising. AnyWoman awakens, blinking with the light in her eyes.

ANYWOMAN: Where am I? It's a garden, with stream and rocks and beautiful flowers and trees. There is the sun just coming up over the distant hills. I hear the whir of a hummingbird's wings, I see fresh dew and smell the fragrance of the rose petals. And look! A beautiful butterfly bursting forth from its bindings. This day feels different. Something is new. And there is a new bead on my bracelet; I never noticed it before.

GRACE: Here I am again, but this time to celebrate with you, to be glad and rejoice. I also want you to meet my special friend. She is a musician and her name is Joy.

JOY: (singing) Morning has broken...

How can I keep from singing?...

Jesu Joy of our desiring...

Alleluia! The strife is over, the battle done...

I know my redeemer lives...

WISE WOMAN: I hear singing, so early in the morning. It must be Joy arriving to join us on our journey.

JOY: There is good news in the town. A mother has just been reunited with her son. She thought he was lost and now he is found. People have been arriving from all over telling stories of meeting him along their way. The whole town is rejoicing.

WISE WOMAN: You go along into the town, AnyWoman, for now I must be on my way. Share with the people the treasures of your journey.

STORYTELLER: As AnyWoman continues to the edge of town she is excited but a little apprehensive.

ANYWOMAN: Where am I? This looks strangely familiar, as though I've been here before. Those people *are* my neighbors. I'm home! I've never seen life like this before. My questions have led me home, and yet I know everything in a new way. It's beautiful! Everywhere I look, it is as though God dwells in all things, the rays coming from the sun, the rain falling from the clouds, all as gift. Look there is a rainbow arching over the whole town. I am so grateful. God, take and receive all I have and possess—all the friends and gifts you've given to me: Wise Woman, Memory, Discernment, Senses, Intellect, Imagination, Will, Joy, all the Graces of this journey. Everything I have and possess you've given to me, and now I want to return all to you. Do with these friends as you wish. Share them with others who also journey. All I ask and desire now, O God, is your love and your grace. You are enough for me.

WISE WOMAN: Good-bye—until we meet the next time.

## Epilogue

STORYTELLER: Thus concludes the story of AnyWoman. Since you now have met her and her companions, take to heart what you have learned from her questions: "How do I name and claim my true self? How and with whom am I in relationship? How deeply can I commit myself? How can I live a life of love and service more fully?" Think about the difference this journey makes in your life. For AnyWoman now knows that love and mutual sharing happens through both words and deeds. Speak and act faithfully, with wisdom and courage and compassion. May AnyWoman, Wise Woman and all their friends accompany you.

# Works Cited

Arbuckle, Gerald A. 1993. *Refounding the church: Dissent for leadership*. Maryknoll, N.Y.: Orbis Books.

Aschenbrenner, George. 1972. Consciousness examen. *Review for Religious* 31 (January): 14–21.

Augustine. 1961. *Confessions*. Translated by R. S. Pine-Coffin. New York: Penguin Books.

Barnes, Michael. 1989. The body in the Spiritual Exercises of Ignatius of Loyola. *Religion* 19 (1989): 263–273.

Barry, William. 1994. *Allowing the Creator to deal with the creature*. New York: Paulist.

Barry, William, and William Connolly. 1982. *The practice of spiritual direction*. New York: Seabury Press.

Bass, Dorothy. 1979. "Their prodigious influence": Women, religion and reform in antebellum America. In *Women of spirit: Female leadership in the Jewish and Christian traditions,* ed. Rosemary Ruether and Eleanor McLaughlin, 279–300. New York: Simon and Schuster.

Belenky, Mary Field, Blythe McVicker Clinchy, Nancy Rule Goldberger and Jill Mattuck Tarule. 1986. *Women's ways of knowing: The development of self, voice and mind*. New York: Basic Books.

Bergan, Jacqueline, and S. Marie Schwan. 1985. *Love: A guide for prayer*. Winona, Minn.: St. Mary's Press.

Berry, Thomas, and Brian Swimme. 1992. *The universe story: An autobiography of planet earth*. New York: Harper and Row.

Blaisdell, Charmarie J. 1988. Calvin's and Loyola's letters to women: Politics and spiritual counsel in the sixteenth century. In *Calviniana: Ideas and influence of John Calvin,* ed. Robert Schnucher, 235–53. *Sixteenth-century essays & studies,* Vol. 10. Kirksville, Mo.: Sixteenth-Century Journal Publishers.

Boyle, Marjorie O'Rourke. 1983. Angels black and white: Loyola's spiritual discernment in historical perspective. *Theological Studies* 44 (June): 241–57.

Bridges, William. 1980. *Transitions: Making sense of life's changes.* Reading, Mass.: Addison-Wesley.

Bryant, Christopher. 1984. Images and the psyche. *The Way* 24 (April): 83–91.

Buckley, Michael. 1995. Ecclesial mysticism in the Spiritual Exercises of Ignatius. *Theological Studies* 56 (September): 441–63.

Burrows, Ruth. 1980. *Guidelines for mystical prayer.* Denville, N.J.: Dimension Books.

Capps, Donald. 1984. *Pastoral care and hermeneutics.* Philadelphia: Fortress Press.

Carr, Anne. 1988, 1996. *Transforming grace: Christian tradition and women's experience.* San Francisco: Harper and Row. 2nd ed., New York: Continuum.

Christ, Carol. 1980. *Diving deep and surfacing: Women writers on the spiritual quest.* Boston: Beacon Press.

Clancy, Thomas. 1978. *The conversational word of God.* St. Louis: Institute of Jesuit Sources.

Clark, Elizabeth A. 1983. *Women in the early church.* Wilmington Del.: Michael Glazier.

Colledge, Edmund, and James Walsh, trans. 1978. *Julian of Norwich: Showings.* Classics of Western Spirituality. New York: Paulist.

Conroy, Maureen. 1995. Prayer and life: Experiencing the fullness of God's love. *The Way Supplement* 82 (spring): 15–26.

Cowan, Marian, and John Futrell. 1993. *Companions in grace: A handbook for directors of the Spiritual Exercises of St. Ignatius of Loyola.* Kansas City: Sheed and Ward. Reprint of *The Spiritual Exercises of St. Ignatius of Loyola: A Handbook for Directors.* Ministry Training Services, 1981.

Cusson, Gilles, S.J. 1988. *Biblical theology and the Spiritual Exercises.* St. Louis: Institute of Jesuit Sources.

Daley, Brian E. 1995. To be more like Christ: The background and implications of "The Three Kinds of Humility." *Studies in the Spirituality of Jesuits* 27 (January 1995): 6–39.

de Dalmases, Candido, S.J. 1985. *Ignatius of Loyola, founder of the Jesuits: His life and work.* Translated by Jerome Aixalá, S.J. St. Louis: Institute of Jesuit Sources.

———. 1991. *Francis Borgia: Grande of Spain, Jesuit, saint.* Translated by Cornelius Michael Buckley, S.J. St. Louis: Institute of Jesuit Sources.

de Mello, Anthony. 1978. *Sadhana: A way to God.* St. Louis: Institute of Jesuit Sources.

Dreyer, Elizabeth A. 1989. *Passionate women: Two medieval mystics.* New York: Paulist.

———. 1996. Narratives of the Spirit. In *Proceedings of the Fifty-first Annual Convention of the Catholic Theological Society of America.* San Diego, 45–90.

Dyke, Doris Jean. 1991. *Crucified women.* Toronto: United Church Publishing House.

*Economic justice for all: Pastoral letter on Catholic social teaching and the U.S. economy.* 1986. Washington D.C.: National Conference of Catholic Bishops.

Egan, Harvey. 1987. *Ignatius the mystic*. Wilmington, Del.: Michael Glazier.

English, John. 1995. *Spiritual freedom*. 2nd ed. Chicago: Loyola University Press.

Fabella, Virginia. 1989. A common methodology for diverse Christologies. In *With passion and compassion: Third-world women doing theology*, ed. Virgina Fabella and Mercy Amba Oduyoye, 108–17. Maryknoll, N.Y.: Orbis.

Farganis, Sondra. 1986. *Social construction of the feminine character*. Totowa, N.J.: Rowman and Littlefield.

Farley, Margaret A. 1986. *Personal commitments: Making, keeping, changing*. San Francisco: Harper.

Fischer, Kathleen. 1988. *Women at the well: Feminist perspectives on spiritual direction*. New York: Paulist.

———. 1989. The imagination in spirituality. *The Way Supplement* 66 (Autumn): 96–105.

Fischer, Kathleen, and Thomas Hart. 1995. *Christian foundations: An introduction to faith in our time*. New York: Paulist.

Flannery, Austin, O.P., ed. 1996. *Vatican Council II: Constitutions, decrees, declarations*. Northport, N.Y.: Costello Publishing Company.

Fleming, David, S.J. 1978. *The Spiritual Exercises of St. Ignatius: A literal translation and a contemporary reading*. St. Louis: Institute of Jesuit Sources.

Frankl, Viktor. 1959. *Man's search for meaning: An introduction to logotherapy*. Pocket Book Edition. New York: Simon and Schuster.

Freedman, David. 1983. Woman, a power equal to man. *Biblical Archeology Review* 9 (January/February): 56–58.

Ganss, George E. 1973. Thinking with the church: The spirit of St. Ignatius's rules. *The Way Supplement* 20 (autumn): 72–82.

————, ed. 1991. *Ignatius of Loyola: "Spiritual Exercises" and selected works*. Classics of Western Spirituality. New York: Paulist.

Gendlin, Eugene. 1981. *Focusing*. 2nd ed. New York: Bantam.

Gilligan, Carol. 1982. *In a different voice: Psychological theory and women's development*. Cambridge: Harvard University Press.

Grant, Jacquelyn. 1993. Come to my help, Lord, for I'm in trouble: Womanist Jesus and the mutual struggle for liberation. In *Reconstructing the Christ symbol: Essays in feminist Christology*, ed. Maryanne Stevens. New York: Paulist.

Gray, Howard. 1993. Changing structures. *The Way Supplement* 76 (Spring): 72–84.

Gula, Richard, S.S. 1989. *Reason informed by faith: Foundations of Catholic morality*. New York: Paulist.

Hart, Ray. 1968. *Unfinished man and the imagination*. New York: Herder and Herder.

Herrera, Marina. 1993. Who do you say Jesus is? Christological reflections from a Hispanic woman's perspective. In *Reconstructing the Christ symbol: Essays in feminist Christology*, ed. Maryanne Stevens. New York: Paulist.

Houdek, Frank. 1995. The limitation of Ignatian prayer. *The Way Supplement* 82 (Spring): 26–34.

Ignatius of Loyola. 1970. *The Constitutions of the Society of Jesus*. Translated by George Ganss. St. Louis: The Institute of Jesuit Sources.

————. 1991a. The Autobiography. In *Ignatius of Loyola: "Spiritual Exercises" and selected works*, 66–111. Translated by Parmananda R. Divarkar. Edited by George E. Ganss, S.J. New York: Paulist.

————. 1991b. The Spiritual Exercises. In *Ignatius of Loyola: "Spiritual Exercises" and selected works*, ed. and trans. George E. Ganss, S.J., 113–214. New York: Paulist.

Ivens, Michael. 1983. The eighteenth annotation and the early Directories. *The Way Supplement* 46 (Spring): 3–10.

Jack, Dana Crowley. 1991. *Silencing the self: Women and depression.* New York: HarperCollins.

Jesuits and the situation of women. 1995. 34th General Congregation, Rome. *Origins* 24 (April 13): 740–42.

Johnson, Elizabeth A. 1991. The maleness of Christ. In *The special nature of women?*, ed. Anne Carr and Elisabeth Schüssler Fiorenza, 108–16. Philadelphia: Trinity Press International.

———. 1992. *She who is: The mystery of God in feminist theological discourse.* New York: Crossroad.

———. 1993. *Women, earth and Creator Spirit.* New York: Paulist.

———. 1996. Turn to the heavens and the earth: Retrieval of the cosmos in theology. In *Proceedings of the Fifty-first Annual Convention of the Catholic Theological Society of America.* San Diego, 11–14.

Johnston, William. 1995. *Mystical theology: The science of love.* London: Harper Collins.

Jordan, Judith, Alexandra Kaplan, Jean Baker Miller, Irene Stiver, and Janet L. Surrey. 1991. *Women's growth in connection.* New York: Guilford Press.

Kaschak, Ellyn. 1992. *Engendered lives: A new psychology of women's experience.* New York: Basic Books.

Kavanaugh, Kieran, and Otillo Rodriguez, trans. 1976. *The collected works of St. Teresa of Avila.* Washington, D.C.: Institute of Carmelite Studies.

Kelly, Justin. 1991. Absence into presence: A theology of imagination. Warren Lecture Series 16. University of Tulsa, September 8, 1991, 12–16.

King, Ursula. 1993. *Women and spirituality: Voices of protest and promise.* 2nd ed. University Park, Pa.: Pennsylvania State University Press.

# Works Cited

LaCugna, Catherine. 1991. *God for us*. San Francisco: Harper.

Levine, Amy-Jill. 1992. Matthew. In *The women's bible commentary*, ed. Carol A. Newsom and Sharon H. Ringe, 261. Louisville: Westminster/John Knox.

Liebert, Elizabeth. 1992. *Changing life patterns: Adult development in spiritual direction*. New York: Paulist.

———. 1996. Coming home to themselves: Spiritual care of women. In *Through the eyes of women: Insights for pastoral care*, ed. Jeanne Stevenson Moessner, 257–84. Minneapolis: Fortress.

Lonsdale, David. 1990. *Eyes to see, ears to hear: An introduction to Ignatian spirituality*. Chicago: Loyola University Press.

———. 1992. *Listening to the music of the Spirit: The art of discernment*. Notre Dame, Ind.: Ave Maria Press.

May, Gerald. 1982a. *Care of mind, care of spirit: A psychiatrist explores spiritual direction*. San Francisco: Harper and Row.

———. 1982b. *Will and spirit: A contemplative psychology*. San Francisco: Harper and Row.

———. 1988. *Addiction and grace*. San Francisco: Harper and Row.

McFague, Sallie. 1993. *The body of God: An ecological theology*. Minneapolis: Fortress Press.

McGrath, Thomas. 1993. The place of desires in the Ignatian Exercises. *The Way Supplement* 76 (Spring): 25–31.

Meissner, W. W., S.J., M.D. 1992. *Ignatius of Loyola: The psychology of a saint*. New Haven: Yale University Press.

Merchant, Carolyn. 1983. *The death of nature: Women, ecology, and the scientific revolution*. San Francisco: Harper.

Miles, Margaret. 1981. *Fullness of life: Historical foundations for a new asceticism*. Philadelphia: Westminster.

———. 1992. *Desire and delight: A new reading of Augustine's "Confessions."* New York: Crossroad.

Morton, Nelle. 1985. *The journey is home.* Boston: Beacon Press.

Nelson, James. 1983. *Between two gardens: Reflections on sexuality and religious experience.* New York: Pilgrim Press.

Neuger, Christie Cozad. 1991. Women's depression: Lives at risk. In *Women in travail and transition: A new pastoral care,* ed. Maxine Glaz and Jeanne Stevenson Moessner, 146–61. Minneapolis: Fortress Press.

———. 1993. A feminist perspective on pastoral counseling. In *Clinical handbook of pastoral Counseling,* vol. 2, ed. Robert J. Wicks and Richard D. Parsons, 195–209. New York: Paulist.

Noffke, Suzanne, ed. and trans. 1980. *Catherine of Siena: "The dialogue."* New York: Paulist.

Norris, Kathleen. 1993. *Dakota: A spiritual geography.* New York: Houghton-Mifflin.

O'Connell, Timothy E. 1990. *Principles for a Catholic morality.* San Francisco: HarperCollins.

O'Malley, John. 1991. Early Jesuit spirituality: Spain and Italy. In *Christian spirituality: Post-reformation and modern,* ed. Louis Dupré and Don E. Saliers, 3–27. New York: Crossroad.

———. 1993. *The first Jesuits.* Cambridge, Mass.: Harvard University Press.

O'Murchu, Diarmuid. 1997. *Quantum theology: Spiritual implications of the new physics.* New York: Crossroad.

Orsy, Ladislas. 1975. On being one with the church today. *Studies in the Spirituality of Jesuits* 8 (January): 21–41.

Padberg, John W., S.J. 1993. Ignatius, the popes, and realistic reverence. *Studies in the Spirituality of Jesuits* 25 (May): 2–38.

Palmer, Martin E., trans. and ed. 1996. *On giving the Spiritual Exercises: The early Jesuit manuscript directories and the official directory of 1599.* St. Louis: Institute of Jesuit Sources.

Pelikan, Jaroslav. 1985. *Jesus through the centuries: His place in the history of culture.* New Haven: Yale University Press.

Peters, William A. M., S.J. 1967. *The Spiritual Exercises of St. Ignatius: exposition and interpretation.* Jersey City, N.J.: Program to Adapt the Spiritual Exercises.

Piercy, Marge. 1996. *City of darkness, city of light.* New York: Fawcet Columbine.

Plaskow, Judith. 1980. *Sex, sin and grace.* Lanham, Md.: University Press of America.

Potter Engel, Mary. 1990. Evil, sin and violation of the vulnerable. In *Lift every voice: Constructing Christian theologies from the underside,* ed. Susan Brooks Thistlethwaite and Mary Potter Engel, 152–64. San Francisco: Harper and Row.

Rahner, Hugo. 1960. *Saint Ignatius Loyola: Letters to women.* Translated by Kathleen Pond and S. A. H. Weetman. Freiburg: Herder KG; New York: Herder and Herder.

————. 1968. *Ignatius the theologian.* Translated by Michael Barry. New York: Herder and Herder.

Rahner, Karl. 1979a. The doctrine of the "spiritual senses" in the Middle Ages. In *Theological Investigations,* vol. 16, *The experience of the Spirit: Source of theology,* 104–34. Translated by David Moreland. New York: Crossroads/Seabury.

————. 1979b. The "spiritual senses" according to Origen. In *Theological Investigations,* vol. 16, *The experience of the Spirit: Source of theology,* 81–103. Translated by David Moreland. New York: Crossroads/Seabury.

————. 1986. *The Practice of Faith.* New York: Crossroad.

Ranft, Patricia. 1996. *Women and the religious life in premodern Europe.* New York: St. Martin's Press.

Roszak, Theodore. 1992. *The voice of the earth.* New York: Simon and Schuster.

Ruether, Rosemary Radford. 1983. *Sexism and God-talk: Toward a feminist theology.* Boston: Beacon Press.

———. 1990. *To change the world: Christology and cultural criticism,* 2nd ed. New York: Crossroad.

Ruffing, Janet. 1995. You fill up my senses. *The Way* 35 (April): 101–10.

Saiving, Valerie. 1992. The human situation: A feminine view. In *WomanSpirit rising: A feminist reader in religion,* 2nd ed., ed. Carol P. Christ and Judith Plaskow, 25–42. San Francisco: Harper.

Schneiders, Sandra. 1991a. *Beyond patching: Faith and feminism in the Catholic Church.* New York: Paulist.

———. 1991b. *The revelatory text: Interpreting the New Testament as sacred scripture.* San Francisco: Harper.

Schüssler Fiorenza, Elisabeth. 1984. *Bread not stone: The challenge of feminist biblical interpretation.* Boston: Beacon Press.

Segarra Pijuan, S.J., Joan. 1992. *Manresa and Saint Ignatius of Loyola.* Manresa: Ajuntament de Manresa.

Sheldrake, Philip. 1983. The principle and foundation and images of God. *The Way Supplement* 48 (Autumn): 90–96.

———. 1987. *Images of holiness.* Notre Dame: Ave Maria Press.

Sisters of Providence. 1990. *The love of Christ impels us: Providence retreat in everyday life.* Spokane, Wash.: Sisters of Providence Provincial Administration.

Suchocki, Marjorie Hewitt. 1995. *The fall to violence: Original sin in relational theology.* New York. Continuum.

Swimme, Brian. 1996. *The hidden heart of the cosmos.* New York: Orbis.

Tellechea Idígoras, José Ignacio. 1994. *Ignatius of Loyola: The pilgrim saint.* Translated by Cornelius Buckley, S.J. Chicago: Loyola University Press.

Works Cited

## Works Cited

Works Cited

# Works Cited

Works Cited

Works Cited

Works Cited

# Works Cited

Works Cited

# Works Cited

Teresa of Avila. 1976. *The book of her life.* In *The collected works of St. Teresa of Avila,* vol. 1, translated by Kieran Kavanaugh, O.C.D. and Otilio Rodriguez, O.C.D., 54–365. Washington, D.C.: ICS Publications.

# Works Cited

Teresa of Avila. 1976. *The book of her life.* In *The collected works of St. Teresa of Avila,* vol. 1, translated by Kieran Kavanaugh, O.C.D. and Otilio Rodriguez, O.C.D., 54–365. Washington, D.C.: ICS Publications.

Teresa of Jesus, Saint. 1950. *Conceptions of the love of God.* In *The complete works,* vol. 2, edited and translated by E. Allison Peers. New York: Sheed and Ward.

Tetlow, Joseph A., S.J. 1989. The fundamentum. *Studies in the Spirituality of Jesuits* 21 (September).

Tillich, Paul. 1957. *The Protestant era.* Abridged edition. Chicago: University of Chicago Press.

Toner, Jules. 1982. *A commentary on Saint Ignatius's rules for the discernment of spirits: A guide to the principles and practice.* St. Louis: Institute of Jesuit Sources.

———. 1991. *Discerning God's will: Ignatius of Loyola's teaching on Christian decision making.* St. Louis: Institute of Jesuit Sources.

Turner, Alice K. 1993. *The history of hell.* New York: Harcourt Brace.

Veale, Joseph. 1995. Manifold gifts. *The Way Supplement* 82 (Spring): 44–53.

Wildiers, N. Max. 1982. *The theologian and his universe: Theology and cosmology from the Middle Ages to the present.* New York: Seabury.

Wink, Walter. 1998. *The powers that be: Theology for a new millennium.* New York: Doubleday.

Young, William J., ed. and trans. 1959. *Letters of Ignatius of Loyola.* Chicago: Loyola University Press.

Zohar, Danah. 1990. *The quantum self: Human nature and consciousness defined by the new physics.* New York: Quill/William Morrow.

Teresa of Avila. 1976. The book of her life. In The collected works of St. Teresa of Avila, vol. 1, translated by Kieran Kavanaugh, O.C.D. and Otilio Rodriguez, O.C.D., 54–365. Washington, D.C.: ICS Publications.

Teresa of Jesus, Saint. 1950. Conception of the love of God. In The complete works, vol. 2, edited and translated by E. Allison Peers. New York: Sheed and Ward.

Tetlow, Joseph A. SJ. 1989. The fundamentum. Studies in the Spirituality of Jesuits 21 (September).

Tillich, Paul. 1957. The Protestant era. Abridged edition. Chicago: University of Chicago Press.

Toner, Jules. 1982. A commentary on Saint Ignatius' rules for the discernment of spirits: A guide to the principles and practice. St. Louis: Institute of Jesuit Sources.

———. 1991. Discerning God's will: Ignatius of Loyola's teaching on Christian decision making. St. Louis: Institute of Jesuit Sources.

Turner, Alice K. 1993. The history of hell. New York: Harcourt Brace.

Veale, Joseph. 1995. Manifold gifts. The Way Supplement 82 (Spring): 44–55.

Wildiers, N. Max. 1982. The theologian and his universe: Theology and cosmology from the Middle Ages to the present. New York: Seabury.

Wink, Walter. 1998. The powers that be: Theology for a new millennium. New York: Doubleday.

Young, William J., ed. and trans. 1959. Letters of Ignatius of Loyola. Chicago: Loyola University Press.

Zohar, Danah. 1990. The quantum self: Human nature and consciousness defined by the new physics. New York: Quill/William Morrow.

# Index of Modern Authors

# About the Authors

**Katherine Dyckman, S.N.J.M.,** is an assistant professor at the School of Theology and Ministry at Seattle University. Active as a retreat and spiritual director, she is also the coauthor of three other books, includ-

ing *Inviting the Mystic, Supporting the Prophet: An Introduction to Spiritual Direction* and *Chaos or Creation: Spirituality in Mid-Life* (both published by Paulist Press). In addition, in 1983 she and a Jesuit colleague began the first eight-month Nineteenth Annotation Retreat program in the United States (Spiritual Exercises in Everyday Life), which utilizes the gifts of the laity as directors and administrators.

**Mary Garvin, S.N.J.M.,** has a doctor of ministry degree from Andover

Newton Theological School and currently serves as an assistant professor in the Religious Studies Department of Gonzaga University in Spokane, Washington. An experienced lecturer and spiritual director, she is also the author of numerous articles on religious life and Ignatian spirituality.

**Elizabeth Liebert, S.N.J.M.,** is professor of spiritual life at San

Francisco Theological Seminary and a member of the doctoral faculty in Christian spirituality of the Graduate Theological Union. She has written numerous scholarly and popular works on spirituality and spiritual direction. Her latest book, written with John Endres, S.J., is entitled *A Retreat with the Psalms: Resources for Personal and Communal Prayer* (Paulist Press).

Additional Praise

for

*The Spiritual Exercises Reclaimed*

"*The Spiritual Exercises Reclaimed* is an extraordinarily lucid and wise reinterpretation of the Spiritual Exercises of St. Ignatius of Loyola. It brilliantly explains key themes and movements in this profound spiritual process, placing the Spiritual Exercises within the historical context in which they originated and illuminating both the problems and possibilities this spiritual pedagogy poses for women who both make and give the Exercises today....Although women will particularly discover creative possibilities for themselves in the Spiritual Exercises through this reinterpretation, so too will men discover many fresh ways of looking at the Exercises as a whole, their processes, themes, and key dynamics. This is one of the best companion volumes on the Spiritual Exercises for all who guide others through the Exercises and the only comprehensive one for women."

Janet K. Ruffing, R.S.M.
Professor in Spirituality and Spiritual Direction
Fordham University

"The authors' bold and confident authorial voice, speaking from deep experience, wisdom, and familiarity with the Spiritual Exercises, will empower every woman who seeks to express her commitment to God in deeds more than in words. Finally, women (and men) who are committed to the inclusion of all people in God's boundless freedom can claim unreservedly and with new energy the legacy left by Ignatius of Loyola and his feminine counterparts."

Elisabeth Koenig
Professor of Ascetical Theology
The General Theological Seminary, New York City